Narrating Heritage

UCL Critical Cultural Heritage Series

Series Editor: Beverley Butler

The aim of this series is to ask new questions about what heritage is and does, and why it is important. Rejecting the idea that there is any one static model, it seeks out as-yet-unconceptualized notions of heritage based on grounded research contexts and cutting-edge methodologies that are global in reach and traverse disciplinary boundaries to draw on diverse perspectives notably, though not limited to, archaeology and museum studies, anthropology, ethnography, political studies, postcolonial studies, cultural memory studies, health humanities and environmental humanities. Published in association with the UCL Institute of Archaeology, the series welcomes submissions for authored and edited volumes from scholars and practitioners worldwide in pursuit of its goals to embrace a plurality of perspectives, increase diversity and representation in the discipline, and exemplify a proactive, responsive and just future for critical cultural heritage studies.

Narrating Heritage

Rights, Abuses and Cultural Resistance

Veysel Apaydin

BLOOMSBURY ACADEMIC
LONDON • NEW YORK • OXFORD • NEW DELHI • SYDNEY

BLOOMSBURY ACADEMIC
Bloomsbury Publishing Plc, 50 Bedford Square, London, WC1B 3DP, UK
Bloomsbury Publishing Inc, 1385 Broadway, New York, NY 10018, USA
Bloomsbury Publishing Ireland, 29 Earlsfort Terrace, Dublin 2, D02 AY28, Ireland

BLOOMSBURY, BLOOMSBURY ACADEMIC and the Diana logo
are trademarks of Bloomsbury Publishing Plc

First published in Great Britain 2024
Paperback edition published 2025

Cover design: Terry Woodley
Cover image © Serkan Çetin / EyeEm via Getty

A catalogue record for this book is available from the British Library.

A catalog record for this book is available from the Library of Congress.

ISBN: HB: 978-1-3503-3463-2
PB: 978-1-3503-3464-9
ePDF: 978-1-3503-3465-6
eBook: 978-1-3503-3466-3

Series: UCL Critical Cultural Heritage Series

Typeset by RefineCatch Limited, Bungay, Suffolk

For product safety related questions contact productsafety@bloomsbury.com.

To find out more about our authors and books visit www.bloomsbury.com
and sign up for our newsletters.

For the oppressed, human and non-human, in this world.

Contents

Illustrations

Preface and Acknowledgements

The idea behind this book first came about during my first ethnographic field work at the contested site of Ani in east Turkey, and the questions and arguments developed over the next ten years. I then conducted ethnographic fieldwork at various UNESCO World Heritage Sites, including Çatalhöyük, Hattusa and Ani in Turkey, to look at the relationships between local communities and these World Heritage Sites. The in-depth ethnographic fieldwork, which included observations, participatory observations and interviews with the local community members, helped me to explore the complex ontology of heritage in which local communities attach, ascribe and develop different values, meanings and memories. I also joined the Ilisu Dam Rescue Archaeological Projects, as an archaeologist and heritage researcher, in southeast Turkey, where one of the biggest dams in Turkey was about to be constructed. Working as part of this team in this highly contested region of Turkey gave me the opportunity to examine the links between the use of landscape and natural resources, conducting cultural activities and heritage making, and the importance of these resources for the Kurdish local communities in this region. Working in this region of Turkey also gave me insights into how the over 40-year conflict in this region affected local communities, ranging from displacement to forced migration, and the loss of sense of belonging and sense of place, which has a great impact on cultural memory and identity of those communities.

While I was interested in finding about how natural heritage is linked to cultural heritage, I also looked at the discourses of why a nation state – in this case, Turkey – was desperately attempting to wipe out the natural and cultural resources of the Kurdish minority groups in southeast Turkey through dam construction and continuous conflicts. This type of authoritarian approach, which is linked to heavy neoliberal policies, can also be seen in many other parts of the world. Additionally, the case of the Ilisu Dam project and conflict in southeast Turkey is not the only example of this in Turkey. In order to unlock this pattern of the Turkish state, whereby it constantly attempts to oppress minority groups whom it considers to be a threat to the state's national unity, I looked at other case studies. One example was in east Turkey, specifically Munzur Valley in Dersim (Tunceli) where predominantly Alevi minorities live. The state planned several dams in this natural valley, which is considered sacred and spiritual for the Alevi communities whose values are attached and memories and collective identities are developed. I also observed one of the biggest environmental protests in the centre of Istanbul against authoritarian policies of the Turkish government, who were attempting to abolish a city garden square.

Many years of research and ethnographic fieldwork in these regions has made me aware of the complex structure of heritage, from construction to transformation and to destruction, and how it can become a tool, a way to resist authoritarian regimes. These case studies and many other examples from all around the world that I researched for this book demonstrated that heritage is social, cultural, political and economic. This is the main reason why I advocate that as critical heritage scholars, we have an ethical and professional responsibility to expose discourses of heritage and to deal with social and political issues that arise through heritage, and to support communities and their sustainability.

A number of the ideas in this book were presented in many international conferences and lectures. Some ideas in Chapter 3 appeared in *International Journal of Heritage Studies*. Throughout these ten years of research and data collection, I benefited a lot from the knowledge of stakeholders, NGO representatives and, most importantly, local communities, who showed me what heritage means at the local level. Therefore, I must thank all of them who made this book possible. I also owe a big thank you to Beverly Butler, the series editor, for her guidance and help throughout all the stages of this work; without her support this book would not be possible. Very special thanks to Michael Rowlands, who read the earlier version of this book and provided extremely valuable, critical and constructive feedback. I must also thank the three anonymous peer reviewers who provided invaluable comments and suggestions. Thanks also to editors of Bloomsbury, Georgina Leighton, Lily Mac Mahon and Zoe Osman for their help and guidance. Over all of these years, I have had a lot of help from many people in academia and thanks must go to Ulrike Sommer, Tim Schadla-Hall and Louise Martin; my colleagues at the Institute of Education, Claire Robins, Annie Davey, Marquard Smith, Andrew Ash, Caroline Marcus, Lesley Burgess, Thomas Jones, Pam Meecham, John Reeve, Josephine Borradaile, Carol Wild, Sophie Huckfield, Ross Head and Johnathan Flint. I would particularly also like to thank the Art, Design and Museology students who helped me to more critically think about heritage over the years. Lastly and most importantly, I would like to thank my friends and family who are always there for me: Jonathan Gardner, Brenna Hassett, Sara Perry and Andrew Bevan, Colin Sterling, Beatrijs de Groot, Rachel King, Gabriel Moshenska, Ian Kirkpatrick, Paul Tourle, Jeff Marks, David Francis, Constance Maurer and Gwendoline Maurer, and of course mum and dad.

Introduction: Performing and Participating

What do nature, landscape, rivers and valleys have to do with heritage, rights and social justice? It is the end of July. I am travelling to east Turkey to Dersim (Tunceli), where the Alevi minorities predominantly live. It is one of those places that is difficult to get to as it is surrounded by mountains in the east, west and north and a river from the south. I take a ferry to cross the river where the megadam was built in the 1970s that completely transformed the landscape and natural environment. The ferry arrives at the shore of Dersim, and I see that there is a checkpoint. This surprises me because I am travelling from one Turkish city to another. I am in a minibus, talking to locals about the route to get to central Dersim. The minibus passes easily and quickly through the checkpoint where there used to be a very strict security check; everyone used to be searched one by one, the locals say. Looking from the window towards the river and mountains, I am amazed by what I see. Against the backdrop of the natural scenery, which is like something out of a novel, the roads are being patrolled by heavily armed military vehicles. It is surreal to me, but the locals in the minibus do not pay any attention. They are used to this.

We finally arrive in the city centre where there are too many people on the streets – shopping, sitting in the coffee shops and drinking in the bars with live music – while on the other side, across the river, at the top of hill, military helicopters land and take off. It is the busiest time of the year; many people come from all around the world to visit their hometown and attend the Munzur Festival that is held every year at the source of the Munzur River and Valley. Although the festival lasts three days, people stay much longer to attend cultural activities and visit Alevi sacred places. The river and valley are significant and sacred to the Alevis (Ronayne 2005; Gezik and Gültekin 2019), whose values and identity construction are strongly attached to, and developed from, the natural characteristics of the Munzur Valley.

I drive from the city centre to the source of the Munzur River. It is more than an hour's journey. The drive is hard; the road curves often, following the bends of the river and the foothills of the mountains. While driving, I see the incredible richness in the valley. The valley is biodiverse and includes a range of flora and fauna, such as mountain goats, eagles and many other kinds of birds that can be seen everywhere under the green blanket of trees and over the powerful flow of the Munzur River. I open the window to listen the rumble of the river, which relaxes me. All along the route, from the city centre to the source of the Munzur River, there are people fishing, swimming, having picnics and drinking. It feels like I am not in east Turkey but somewhere on the Mediterranean or Aegean coast.

As I near the source of the Munzur River, I hear music that comes from very far away. When I arrive, music is coming from everywhere. People are having picnics and dancing and children are playing. Although there is extreme heat at this time of the year, the Munzur River cools the valley down. I walk up to the source and I see people are swimming and walking in the water. Many people are also camping under the trees around the source. I talk with local community members and with people who live in Europe and come to join the annual festival, which was organized by the solidarity campaign against dam constructions in the Munzur Valley. They start by telling me how significant the Munzur Valley is for their belief system and cultural practices and how it is a resource for their collective identity and memory. In this discussion it becomes clear that their cultural production or, in other words, their tangible and intangible heritage is highly linked to this valley, which serves as a resource through its river and mountains, and through its floral and faunal diversity, much of which is unique to this valley.

I walk down to the river towards the other end of the festival where locals are making food and selling souvenirs. I stop and start talking to one of the locals who is selling jewellery. He says, 'all these trees and spiritual valley play a significant role for Alevism and our community but they are under threat becuase of the conflict between Turkish military and Marxist armed groups'.

Although the Alevis of Dersim try very hard to run the festival every year, the Munzur Festival is often banned for security reasons. The people of the Munzur Valley and the Alevi people are a demonstration of the fact that heritage is not only about the material culture of the past but that it is also a process, and this process is continuously developed, formed and reshaped by the people who have been performing these cultural activities for generations. Therefore, if heritage is to be protected, these rights to cultural production of heritage must be exercised freely. While I walk around and meet people, including local people who live in the villages and towns around the Munzur Valley, the older women and men of the community tell stories to the younger generations that are highly linked to identity constructions and a sense of belonging that contribute and develop a new heritage, as part of an overall heritage process. The high attendance and passion of the people towards this very unique festival also makes me realize that heritage is a process that develops tangible and intangible aspects, and that it is highly linked to people's emotions. These emotions can be individual, of course, but also in more of a collective sense of communities (see Smith 2020) because they share memories and stories, and preserve meanings and attach new meanings to cultural heritage through cultural performance.

An example of the uses of heritage, producing both intangible and tangible heritage, developing cultural memories, community resilience and persistence, as well as the restriction on performing cultural heritage and cultural rights can be clearly seen in the activities of the the Munzur Festival. It is not only cultural life that is linked to natural heritage but also social and daily lives. These connections demonstrate to me that heritage, as a field, is very deep and diverse because it can reflect on any facet of life that has a connection with humans and nature, and as a science, heritage can have a large impact on social and political life. The case of the Munzur Valley also demonstrates what this book is about and how the essence of heritage can be used for different purposes, particularly to (re)construct, to abuse rights, to restrict, to increase resilience, to perform and produce culture and to persist for social justice.

The Munzur Valley will be discussed in more detail in Chapter 5, and it is certainly not the first or only case of its kind. Examples can be seen in many parts of the world. For those specific groups, performing cultural heritage is deliberately restricted by the dominant group or state authority, and the landscape and natural environment intrinsically linked to this production of heritage by minority and indigenous groups have been transformed through strong neoliberal policies (Harvey 2005; King 2020; Eoin and King 2013; King and Eoin 2014; Nixon 2011). In other cases, because of conflict or security reasons, communities cannot exercise cultural performances to develop their heritage (Bevan 2016; Herscher 2010; Estes 2019; see Walasek 2015 for the 1990s Bosnian conflict; see Butler 2009 for the Palestinian case; see Harrison 2008 for the Armenia and Azerbaijan case). Cultural heritage is often targeted for elimination by oppressive groups because of these social conflicts. In the worst cases, people are being displaced and having traumatic experiences, as in the case of the recent conflict in Syria (Fiddian-Qasmiyeh 2020).

Indeed, the idea and concept of heritage is significant for every individual, group and community, particularly from collective identity and sense of belonging perspectives. In this book, I define heritage as any tangible and intangible outcome of social and cultural interactions of groups who share or develop similar values and, based on this, make memories, create a sense of belonging and collective identity. In other words, heritage emerges from the daily social and cultural practices of communities. This is also the main reason that one singular definition of heritage is difficult, as practices of communities are also shaped with unique cultural dynamics that differ in every part of the world. In this book it is stressed that heritage is a cultural and social process, which is actively engaged in by people and considered in a 'positive manner' and that every person, group and community has the right to perform heritage and learn about it freely; it is thus a basic human right and so cannot and should not be restricted.

However, heritage is also an ontology that has a negative impact that leads to conflict and creates division between communities within a society. Or, in other words, heritage is a space and material culture that is used by different claimants, who develop memories, attach values and meanings as well as develop tangible and intangible forms of heritage; because of this it often becomes a battleground between different identity groups. What I am emphasizing here is that the essence of heritage, which has different uses, has both positive and negative consequences, which is evident throughout history and into the modern period. While being able to exercise, perform and develop heritage is certainly a 'basic human right', it is also true that aspects of heritage can be considered an existential threat for other groups. We see this particularly in undemocratic countries, in conflicted and contested regions, as well as where authoritarianism has taken over.

While some sites, objects, monuments and intangible aspects are considered heritage by certain groups, they are also dismissed and not recognized by other groups, and furthermore can be considered as a threat that leads to conflict. This is also one of the discourses behind heritage destruction, as can be seen in many parts of the world throughout history. Although heritage can be a reason for conflict, leading to destruction of material culture that is significant for certain groups, in many cases the impact of the destruction is much greater on people themselves. This is one of the main reasons that this book focuses on the people who perform, develop and transform heritage, rather than heritage as an ontology. This is also why I argue that, as heritage scholars, we need to engage more critically with the changing parameters of social, cultural, economic and political issues that greatly affect people and are being created through historical narratives and implemented in the present day.

Book approach

In this book, I do not consider cultural heritage as only past objects, monuments or something to do with materiality and material culture. I consider cultural heritage as a cultural performance that develops memories and values; that forms, shapes, constructs and transforms cultural identity as well as a sense of belonging for communities. Through several case studies I attempt to demonstrate how cultural heritage can be used in different ways: abused by a dominant power or used to build community resilience and persistence for social justice. In doing so, I draw on a range of ideas and case studies based on extensive research and ethnographic fieldwork over ten years, mainly from Turkey, and consistently compare them in a global context. In each chapter, I contextualize and compare my own field research with other case studies from other parts of the world where similar attitudes to heritage have been enacted to demonstrate different parameters and paradoxes of cultural heritage, and different aspects of negativity and positivity.

Throughout the book, I critically examine the links between heritage, rights and social justice. I bring together unique case studies in a coherent and cohesive sense to examine patterns and differences of approaches to heritage to expose discourses of uses and abuses of heritage and narratives of persistence, and its importance for human rights and social justice. I delve more into social justice with details in the next chapter – but very briefly, social justice is a concept that advocates equal share of resources and wealth, recognizing everyone with their backgrounds and identities, and giving voice to people in decision-making processes (Fraser 1998, 2003, 2009). In the concluding chapter, I place these case studies within a theoretical context by taking a critical approach, arguing that exercising the right to use space, landscape or the natural environment to develop heritage is highly linked to human rights, and that this is significant to the cause of social justice and the path to sustainable societies. I make the case that social equality is only possible when people are able to freely exercise the right to culture.

The case studies presented here focus on Turkey, a region of complex history and complicated relationships as well as contested territory between modern-day ethnic and identity groups. It is a country in political turmoil, being transformed from democracy to authoritarianism (Brown 2019). It uses strong right-wing populist and neoliberal policies to oppress minority groups, resulting in restricted freedom of expression, restrictions on human rights and restrictions on the right of communities to their culture and heritage and consuming landscape and environment to make profit. In recent years, authoritarian practice through heavy use of neoliberal policies in rural areas and conflicts in the urban areas of southeast Turkey (Göçek 2018) has led to a displacement of minority communities and destructively affected heritage sites, landscapes and material culture. This has significant effects on these minority groups' ability to form and embody collective identity, memory and sense of belonging through using landscape and natural environment as a space.

Turkey is a very multicultural state where large numbers of minority groups have lived, including groups such as Greeks and Armenians, which are officially recognized as minorities, and not-recognized Kurds and Alevis, whose cultural rights have often been undermined, restricted and neglected. In many cases, their heritage is neglected to conserve and preserve national unity. This has generated resistance and persistence in some cases. For instance, in southeast Turkey, the Kurdish ethnic minority has used heritage and attachments to the landscape to claim ownership rights over territory and to conserve Kurdish identity. In the region of eastern Turkey discussed above, in Dersim (Tunceli) province, the majority of the population is from the Alevi cultural group and their heritage has been under threat from both conflict and large-scale state dam constructions. There is also the issue of Armenian heritage in many parts of Turkey, which has often been neglected or ignored for political reasons (Üngör 2011).

These minority groups have actively engaged with the landscape and nature and developed a heritage that is highly linked to memory and collective identity (Ricoeur 2004, 93), but their heritage is neglected by the Turkish state. Following Smith (2006), in Turkey, we find there is a 'hegemonic authorized heritage discourse which takes its power from the grand narratives of nation and class . . . and privileges monumentality . . .' (2006, 11) as well as some material culture and heritage that is linked to national narratives. There are many other minority groups and traditions whose heritage is not favoured by the authorized heritage discourse and official heritage practice of Turkey; privilege is primarily given to the heritage of the dominant (Turkish) ethnicity (Zencirci 2014). In Turkey, from the heritage perspective, the process of violating the rights of people, abusing power and resources, as well as misrecognition and exclusion of diversities, can take the form of persecution that can be seen in many ways: intentional destruction, neglect of heritage sites, destruction of landscape through large-scale constructions such as dams under the guise of 'economic development', restriction of access to land and heritage, forced migration, displacement and dispersing communities, neglect of diverse history in formal education, developing negative discourses in textbooks against different identity groups, presenting cultural heritage as singular and mono-ethnic, and linking only the identity and history of the majority into everyday life.

This kind of persecution can be explained through a non-violent approach and 'scopes of violence', which I divide into two dimensions and demonstrate with case studies in this book. The non-violent approach has been used by the Turkish state since it was established. It has been used in all state communication tools, but most importantly in formal and informal education – for example, in schools and museums, where minority groups' history, past and heritage is omitted and neglected. Instead a singular version of the past is presented to the public, parallel to the Turkish state's official ideology based on Turkish ethnicity and Islamic identity. The state has used schools and museums or public informal learning places to assimilate ethnic minority groups by imposing its authorized heritage discourse. This form of ideological use of education has been commonly used in many parts of the world to create 'legitimate knowledge' to conserve the state's ideology (Apple 2004).

A first scope of violence is 'direct violence', using the state's armed forces. Hannah Arendt, in her classic work *The Origins of Totalitarianism* (1958), notes that once complete power over all state institutions is seized by a new government and ideology, the new regime turns its attention and all resources, including its armed forces, towards the potential threat to new regimes' power in the future of the domestic masses. The Republic of Turkey was established in 1923 following years of fighting for independence and war against external powers. During this time, all groups, including some minority groups such as the Kurdish ethnic minority, joined and fought for the Turkish Republic. However, after that, what we have seen is decades of violence against minorities – in the case of Kurdish communities, direct violence for almost a century.

The second aspect of violence, 'slow violence', is based on environmental destruction, including destroying, for example, the landscape, nature, biodiversity, or polluting the air. For instance, the nuclear incident at Chernobyl in the former Soviet Union in 1986 has affected the environment and health of people in large proximity in the region of the Black Sea (Nixon 2009). There are many examples in many parts of the world of this kind of slow violence but, since the introduction of neoliberalism, 'slow violence' has increased, especially in the poorest parts of the world (Nixon 2009, 2011), as developed countries in the Global North use poorer countries in the Global South to dump their garbage, which has long-term impacts on the environment and people of the region.

Rob Nixon (2011, 2) calls 'slow violence' a 'violence that occurs gradually and out of sight, a violence of delayed destruction that is dispersed across time and space, an attritional violence that is typically not viewed as violence at all'. Environmental slow violence does not only occur through toxic garbage but also comes about through large-scale infrastructure projects in many parts of the world (Nixon 2011). This is particularly the case for Turkey, where hundreds of megadams have been built that have extreme impacts on the environment as well as on local communities. This form of slow violence also results in forced migration, with particular impact, as is the case in Turkey, on the assimilation of minority groups who have lost their landscape, cultural space, nature where they developed collective identity, sense of belonging and place, and an attendant ability to construct a cultural heritage.

The non-violent approach, direct violence and slow violence directly impact on cultural activity and heritage making for those who are affected. They have strong effects on social, cultural, economic and political discourses and because of this are inextricably linked to human rights and social justice. This is why I argue that the question of what makes 'heritage' needs more effective, critical and creative engagement by heritage academics and professionals with social, political and economic issues. This is even more crucial for the field of 'critical heritage'. Years of intensive ethnographic field work with several case studies and communities have demonstrated that heritage is more than only material culture; it exists within existing social, political and economic discourses.

In this book, I attempt to expose links between the cultural performance and activities of people with the construction of collective identity and sense of belonging; the role of education as an institution in learning about cultures and human rights as well as the nationalist use of education to reshape public life and communities; the relationship between access to space and landscape for performing cultural activities in heritage construction; and the exclusion and restriction of access to perform cultural activities in relation to developing heritage as a breach of human rights. Who decides what to perform and who has the right to give access for heritage making is closely related to human rights, and I will examine how exclusion and restriction affect heritage and how the breaching of human rights has often been practised in authoritarian regimes and protected by national policies. I will critically examine these nationalist and authoritarian policies and look at how they are practised to restrict participating in heritage making, and the link between use of neoliberal policies, environmental deterioration and erasing minority heritage in contested land. I will analyse how communities resist intense forms of persecution with different methods to protect and preserve their right to heritage.

Case studies and local communities

In order to expose the discourses of heritage making, heritage rights, uses and abuses of heritage as well as examples of breaching human rights through exclusion and restriction, as well as expose violence and resistance to persecution, I selected several case studies from different regions of Turkey. These case studies were selected deliberately to analyse discourses of uses and abuses of heritage in relation to contemporary politics, to reflect on the multicultural past and present of Turkey's community structure, as well as measuring the impact of strong nationalist discourses that have been implemented through institutions of education. Through these case studies (see Figure 0.1) I have also aimed to demonstrate the complex structure of heritage that is strongly linked to the social, cultural and economic life of communities as well as landscape, valley, river and other forms of natural heritage. The case studies demonstrate and develop arguments about how tangible, intangible and natural heritage are significant for cultural memory and identity, sense of belonging and sense of place, and how they are strongly linked to each other.

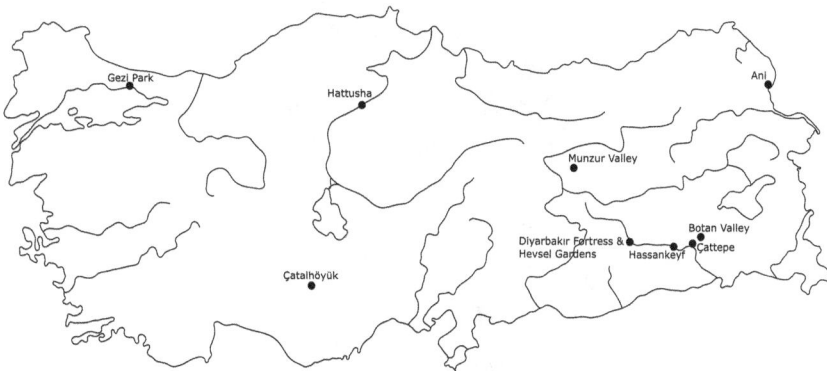

Figure 0.1 Locations of case studies. © Veysel Apaydin.

Ani: A Medieval Armenian heritage site

Ani is not only interesting and stunning for its architecture and monumental remains but also for its location; it is right on the border of Turkey and Armenia, in eastern Turkey. The site itself used to be a reason for tension between Turks and Armenians in the past and it still represents this tension as a borderland heritage site since the Republic of Turkey was established in 1923 and drew its modern borders. The heritage site and surrounding area were off limits for a long time, until 2006, because the region is highly contested between Turkish and Armenian states; the region is called 'western Armenia' by nationalist Armenians. The site was neglected for a long time by the Turkish state because of its Armenian architectural remains.

The site does not only have Armenian heritage but also contains some Byzantine, Islamic, Seljuk, Arabic and Georgian archaeological remains. However the site's monumental architecture is mainly from the Medieval Armenian Kingdom period (Cowe 2001). The site was mainly developed during the tenth and eleventh centuries AD and was capital of the Armenian Kingdom. The province of Ani has always been very multicultural with groups including Armenians, Yezidis, Assyrians, Malakans (Akçayöz et al. 2007). However, following the 1915 Armenian genocide and ethnic cleansing, as well as decades of purification process, the population of this region now mostly consists of Turkish and Kurdish communities which were repopulated following the 1915 genocide and ethnic cleansing.

In contrast to other case studies in this book, Ani also demonstrates the religious side of heritage. Most of Ani's standing monumental architecture and remains are churches and cathedrals which are very significant for Orthodox Armenians who are part of the Armenian Apostolic Church, which is one of the oldest Christian institutions. Along with nationalistic contestations between Turkey and Armenia, issues of religious heritage also increased the tension in the past; for instance, some Armenian churches were converted into mosques in the city of Kars. However, the Turkish government has increased access, and helped to restore and conserve some of the monumental heritage in the site, in order to inscribe it to the UNESCO list of World Heritage in 2015 as part of its strong neoliberal policy to make more profit through tourism.

Sur: Diyarbakir Fortress and Hevsel Gardens

The fortress and Sur (inner city of Diyarbakir inside the fortress) as well as Hevsel Gardens have been a crucial site for thousands of years from ancient civilizations to modern day communities and different identity groups. The remaining archaeological architecture demonstrates its multicultural past and heritage. The inner city was important because of its location, as in the case of Ani, and it was the regional capital of many empires including the Persian, Roman, Sassanian and Byzantine. The site contains significant religious buildings including Armenian churches as well as mosques. The Sur district has/had 595 registered heritage sites and many of them are architectural and monumental buildings from those periods. Diyarbakir Fortress and Hevsel Gardens also became a World Heritage Site in 2015.

The site has considerable importance for Kurdish communities who have developed memory and collective identity within the space of Sur and attached meanings to its material culture and developed a sense of belonging over time. Historically, Sur and Diyarbakir are also considered as the centre of Kurdish struggle for independence that has continued since the 1980s, led by the Kurdistan Workers' Party. The city of Diyarbakir as a whole is the largest Kurdish populated city in Turkey and has supported the Kurdish movement for a long time (Watts 2010). In 2015, the inner city became the centre space for the Kurdish movement as it declared self-autonomy (Saadi 2021), which resulted in armed conflict with the Turkish armed forces. The Kurdish movement chose the Sur to declare autonomy because of its Kurdish population and historical attachment. For the same reason, the inner city was heavily targeted by Turkish armed forces to erase tangible Kurdish heritage.

Botan Valley: Çattepe

The Botan Valley is located in southeast Turkey in the province of predominantly Kurdish city Siirt. Similar to Ani and Sur, the Botan Valley is historically significant because of its location and the Botan River, which was a natural route to connect civilizations in the past. The valley, with its natural water resources, had a significant role for the local population, whose economy was dependent on farming. The valley contains many archaeological sites that are dated to prehistoric times as well as modern villages that were mostly occupied by Kurdish communities for generations. The archaeological site of Çattepe, which sits on the intersection of the Botan and Tigris rivers, is a good example to demonstrate the merging of a modern village and an archaeological site that goes back to prehistoric times and includes a large late Roman component (Saglamtimur 2014). There has been occupation of a village constructed on top of the archaeological site for some time.

While Çattepe as an archaeological heritage site sheds light on historical events and civilizations (Saglamtimur 2014), modern Çattepe village also represents recent historical events that have shaped the region demographically, politically and economically. First, the villagers of Çattepe were affected by the conflict between the Kurdistan Workers' Party and the Turkish armed forces during the 1990s, which led to displacement and forced migration to nearby cities. While some villagers returned to their homes and villages in the 2000s, the Ilisu Dam project, which flooded the valley, lands and villages in 2019, led to a second wave of forced migration. The completion of the dam project resulted in the complete destruction of Çattepe and both its archaeological and modern heritage.

Hasankeyf

A small medieval town on the Tigris River, near the city of Batman, with a stunning history that goes back to Neolithic periods, had the same destiny as Çattape, and was flooded following the completion of the Ilisu Dam. The site became a symbol of resistance against dam construction and its devastating impact on the landscape, heritage and people. Similar to other case studies mentioned above, Hasankeyf also had a very rich and multicultural past and heritage with its archaeological remains from Armenians, Arabs, Yezidis and Islamic and Christian periods. The recent history of Hasankeyf is significant as the communities of Hasankeyf were heavily affected by the conflict between the Kurdistan Workers' Party and the Turkish armed forces as well as the impact of dam construction, both of which led to forced migration.

The Munzur Valley

The Munzur Valley is located in the east of Turkey, within the predominantly Alevi and ethnically Kurdish region, Dersim. The official name of the region is Tunceli, but people from this region call it by its original Kurdish name 'Dersim'. Therefore, I will also call it Dersim, following the people of this region. The Munzur Valley gained the status of National Park in 1971 because of its unique biodiverse landscape. It is one of Turkey's largest nature reserves, having over 100 endemic plant species. The valley is also home to unique types of animals including wild cats, wolves, bears, ibex, wild pigs and mountain goats.

While the Munzur Valley and surrounding region were home to early civilizations, as archaeological surveys and excavations indicate (Erdogan and Sezgin 2020), for hundreds of years the valley has also been home to Alevi Kurds, who managed to preserve their identity against decades of the 'purification' process of Turkish official ideology resulting from a combination of Turkish nationalism and Islamic motives (see Zencirci 2014). Their ethnic background and belief system are different from the majority of Turkey's Islamic belief system and Turkish ethnic background. These differences also made them targets in the past of both the Ottoman Empire and the Turkish State. In 1938, tens of thousands of Alevi Kurds were massacred in Dersim (Van Bruinessen 1994) because of these differences. Dersim and the surrounding area were also home to many Armenians until the 1915 genocide and ethnic cleansing. The Munzur Valley case study demonstrates centuries of state oppression against a minority group through massacres, deprivation from education and justice, and construction of dam projects that aim to disperse communities under the idea of 'economic development'. However, the main reason for selecting it as a case study for this book is that it also demonstrates embedded discourses of resistance of people who protect their sense of belonging, sense of place, collective memory and identity embedded and developed through this natural valley.

Gezi Park

In contrast to the rest of the case studies in this book, Gezi Park is located on the European side of Turkey, in the city centre of Istanbul. The park sits in the centre of Taksim Square, which has symbolic importance for secularists of Turkey as well as left-wing labour movements who carried out their historical protests and marches in the square. The park is also significant for Armenians because of the presence of Armenian graveyards which were previously destroyed but still carry symbolic importance for the Armenian community. The location of the park also housed Ottoman barracks in Ottoman times. The whole area, including the square and the surrounding neighbourhoods, was also home to many ethnic Greeks (until 1920s population exchange) and Armenians (until 1915 Armenian genocide and ethnic cleansing); therefore the park and Taksim Square are significant for many political and ethnic groups.

In May 2013, the above narratives embodied themselves in one of the world's biggest protests against a planned demolition of Gezi Park and reconstruction of the Ottoman barracks with a shopping mall. This move of the governing party (the Justice and Development Party, or AKP in Turkish), which has ruled Turkey for twenty years, was strongly linked towards a shift in Turkey's official ideology further towards nationalism and Islamic values, as well as neoliberalism and the profit motive. However, this move met with an intense backlash, resulting in strong protests which brought together different ethnic and identity groups to resist this nationalist, ideologic and neoliberal move.

Methodological approach

As shown in the above introductions to the main case studies of this book, these are extremely complex sites and communities in terms of their links to historical as well as contemporary politics. Therefore, I approached those sites and communities from a very strong anthropological perspective by applying critical ethnography to each site and community to access a deep knowledge about the culture and cultural settings of each region; to get to know community dynamics and the importance and value of sites and landscapes at a local level; to see how heritage making is linked to cultural activities, landscapes and natural environment; to identify how these communities have developed a relationship with these sites and landscapes over time and how they have developed memory and collective identity.

The critical ethnography approach included methods of semi-structured interviews, participant observations and observations. For semi-structured interviews, I interviewed local community members, NGO representatives and politicians. Semi-structured interview questions aimed to find more about the relationship of local communities with the heritage sites, landscape and natural heritage; meanings and values of these sites for their daily, social, cultural and economic life, as well as their significance for collective identity and cultural memory of local communities. Interview participants' ages ranged from eighteen to eighty years old. The total number of interviewees was over 100.

Although all methods contributed widely to the data collection, participant observations and observations in particular helped me to understand community cohesions and dynamics as well as how a community's life, culture and heritage were affected by dam constructions, conflict and heavy nationalist and neoliberal policies. In the case of Botan and Munzur valleys and Gezi Park, both observations also helped me to understand people's collective attitude towards authoritarianism and their persistence in protecting and preserving their heritage and therefore collective identity, memory and sense of belonging. Most importantly, being in each site and observing community life and participating in it demonstrated a clear picture about how heritage is, on one hand, a complex ontology but, on the other, crucial for individual and community survival.

In some case studies, for instance in the case of Botan Valley, ethnographic fieldwork was not straightforward. This was due to ongoing conflict between the

Turkish armed forces and the Kurdistan Workers' Party. In the meantime, I was also working as an archaeologist and heritage researcher as part of ongoing rescue archaeological projects for Ilisu Dam. For years, being part of this project provided me with many resources, developing relationships with local communities as well as working with them in the archaeological sites. However, our work was often interrupted when conflict intensified. The archaeological site and the modern village Çattepe were often in the middle of this conflict. It was a one-hour drive from the city centre through the mountains and Botan Valley. While we were at the site, we were often able to see fighter jets or army helicopters flying above us or hear hours of conflict sounds. This without doubt was creating anxiety and tension in the archaeological team as well as, of course, villagers whose lives had been affected by conflict for decades. Therefore, developing trust with the local communities of Çattepe and Botan Valley was very important to get deeper knowledge and give them voice first-hand as part of the people-centred approach that I applied in each case study of this book.

In contrast to conducting intense ethnographic fieldwork in these case studies and communities, the case study of Sur is limited in terms of bringing views of residents of Sur regarding their heritage and conflict. Although I went to Diyarbakir for years and have had talks with community members and NGOs, in 2015 when the Sur conflict began and afterwards it was difficult to interview local people of Sur and conduct any observations or participant observations. This was mainly due to security reasons, as no one was allowed to get into Sur during the conflict and the following several years. Therefore, my main resources regarding Sur are based on reports of international organizations such as Amnesty International and OHCHR (United Nations Human Rights Office), which had a permit to observe the conflict and measure the impact of this conflict on communities.

Book structure

In Chapter 1, I explore and reflect on the idea of critical heritage, rights and social justice from a theoretical perspective and attempt to contextualize them in heritage settings. In this chapter, I particularly focus on current approaches in critical heritage, international human rights law in relation to cultural rights and their link to social justice, which I analyse from theoretical and praxis perspectives. In Chapter 2, I explore the relationship between the nationalist and populist use of formal education to develop and preserve national narratives that are based on a single, dominant ethnic group. I theorize about education in the context of the nationalist use and significance for nation building and conserving the national unity of nation states. I delve into the case of Turkish education and use of history textbooks in formal education since the modern state of Turkey was established in 1923 and demonstrate how education is used to create an 'imaginary community' by excluding other histories and heritages, including ethnic minorities, and neglecting the ancient and prehistoric past. Particularly, in this chapter, I look at history textbooks of primary, secondary and high schools, through critical discourse analysis, to expose how national and nationalist imaginary narratives are presented to students, how heritage of minorities is neglected, how minority groups are presented and othered through hate speech in the textbooks, and how the ancient and prehistoric past are neglected. Finally, to demonstrate the impact of the heavy use of nationalist discourses in the textbooks, I present the result of intense ethnographic fieldwork in three culturally distinct modern communities who live around three significant UNESCO World Heritage Sites that are either contested, not recognized as heritage or considered as part of national heritage.

I link the impact of Chapter 2 to Chapter 3 by analysing the medieval and monumental heritage site of Ani in east Turkey. I particularly look at the ways in which heritage as a practice and concept has been used, and the diverse meanings and values ascribed to heritage by different claimants. I look at the abuses of heritage to establish hegemony, oppress others, and how it is used for nationalist agendas and making national narratives. The site marks a point of conflict between Turks and Armenians, with the heritage and the past of the site playing a significant role for identity making and construction of national narratives and conserving national unity. The abuse of cultural heritage and landscape of the region have contributed to political tension and led to the unsustainability of the region where two neighbouring communities, who have been affected by political tension, have not been able to trade or establish relationships for decades. The site, as a local landscape, has been intensely used by local people who have ascribed meanings and values over a time at a grassroots level, away from political agendas. I consider, in this chapter, to what extent the built environment in particular can play a role in identity making and add to the political tension as well as alleviate the tension by using the multicultural past of the site for reconciliation and creating a sustainable future for the groups in conflict and how local meanings and values can be different from political meanings.

While some cultural heritage sites or landscapes have been contested between groups and have alleviated political tension in some cases, this kind of political tension can lead to armed conflict, devastation, destruction of heritage and displacement of communities. I link Chapter 3 to Chapter 4 by focusing on how the material culture of the past and present can play a significant role to claim lands as well as lead to armed conflict over ownership rights of the lands. I demonstrate material culture is not always a positive concept but it also often creates division and leads to conflict. I discuss that while heritage is a positive aspect for some communities, it is also a negative concept and threat for others. In this chapter, I analyse discourses of targeting cultural heritage during times of war and conflict and how groups use material culture as a resilience tool through a case study of the UNESCO World Heritage Site of the Sur city walls in southeast Turkey. The site became a battleground between the Turkish armed forces and Kurdish militias, who both claimed ownership of the land (Amnesty International 2016; OHCHR 2016). The site has a long and diverse history that includes Christian, Islamic, Armenian, Turkish and Kurdish occupations. During the conflict, which took months, most of the monuments in the site were damaged or destroyed and, following the conflict, a large percentage of Sur was levelled by authorities to develop 'new Sur'. Both the conflict and gentrification led to displacement and dispersed the communities of Sur. In this chapter, I explore discourses of heritage and material culture, with negative and positive sides, that led to conflict, displacement and authoritarian decision-making process following the conflict, by building 'new Sur'.

While I tackle the discourses of heavy breaches of human rights through armed conflict from a heritage perspective, in Chapter 5 I analyse the ways the landscape and natural environment is used as a resource for heritage making and explore the links between landscape, rights and social justice. I attempt to unlock the discourses of the use of neoliberal policies to make a profit as well as to erase heritage resources under the authoritarian approach. I focus on two case studies, Botan and Munzur valleys in southeast and east Turkey, to illustrate why and how the landscape and the natural environment, with all their characteristics, play a substantial role as a resource for minority communities' sense of belonging and identity constructions. I also discuss embedded discourses of building dams under the idea of 'economic development' and to show the power of the nation state to minority groups who were considered to be a threat to national unity. Botan Valley is located in southeast Turkey and had been under threat by the Ilisu megadam project. The valley was home to Kurds and was used as a resource for tangible and intangible heritage making, which had a great significance for Kurdish communities whose rights were undermined. The second case study presents Munzur Valley, which has been under threat by multiple dam projects and is significant for especially intangible heritage making for the Alevi communities, whose values are not parallel to Turkish ideology, which is based on Turkishness and religious values. Through these case studies, in this chapter I analyse the importance of the landscape and natural environment for cultural participation and activities to make heritage and consolidate a collective identity and cultural memory and to demonstrate resilience and persistence against authoritarian decision-making processes.

The heavy use of neoliberal policies in practice through the authoritarian approach is not only seen in rural areas through dam projects but elsewhere, such as in urban cities through gentrification or other means that can be seen in different parts of the world (see Harvey 2005). Without question, the top-down transformation in cities also breaches the rights of people, who attach values to those spaces (see Lefebvre 1991) and again, they are totally excluded from the decision-making process. In Chapter 6, I focus on the significance of urban space for diverse identity groups, who use space for heritage making and values from different historical as well as social and daily perspectives. I analyse one of the biggest environmental demonstrations against the authoritarian approach of using space in an attempt to transform the identity of the space in parallel to hegemonic ideology by using top-down neoliberal policy. The case study of this chapter is Gezi Park, located in the centre of Istanbul, where large numbers of protestors occupied the park and Taksim Square to protect them from demolition. The Turkish government wanted to reconstruct the Ottoman barracks with a planned shopping mall. While Gezi Park as a space demonstrates how different and modern identity groups valued and developed memories historically and therefore attached meanings, weeks of protests and occupation also presents how protests become heritage for those who participated in the protests and transformed the meaning and values of space at a grassroots level, through strong resistance and persistence. In this chapter, I analyse and expose the importance of space as a social production and for social justice. I delve into the discourses of hegemonic top-down decision making and look at how authoritarian decision making can lead to persistence at a grassroots level and how protest becomes heritage itself.

In Chapter 7, the concluding chapter, based on the case studies of this book, I theorize about rights and social justice in the heritage context. I particularly focus on discourses of the right to learn, right to recognition, right to landscape, right to resistance and right to participate and develop heritage as well as the reasons for developing oppression by dominant power. I take and analyse theories of Paulo Freire, Pierre Bourdieu, Gordon Allport, James Scott and

Gramsci model to reflect on hegemonic discourses and discuss how it leads to resistance and counter-hegemony, then discuss discourses of oppression of authoritarian nation states through demonstrating the use of education, ownership rights and megadam projects in contested lands of Turkey. This also links the significance of space and its use (Harvey 2007; Lefebvre 1991) for people who use it in heritage making as well as the authoritarian state that uses heavy neoliberal policies to make profit and erase the history and heritage resources of minority groups who value the landscape and natural environment from a local perspective. This brings us to Arjun Appadurai's locality and nationality concepts which oppose each other, but also this kind of opposition motivates other groups.

Through these case studies, I aim to unlock the discourses behind the abuses of heritage and the ways in which it is used to oppress. Exposing those discourses, discussing them widely and disseminating knowledge of them to academia and the public is significant for not only protecting material culture, but also for preserving and sustaining diversity in societies. The findings of this book are significant for the heritage field in two ways. First, although scholars in heritage studies have long researched the uses and abuses of heritage, it is still important to expose and discuss ongoing case studies to develop public awareness and effective professional approach to heritage management and preservation. In this book, I explicitly expose the discourses used by dominant groups. Second, the social and political role of heritage as a profession and social science is stressed as I critically reflect on the role of heritage and its capacity that can provide ground to raise larger world issues.

1

Reflections

Critical heritage

Why critical heritage? This question has been intensely discussed in heritage studies in the last decade. Since this book is about 'criticality', with its own approach and methodology, I would like to delve into and justify why criticality is important in heritage studies. Critical heritage has been around for the last couple of decades. It is built on the preexisting work in social sciences and of scholars who reflected on global and regional social, cultural, economic and political issues from critical perspectives with links to heritage studies. Some examples of research in critical heritage include Henry Lefebvre (*The Production of Space*, 1991), David Harvey (*Social Justice and the City*, 2009), Benedict Anderson (*Imagined Communities*, 1983), David Lowenthal (*The Past is a Foreign Country*, 1985, 2006; *Heritage Crusade and Spoils of History*, 1996) and Arjun Appadurai (*Social Life of Things*, 1986).

Smith's (2006) *Uses of Heritage* perhaps opened up new ways for heritage studies to engage critically in the field and many scholars discussed the way a 'critical' heritage should work. The Association of Critical Heritage Studies manifesto also brought powerful approaches to the field (ACHS 2011). As examples, Gentry and Smith (2019) discussed and compared traditional heritage studies and critical heritage studies and examined the development of critical heritage studies in the late twentieth century. Several other scholars have reflected on how and what direction critical heritage should go and how it should work in theory and practice. Witcomb and Buckley (2013) discussed the directions of critical heritage. Sterling (2020) pointed out the theoretical side of critical heritage. Winter (2013), Winter and Waterton (2013) and Harrison (2013a) discussed the direction and the sociopolitical elements of critical heritage.

It is important to mention that heritage as a concept is very abstract and difficult to define. However, for this book, I will define heritage as any tangible or intangible cultural production that has social and cultural value for communities: this includes elements of landscape, river, mountain, flora and fauna; any material culture, home, food, poetry, or songs that bind communities who develop shared memory and values, construct collective identity, and ascribe meaning to these cultural productions. Heritage has many aspects and linkages which can include social, political, cultural and economic characteristics (Butler 2006) and therefore it is necessary for critical heritage scholars to engage with these features.

As this book deals with economic, social, cultural and political issues linked to heritage, and while I agree with the views of critical heritage scholars, I see heritage not only as a theory and approach but also as a narrative. In practice, I consider heritage as a progressive force that can deal with social and political injustices, inequality, poverty, as well as support and be the voice of the under-voiced, oppressed, minority, local and indigenous groups. I consider heritage as a narrative but also as a resource that can have impact in present and future. Butler (2006, 463) emphasizes:

> heritage as a powerful resource for 'creating a future' and to the recognition of how a fundamental recentralization of heritage is uniquely placed not only to address claims about identity, ancestry and cultural transmission but to engage with key moral-ethical issues to our times.

In today's world we have many 'key moral-ethical issues', for example, inequality, poverty, all forms of racism and discrimination, that we have the responsibility to reflect on. In agreement with other critical heritage scholars, I argue, we need to keep questioning our role and responsibility and to ask how and to what extent can heritage studies offer and provide support for people who have been oppressed through social, economic, undemocratic and authoritarian paradoxes that lead to injustices in every part of life. Cornelius Holtorf (2020, 310), who is an archaeologist and holds a UNESCO chair on Heritage Futures, stresses that as professionals of heritage studies we need to be careful about 'overt political motivation'. I agree that not everything should be overtly politicized, but I argue that everything is also political and we need to engage with this changing parameter of life, because social, cultural and economic circumstances have many dynamics and we need to consider both causes and consequences, and we certainly need to take a constructivist approach to respond to those narratives as well as offer alternative future heritage-making solutions. From an ethical perspective, as a critical heritage scholar, I see our role as to expose the 'truth' and this should be a main principal, as Badiou (2001) suggests, whether or not exposing this truth leads to engaging with political paradoxes. What I mean by 'exposing the truth' is taking people and communities, i.e. those we work with, and their issues seriously and empowering them to discuss their own truth in the research we conduct and collect data based on people's truth. In the words of the French philosopher, anthropologist and sociologist Bruno Latour (2004a, 246):

> The critic is not the one who debunks, but the one who assembles. The critic is not the one who lifts the rugs from under the feet of the naive believers, but the one who offers the participants arenas in which to gather. The critic is not the one who alternates haphazardly between antifetishism and positivism . . . but the one for whom, if something is constructed, then it means it is fragile and thus in great need of care and caution.

Therefore, the main question for critical heritage should be how we reach the truth that also shapes the level of criticality of research. As Witcomb and Buckley (2013, 562) say, reflecting on the Association of Critical Heritage Studies' manifesto (2011):

> We want to challenge you to . . . question the received wisdom of what heritage is, energise heritage studies by drawing on wider intellectual sources, vigorously question the conservative cultural and economic power relations that outdated understandings of heritage seem to underpin and invite the active participation of people and communities who to date have been marginalised in the creation and management of 'heritage'. Above all, we want you to critically engage with the proposition that heritage studies need to be rebuilt from the ground up, which requires the 'ruthless criticism of everything existing'.

Witcomb and Buckley (2013) suggest that critical heritage practices should engage and address social issues that are linked to heritage. Having agreed with their point, of course, the most important question for us, as critical heritage researchers, should be how we can be critical and can this criticality make us more creative in terms of addressing world issues and be the voice of the people. I argue that we need to expose the concept of 'criticality' in the heritage context first, rather than drawing conclusions. Being critical is, of course, significant in exposing the 'truth'; however, 'ruthless criticism of everything existing' should not be an approach and should not shape research. Research should be developed depending on the process that leads to it being critical. In theory, any research can be critical, but in practice – or, in other words, on the ground – an overt theoretical approach may clash with actual practice. I am not arguing that we should avoid theory. On the contrary, as critical theories are strictly linked to politics (Apple 2004, 2009), I argue that theory should be drawn in practice by considering dynamics of the cultural settings in which we research, or, in other words, theory should be developed in the process of the research that will lead to criticality as well as creativity, which will provide the ground to reflect on world issues.

What I would like to propose and argue here is that 'criticality' is not a theory or an approach in the heritage context but rather, a 'process' and 'method' that we apply in practice. As can be seen from each chapter of this book, criticality, or the reflexive interrogation of heritage research, acts as a process that frames every case study. My years of ethnographic fieldwork in these case studies have led me to being critical – I reflect on sociopolitical issues to cultural paradoxes, as well as political and economic decisions, and expose and critique injustices from a heritage perspective. However, this critical inquiry was developed through taking the views of participants in my ethnographic work seriously and making those views central in the research rather than enforcing my own assumptions.

I certainly argue that heritage studies are highly political and can reflect on world issues and provide ground for sustainability (Winter 2013); heritage studies itself is political as all of its data is collected from people. However, in order to be accurately critical and fully reflect on social and political issues, the methodological approach that we take (Apaydin 2018a, 2018b) and the methods we apply in practice should be designed by taking a 'people-centred process' through extensive and detailed ethnographic fieldwork. To achieve criticality, the process of the research is the utmost important stage. What the people-centred method brings to the process of research is a scope of reflexivity to and awareness of issues at the individual level that makes heritage research truly critical. In the case of this book, the people-centred processes certainly brought important benefits to the critical study of heritage and resulted in a malleable and creative approach to heritage discourses that involve social, political, economic and cultural parameters based on people's own experiences.

Theory and practice often create tension together as theoretical approaches to some practical cases seem not to apply, or vice versa. In fact, having a reflexive theoretical position (Davies 2012) on the ground, in the process of research itself, can help ease the tension between idea and practice and lead to the development of new theoretical approaches through the dynamics of specific research. Reflexivity in the process of research is at the heart of criticality, situating research inside the dynamics of the cultural settings in which we research. This kind of theoretical criticality cannot be separated from practice (Mason 2004); they feed on each other, which leads to constantly developing theoretical approaches. These depend also to some extent on the methods we apply on the ground, how they reflect on the locality of research, to what extent this locality is allowed to affect the research, and to what extent the researcher is reflecting on the locality in the result.

In many cases, locality is neglected by many researchers, who often take a top-down or colonial approach (McGuire 2008), but locality is everything for heritage studies – as it is, perhaps, for many other social sciences. Bakhtin (1981, 84), the philosopher of language and cultural historian, in his essays on *The Dialogic Imagination*, points out the importance of subjectivities and how they can emerge through narrating time and space in his concept of the *chronotope*: 'In the literary artistic chronotope ... time ... thickens, takes on flesh, becomes artistically visible; likewise, space becomes charged and responsive to the movements of time, plot and history.' This has inspired many scholars in postcolonial studies (Binter 2019) and has a clear application in heritage studies.

In the heritage context, I consider locality as a necessary of recognizing diversities, as in the concept of social justice (Fraser 1998). Recognizing locality means also taking into account the under-voiced, the minority and the oppressed groups in a time and place, or, in other words, all diversities. The application to social justice will become more apparent when I delve into more detail below and link it to material culture and human rights. Locality exposes, as seen in the case studies in this book, the authoritarian policies of undemocratic nation states that oppress local communities whose rights have been undermined, restricted and violated. A dominant power cannot recognize these fine-grained aspects of locality as they are a threat to national unity. The concept of locality itself clashes with the idea of nation (Appadurai 1995). Locality highlights values that communities develop through their relationship with the landscape, environment and material culture. Exposing locality is crucial as it brings local values and diminishes 'universal values' that are developed through the top-down approach of experts or elites. UNESCO's 'Outstanding Universal Value' is a good example to illustrate this type of approach: it is a part of the top-down process that prevents the incorporation of local meanings and local interpretation(s) of heritage.

Decolonization. This is, perhaps, one of the most significant subjects of critical heritage – reflecting on the colonial attitude in the heritage context (Smith 2005; Bennett 2004; Bennett et al. 2014). Although researchers in heritage studies have been tackling this issue for decades, there are still many academics and researchers whose research and work is still tainted by colonialism, where local knowledge and ideas are subsumed and hidden, as in the case of American archaeologists who worked in Mexico and approached their research with a Western, colonial outlook (McGuire 2008).

The case of southeast Turkey, home to Turkey's Kurdish ethnic minority but also a number of other ethnic identities, is one of the examples that demonstrate regional colonization that violates every right of local people, and how the Turkish state imposes knowledge, values and meanings on a region in a heritage context. For instance, all state museums' displays are designed only by experts and local interpretations of heritage are excluded. Similarly, although many archaeological projects are run in this region by archaeologists, locals are only used as labour. In heritage studies, one of the reasons that some institutions and academics still have a colonial attitude and use a top-down approach (deliberately or not) is that the methodological approach used does not allow them to decolonize knowledge and ideas, because this approach uses a top-down perspective that excludes locality and local interpretation as well as local values. By contrast, taking a people-centred approach during the research process provides ground for the decolonization of knowledge and ideas by acknowledging local values, meanings and interpretation. There are several critical components of a people-centred approach to heritage.

Redistribution of knowledge. A people-centred approach to heritage involves not only researchers themselves but also local people who are empowered to take roles and responsibilities that shape the research process. In other words, they play a main role, along with researchers, in data collection and interpretation. However, in many cases, the data collected is not accessible to local communities. Smith et al. (2018) demonstrate this with the case of indigenous intellectual property that was not accessible by indigenous people in Australia. While sharing and disseminating knowledge collected on the ground helps researchers and is ethical, it also helps the creativity and sustainability of local communities who can preserve, reconstruct and transform this knowledge for future generations.

Dialogue. Redistribution of knowledge itself is a necessary part of a people-centred approach. Within this sphere of research, there needs to be a dialogue between researchers and communities – this is the only way to democratize the research and make it multivocal. The dialogue involved in the research process is not what is currently used in archaeological, heritage and museum studies, which takes participatory engagement strategies in order to involve the public in the interpretation of material culture. Instead, the dialogue in the heritage research process that I am arguing for here is based on the ideas and methods of John Dewey (1997) and Paul Freire (1970). Both philosophers argue that learning is based on experiential process and conversational education. These terms, 'experiential' and 'conversational' processes, which can be understood as critical dialogue, have often been neglected in heritage studies when delving into the material culture to learn more about local values. In order to democratize the research process and create a bridge between heritage researchers and communities, as well as professionals and stakeholders, one should not be acting on another but in praxis as an action: 'people should be working with each other' (Freire 1970); this includes heritage researchers and local communities.

An example of these processes in action can be seen in collaborative projects, and have evident benefits, e.g. carrying out ethnographic studies together with local members will allow them to collect more accurate data. One such case was a study conducted in the Caltham Islands, where researchers were in 'dialogue' with 'the Moriori people' to develop a cultural database and heritage management plan (see Hollowell and Nicholas 2009). In the case of my own research with the Emotive project in Çatalhöyük, Turkey, we trained young locals to collaborate and conduct research together with us to contribute and a develop digital education kit for the public (Apaydin 2022). Dialogue is not only about understanding history, culture and heritage, but it is also an 'informed action' that is developed mutually to enhance local sustainability and, as a result, makes heritage research critical and creative as well as ethical.

Ethics. This is perhaps one of the most significant areas of heritage studies and as professionals, we often struggle to identify ethics in a heritage context (see more on ethics and heritage in Meskell and Pells 2005; Silverman and Ruggles 2007; Hamilakis and Duke 2008; Meskell 2010; Ireland and Schofield 2015; Schofield 2015). All research has to have a principle of ethics and researchers must identify and take actions on any ethical issues that our research faces (Ricoeur 1973, 2004). The issue of ethics is, of course, very complicated and has a long history. Since heritage is strongly linked to culture and people we, as heritage researchers, need to pay more attention to ethics in our work. Ethics can also be understood as the values those professionals or researchers have and their responsibility to lead research to improve sustainability. From a professional perspective, ethical practice is not imposing values onto communities but learning about community values that are ascribed to tangible and intangible heritage. Most importantly, from a professional perspective, ethics in process involves 'exposing the truth', which makes the level of criticality of research or, in other words, critical heritage. The concept of the research process needs to be established on the basis of 'truth' or, in other words, ethics must be of the utmost importance in the research. From a heritage research perspective, exposing truth can be explained by revealing all dynamics and discourses, and informing public about the research. In the 2010 World Archaeological Congress, Shepherd and Haber (2011, 109) made a significant point in their paper, 'What's up with WAC?', arguing that archaeological practice should be 'thoughtful, creative and politically informed modes of engagement between disciplinary discourses and local context'. This very much depends on the extent to which researchers or professionals apply ethics in their research, whether this is archaeological or heritage research or any that significantly involves people and material culture.

In heritage we should consider ethics not just as something that can be used as a tool but as the main framing device of our research in this field. Badiou (2001) points out that 'It is the principle that enables the continuation of a truth-process – or, to be more precise and complex, that which lends consistency to the presence of someone in the composition of the subject induced by the process of this truth.' The process of this truth in the heritage context can be considered as enabling and empowering people to actively and freely exercise their cultural activities and learn about their cultural background and heritage of the past and present. The ethical role of heritage professionals (Ireland and Schofield 2015) in the process of research is to encourage local and indigenous people to manage their own heritage at every stage and to provide the necessary resources. Enabling people to manage their own heritage is also very important, because heritage is a critical element of society and culture. It is also highly economic and political because it is a source for identity, belonging and memory that is vital for community survival.

In Chapter 5, I provide a case study for heritage of this ethical process and discuss dam constructions and their subversion of history, heritage, material culture and, most importantly, their impact on local communities who have been displaced and lost access to their lands and homes. In the case of the Ilisu Dam project in the Kurdish populated region of southeast Turkey (Ronayne 2006; Shoup 2006; Apaydin and Hassett 2019), hundreds of archaeologists from both local and international institutions were involved in saving archaeological objects and remains for more than twenty years. The twenty years of work and research largely neglected local heritage, values, identity and meaning of those lands that were flooded. The role and participation of those academics and professionals only served to save some archaeological objects while the destruction of the dam projects on people has never been discussed or questioned (also see Shoup 2006). This object- and material-based approach not only has clear ethical issues but also, as Noam Chomsky (2003, 3) in his book *Objectivity and Liberal Scholarship* emphasizes, 'the subversion of scholarship may pose a threat to society at large' and may be understood as an 'abuse of knowledge' when the knowledge gained from material culture is not used for the benefit of communities and instead just the academics themselves.

All in all, the question should not be whether critical heritage should be political, whether we should be criticizing everything that has come before and whether heritage's responsibility is to reflect on the world's social, cultural and economic issues. Rather, the question should be how the research process should be framed and how researchers should approach research, who benefits from the research, to what extent does heritage research reflect on people's and world issues at large, and how the research can be more beneficial for people. Heritage itself is overtly political already and there is no avoiding a critical approach, alongside critical theory and social, political, economic and cultural issues. All research is political and, of course, academics and professionals have a responsibility to reflect on the issues in the world through research without the 'subversion of scholarship'. As I pointed out above, many scholars do put this into practice (Butler 2006; Smith 2006; Winter 2013; Witcomb and Buckley 2013 and many more), but as cultural heritage itself is already involved in aspects of the political, social, cultural and economic life. Researchers within this field have a responsibility to reflect on these issues critically and creatively in their research.

Heritage emerges through the past and present actions of people, therefore heritage research should engage with contemporary issues from all angles – for example, contemporary politics and economics as well as long-term impacts of political and economic decisions that diminish cultural, natural and intangible heritage and, most importantly, communities. For instance, engaging with heritage and climate change also requires engaging with many social and political parameters that research and researchers cannot ethically ignore; they have a responsibility to question them. The destructive consequences of large infrastructure projects, such as the dam projects, can be seen as part of intense global neoliberal policies. This, of course, not only has social consequences but also environmental and ecological ones: these activities accelerate climate change because they transform landscapes and destroy the natural environment and processes (Harvey 2005; Parr 2013). Although climate change-related research has been conducted in heritage and museum studies from a critical perspective, this engagement should also offer solutions by putting forward action plans to tackle climate change and other issues, as the Horniman Museum London[1] has done recently by reflecting on what museums can do against increasing climate change. As critical heritage scholars, we need to critically approach the issue of climate change and question embedded discourses that lead to climate change and we need to question and investigate the political and economic decisions that lead to climate change. Particularly, intense neoliberal policies along with authoritarian approaches that transform nature and landscapes are accelerating climate change (Parr 2013) which affects heritage, as seen in the examples of southeast Turkey (see Chapter 5) and Brazil (Da Rocha 2017).

Politics, economics, culture and climate change are topics that cannot be ignored as they all intensely affect the lives of people who construct and transform cultural heritage, and they play a large role in increasing injustice, inequality and poverty. All of these impacts are also highly linked to rights and social justice, which are the main subjects of this book. Therefore, throughout this book, I attempt to contextualize the concepts of rights and social justice in relation to heritage making through using space, landscape and natural resources.

Rights

The concept of the rights of individuals or groups has been debated for a long time (Donnell 2013). There are still many issues that need to be discussed and resolved, particularly in relation to the rights associated with heritage: the right to access of land, the right to participate in cultural activities and to develop heritage, the right to learn, the right to distribute knowledge, and the right to be recognized (Logan 2012; Jokilehto 2012; Silberman 2012; Assi 2012; Ekern et al. 2012). Although discussions regarding human rights goes back to the eighteenth and nineteenth centuries (Ishay 2004), heritage was not considered part of human rights until the mid-twentieth century. The world wars in the first half of the twentieth century had destructive impacts on people, including their rights to heritage and cultural activities. These aspects were considered to be highly linked to each other in the 1948 Human Rights Declaration.

Just after the Second World War, the Universal Declaration of Human Rights in 1948, drafted by René Cassin, mostly focused on aspects of basic liberties, freedom of life and security of the people, expressing people's thoughts freely in any place in society, and practising religions freely (Ishay 2004). The main aspects were classified as 'dignity, liberty, equality and brotherhood' (Ishay 2004: 359) for individuals, groups and communities. The declaration essentially highlighted very basic human rights concepts, such as liberty, freedom of movement, freedom from torture and slavery, freedom of expression, conscience, religion, beliefs and cultural practices. Article 27, particularly, was a declaration more related to cultural heritage: 'everyone has the right freely to participate in the cultural life of the community, to enjoy the arts and to share in scientific advancement and its benefits' (Silverman and Ruggles 2007; Logan 2012, 2014).

Article 27, for the first time, introduced the notion that culture and cultural activity is a basic human right and should be protected through international agreements and international laws. This was, perhaps, the first time cultural heritage was protected by international law. It is always very problematic to define what 'heritage' is, because heritage varies in different parts of the world, as the meanings and values that are ascribed to it differ from one culture to another. However, what we are certain about is the processes by which heritage is developed and to what extent it is significant for people. Cultural heritage is developed through the interaction of people with nature, including for example the landscape, rivers, forests, as well as the participation of more than two people in a daily life or cultural activity that leads to developing a cultural identity, values, belonging and meanings. The cultural activity of more than two people's interaction with nature also develops a material culture that stores memories and acts as a symbol. Article 27 established that the right to freely engage in these is highly related to human rights. These rights are often breached and violated, both in peaceful times and also during times of armed conflicts and wars (Stone 2012). In 1954, after the traumatic experience of the Second World War, when many monumental objects of cultural life had been destroyed (as had also happened after the First World War), the United Nations Educational, Scientific and Cultural Organization (UNESCO) declared The Hague Convention[2] for the Protection of Cultural Property. In the event of armed conflict, the convention emphasized that cultural property, which is the universal heritage of humanity, must be protected.

The 1948 Human Rights Declaration and 1954 Hague Convention were generated after specific events, such as ethnic cleansing of many groups and the destruction of cultural heritage during the First and Second World Wars. However, conflicts developed over these declarations focused on the rights of culturally different peoples and communities. Therefore, in 1966, the UNESCO Declarations on the Principles of International Cultural Cooperation (Langfield et al. 2010, 5) stated more explicitly that in relation to human rights, human dignity and culture:

> Each culture has a dignity and value which must be respected and preserved. Every people has the right and duty to develop its culture . . . In their rich variety and diversity . . . all cultures form part of the common heritage belonging to all mankind.

These basic rights were also emphasized in the 1966 International Covenant on Economic, Social and Cultural Rights[3] (ICESCR). Article 1 explicitly stated:

> All peoples have the right of self-determination. By virtue of that right they freely determine their political status and freely pursue their economic, social and cultural development. (ICESCR Article 1, 1966)

Although many countries from all over the world, as part of the United Nations (UN), signed these declarations, these statements have not been effective in practice in many places where the rights and heritage of minority groups were neglected, and where local people have been excluded from the decision-making process. As in the case studies from Turkey discussed in this book, those minority groups' economic, social and cultural development rights have been barred. Here, the main reason for this is that those minority groups with their unique culture and values do not fit the official ideology and national narrative of Turkey, which sees those groups as a threat to national unity. Along with Turkey, many undemocratic nation states implement similar methodology to prevent those minority groups exercising and performing cultural activities (see Silverman and Ruggles 2007 for the examples of South America and many others). Perhaps, most importantly, the right to perform cultural heritage has been restricted through banning access to the lands for local communities (see Chapters 4 and 5 for the Kurdish case in southeast Turkey).

After the construction of modern nation states, consciously or unconsciously, much of minority heritage was either destroyed, not identified as cultural heritage, or their locality given a different identity that is assimilated under national identity and heritage. Philp (2010) demonstrates this with the case study of Myanmar where the military rule of the State Peace and Development Council ignored sub-national heritage, or in other words heritage of the minority groups to create a national heritage (Logan 2012, 237, 38). In 1972, the World Heritage Convention was declared (Langfield et al. 2010, 6), which more clearly elucidated aspects of cultural heritage in relation to the concept of 'rights'. However, some have argued that local heritage was not critically considered or given attention (Harrison 2013a, 145; Labadi 2007). In 2003, with the Convention for the Safeguarding of Intangible Heritage[4] (ICH) (Langfield et al. 2010, 6), intangible practices such as oral histories, traditions, skills, knowledge, songs, dance and music were also included in the heritage concept. Prior even to this, in 1960, UNESCO adopted 'Discrimination in Education'[5] and aimed to challenge the discrimination of minority groups and their access to equal learning about their own culture and history. The Universal Declaration of

Human Rights Article 26 stated that 'every individual has the right to learn their background and has the right to education'.[6] In other words, the rights to have an education and to learn about their own history and heritage became a part of human rights. However, these rights – performing cultural heritage, participating in cultural events, recognition of local and ethnic heritage and history, protecting and preserving heritage – have the right to transform the heritage and make new heritage, and the opportunity to learn about heritage has often been violated in particularly undemocratic and authoritarian nation states.

The early declarations and statements that were signed by many state parties were vague because cultural heritage was never clearly defined. However, in 2005, the Faro Convention or the Council of Europe Framework Convention on the Value of Cultural Heritage for Society,[7] as a treaty, more clearly defined cultural heritage. Article 1 states that 'rights relating to cultural heritage are inherent in the right to participate in cultural life' and Article 4 of the treaty states that 'everyone has the right to benefit from the cultural heritage and to contribute towards its enrichment'. Although all these international treaties and conventions aim at protecting the rights of people and many states signed these treaties and conventions, they mainly stay in the theoretical realm and, in many parts of the world, they are not applied in practice. This is one of the greatest failings of these treaties: they are weak in the implementation of those articles in practice.

There remain many nation states that refuse to recognize the cultural rights of minorities – for example, the case of the Kurds and Alevis in Turkey, which denies cultural rights definable as anything that is valuable to the Kurdish people, such as language, lifestyle, traditions or intangible and tangible heritage such as monuments, houses or the natural landscapes of mountains or rivers (discussed further in Chapter 5). This is despite being a signatory to the International Covenant on Civil and Political Rights[8] (ICCPR), Article 27, in 1966, which states:

> in those States in which ethnic, religious or linguistic minorities exist, persons belonging to such minorities shall not be denied the right, in community with other members of their group, to enjoy their own culture, to profess their own religion, or to use their own language.

Of course, there are many discourses hidden under the denial of minority groups' heritage and rights in nation states because of the strong link with 'the protection of traditional territories' (Logan et al. 2010, 10), because the territories are a source and are representative of sociocultural identities (Gilbert 2010, 31) and because the landscapes are 'heritage resources' (Harvey 2011) for communities.

Another significant issue of human rights that is strongly linked to heritage is 'access and exclusion' (Silverman and Ruggles 2007, 9). Obstructing the access of communities to their heritage is a breach of the 1948 Human Rights declaration, which stated that everybody should be able to enjoy and to practise their cultural life without any restrictions (Silverman and Ruggles 2007, 4). This is often implemented in specific regions of Turkey. For instance, Sur, as part of the Diyarbakir Fortress and Hevsel Gardens UNESCO World Heritage Site in southeast Turkey, is culturally significant for local communities. The site of Sur, which has monumental architecture containing memories for many identity groups, was off limits for locals during the period of conflict between the state and the Kurdistan Workers' Party in 2015 and afterwards, and previous residents were displaced. Until recently, many evicted Kurdish people were also not allowed to come back to their villages and land, where they had attached meanings and developed memories and values, because of the conflict in the region. There are many other examples from all over the world. However, it has to be pointed out that cultural heritage is a basic human need, and the destruction, expulsion and exclusion from access and practice or restriction of performing cultural heritage is certainly a breach of human rights that should be recognized and confronted everywhere in the world.

Most research and publications that focus on heritage and rights consider human rights and heritage from a very object- and material-based perspective and only focus on the preservation and protection of material culture. I do not argue that preservation is not important, but what is more important is the rights of individuals and groups who construct material culture and who have the right to preserve or transform or even destroy their own heritage. Therefore, the concept of rights should include first the protection of people. Without people, who may be displaced or forced to leave their lands, heritage cannot be performed and material culture cannot be developed.

Particularly in many authoritarian and undemocratic nation states, many communities and individuals have been prevented from learning about their own culture and exercising diverse cultural activities; access to cultural sites have been restricted; and cultural spaces where people carry on cultural activities and develop heritage have been destroyed through large developments, such as dams or gentrification projects (Apaydin 2020a). The list goes on – but the question is that while the interconnection of cultural heritage and human rights is clear and there have been attempts to protect these under international laws, what is the relationship between social justice, heritage and human rights?

Social justice

In heritage studies, the concept of social justice has been tackled very recently and it is an area of study that needs more reflection and narration to contextualize it. Although scholars, such as Baird (2014), Labadi (2018), Sandell and Nightingale (2019), Waterton and Smith (2010) and Joy (2020) have attempted to explore the subject, the questions of how we perceive social justice as heritage scholars, how it can be placed in theory, what it represents from a heritage perspective in grassroot level, and how heritage scholars can apply this concept in heritage practice to promote social justice still need to be explored and delved into more deeply with more research and case studies. Nancy Fraser (1989, 1998, 2000, 2003, 2009), a critical theorist, defines social justice through three dimensions, namely 'redistribution', 'recognition', and 'representation'.

The first type, 'redistribution' (Fraser, 1998) makes a redistributive claim and seeks equal distribution of wealth from the North to the South. Here, the North refers to northern parts of the world that hold much of the wealth and control the resources and the South refers to southern parts of the world that have the resources but are not given enough wealth and resources or rights to control the resources. The redistribution is from the rich to the poor and from owners to workers, to use a different example. Or, in other words, the redistribution concept seeks the egalitarian distribution of resources. Cultural heritage is considered a cultural production which provides resources and knowledge to communities. The basic and effective way of redistributing this knowledge is education in every part of the world where communities can transform their heritage and knowledge to their members and future generations. However, this basic right – to be able to redistribute heritage knowledge and learning – has been restricted in many authoritarian regimes in which breaches occur in Article 27 of the Universal Declaration of Human Rights, The Hague Convention, as well the UNESCO declaration on 'Discrimination in Education'. This intentional breach of human rights in learning about their own past, history and heritage is also strongly linked to the second dimension of social justice.

Fraser (1998, also see 2000, 2003) goes further and argues that what we see today is a second type of claim for social justice, which is also related to earlier definitions of social justice but in different contexts. Fraser terms it 'political recognition'. The aim and purpose of political recognition is 'recognition of differences and diversities of the world'; this is strongly linked to Article 27 of the Universal Declaration of Human Rights in 1948 and the ICCPR declaration in 1966 that both emphasized the importance of diversities and protection of minority rights, which is linked to the concept of recognition. This is severely neglected by undemocratic nation states and that has undermined diversities. I will get back to nationalism in detail in Chapter 2, but it is important to point out that the use of nationalism increased in the second half of the twentieth century. Following the Second World War, most nation states aimed to consolidate their power through increasing nationalist policies that have undermined or neglected identity of religious and ethnic minority groups (Anderson 1983). Within this period, we have seen the increasing assimilation of minorities and different ethnic backgrounds (Panayi 2000), as well as discrimination based on sexuality and gender which remain big issues in many parts of the world. In this very sensitive context, political recognition seeks justice for all those groups and individuals who have been undermined and oppressed, and who have had their rights breached. In other words, political recognition claims recognition and equal treatment for the distinct ethnic, racial and sexual minorities and gender differences (Fraser 1998, 2013) that are also protected with the Universal Declaration of Human Rights, ICCPR, UNESCO and in many other international charters and institutions.

Social justice is also strongly linked to human rights from the point where the communities themselves should be the ones who make their own decisions regarding managing, transforming and performing social, cultural and economic development as well as cultural heritage. This has been neglected in most declarations and conventions as well as museums and heritage sites where communities are either represented at a low level or totally excluded. This is linked to the 'representation' dimension of social justice, according to Nancy Fraser (2009), who emphasizes the importance of representation in order to decrease inequalities. Her focus here is inclusion or exclusion of communities in the decision-making process, especially at a political level. In other words, she discusses possibilities of people-centred decision-making process by giving voice to people. Fraser (2009) further explores the representation dimension of social justice by dividing into three sub-dimensions: 'ordinary-political, framing, and metapolitical'. The three sub-dimensions are strongly linked to the heritage and museum decision-making process and have the potential to direct research towards more inclusive and people-centred practice. For instance, ordinary-political representation focuses on the process of decision making, such as 'inclusion', and how diverse voices can be included in the decision-making process, which has been discussed but is still a major issue in heritage and museum practices.

The second sub-dimension, 'framing', focuses on how this process can be collaborative (Calvert and Warren 2014) by discussing who is recognized and allowed into the decision-making process. We in heritage and museum practice very often experience this dilemma while developing heritage management plans or museum exhibitions and displays. Also when working with only some community members or only a certain representative of communities (or when communities are totally excluded, as in many cases), and some people are excluded from the decision-making process. This creates further ethical questions, as community leaders or representatives may not be able to voice the whole community and may bring their own agendas. In other words, they may act as the agent of exclusion itself.

Linked to the first and second, the third sub-dimension, 'metapolitical', seeks to expose where and how participation in decision making takes place, how the power of decision making shifts from state level to institutions. While this dimension may vary for different parts of the world, as some museums and heritage sites are managed centrally by the state and decisions are taken through top-down approach, for some countries, such as the UK, museums and heritage sites are able to act independently in their decision making. However, for such cases the question should be how decision making should shift from the museums as institutions and heritage sites to people and communities.

The three dimensions of social justice raises an important question for heritage context: why do we need an approach to practice that is strongly linked to human rights and concerns itself with equality and diversity? Heritage and museums have a large role in materializing these concepts and in closing the gap that was created in the last couple of decades. The gap was created through traditional understanding of heritage and museum and/or old museology studies which was only object-based, avoided engaging with sociopolitical issues and excluded communities from interpreting their own heritage and material culture as well as any decision-making process rather than including and supporting communities. This is the main reason that heritage has an important role in cultural and political life and must stand for these values. Museums and cultural heritage institutions cannot be 'neutral' (Tourle 2020) as they store the knowledge of people through material culture of the past and present, and this knowledge also frames certain themes that are linked to human rights and ethics.

Some of these themes can be explored through these questions: How can heritage create a ground for knowledge making and identity construction for individuals and communities? How has specific heritage been privileged by elites of the society and some heritage has been 'othered'? What are the discourses of neglect of some specific heritage? What would be the best way for equal distribution of heritage knowledge to claimants? What are the obstacles around this? How can all diverse heritage be recognized and threated equally? What are the discourses of heritage policies that neglect some of the heritage and privilege some? What is the best way of developing ground for diverse groups and individuals to take roles, control and make their own decisions in managing their heritage?

Certainly, heritage needs to be more diverse, inclusive and people-centred, and the issues of the social justice concepts of 'redistribution', '(mis)recognition' and 'representation' need to be overcome. In practice, to overcome these issues, different methods should be applied, for example, participatory action research, people-centred research and many more. These issues and questions can be dealt with at heritage sites and museums which can more effectively reflect on justice and rights issues. In recent decades we have seen a rapid increase in community engagement and community education programmes (Merriman 2004; Moshenska 2017; Apaydin 2018a, 2018b). These programmes can serve to close the gap that developed through formal education, which many undemocratic and democratic nation states use to implement and conserve their own official ideology. However, this is also only possible (and to a variable extent) if these programmes are critical, inclusive, participatory and people-centred (Apaydin 2018a, 2018b). In other words, it depends on the goal and process of these programmes, the extent that we are reflexive and what we know about the community and audience that we work with, because the community is a complex and powerful concept (Bauman 2001; Waterton and Smith 2010; Merriman 2004; Wetherell 2007). As Cohen (1985, 98) pointed out:

> Community exists in the minds of its members, and should not be confused with geographic or sociographic assertions of fact. By extension, the distinctiveness of communities and, thus, the reality of their boundaries, similarly lies in the mind, in the meanings which people attach to them, not in the structural forms.

Within this complex but powerful structure of community, community engagement programmes need to be designed to reflect, in parallel, each community's differences and needs. This design is a process that has links to theory and practice, decolonization, locality, redistribution of knowledge and ethics. The link between heritage and social justice is not only about inclusion and representation (Baird 2014) but also it is an equal distribution of knowledge that we get from material culture, which also often creates inequality (Smith et al. 2022). Recognition of community cohesion and values, as well as giving a voice to community members, is particularly crucial for the people-centred approach. In other words, social justice concepts in heritage should be in action (Johnston and Marwood 2017). All research needs to engage politically and critically with issues, and as Waterton and Smith (2010, 12) point out, we need to seek 'to deinstitutionalize patterns of cultural participation, particularly those directed by an uncritical and unhelpful notion of "community"'. People should have the opportunity and ground to engage however they wish to, as Rachel Kiddey (2017, 4) points out:

> People have the right to engage with the pasts with which they identify, and it is therefore important that the processes by which they are engaged are genuine and flexible enough that everyone may be included ... The task of the heritage professional is, [therefore], to work with diverse groups to establish narratives representative of all ways to be human, past and present.

As in the education context social justice should be a 'process and goal' (Bell 2016; Hackman 2005), this is true in the heritage context as well, because heritage is a process developed alongside the needs and purposes of people. In this process, community participation must be of utmost importance while research is conducted (May 2019; Johnston and Marwood 2017). Community-based research – or as I call it, a 'people-centred research process' – collaborates with community members, includes them in every stage of the research, avoids tokenistic approach, centres citizen power in the research and enables community members to interpret data that is collected. While the 'people-centred research process' provides ground for the recognition of different and under-voiced communities, it also provides ground for an ethical interpretation that is based on people's voices (Kamash 2019). Since the data is collected through people, the knowledge produced through this data collection will be equally redistributed and managed by community-based researchers again.

A good example of a case study that illustrates people-centred research in a heritage context and how it works from an ethical perspective and links to social justice, is a study of collaborating with Aboriginal communities of Australia regarding their heritage. The Barunga Community Archaeology Field School, which has been running over twenty years, provides knowledge to students about Aboriginal culture. This kind of archaeology school is common in many parts of the world, but the difference here is that the students of Barunga schools learn Aboriginal knowledge and culture from Aboriginal people who also collaborate with archaeologists (Smith et al. 2021). Another good case study that shows community action research which is also based on the people-centred approach is Research for Community Heritage in Sheffield and Rotherham in the UK. In this project, researchers actively engage with community members and NGOs (Johnston and Marwood 2017). The aim of one of their research projects is to look at the history of a specific building dating from the 1700s and today used as a hostel for young homeless people. They work with the residents of the hostel and give them training in how to do research and this is the main aim of the project, not reaching some conclusion or knowledge outcome. This is not only significant from a people-centred research perspective but also from social justice, as they also provide a skill development opportunity to young homeless people, which they can use to take a role in social and cultural life.

While the design of heritage programmes or research is significant for engaging with communities to place social justice concepts in heritage practice, it is also significant to approach the links between social justice and human rights, expose these links and apply them ethically in heritage practice. In the heritage context, from the redistribution and recognition perspectives, social justice can be centred in many areas of heritage, which are also directly linked to human rights and ethics. For instance, in many nation states that are centred round a specific ethnicity and identity, the minority groups' heritage and history are often neglected and undermined in the history textbooks used in schools (see Chapter 2 for the Turkish case; see Bilmez et al. 2017 for the Armenian case).

Since schools are the most effective way for learning and the distribution of knowledge, which has a large role in transforming knowledge for future generations, most of the minority groups or marginalized groups do not get an equal share to the dominant groups or identity groups. This is because the authorized heritage discourse of those countries that are controlled by specific ethnic and identity groups, who have the power, do not recognize those minority groups' existence and therefore their heritage and identity. This is one of the areas in which human rights, social justice and ethics are highly linked to each other. I will demonstrate this linkage further with the case studies in the rest of this book, but it is crucial to point out that this kind of neglect is a breach of human rights, according to the UNESCO and ICCPR declarations that strongly reflect on the diversities of culture, recognition and protection.

Considering the first concept of social justice, 'redistribution', in a heritage context, the knowledge that is gained from material culture, natural heritage and intangible heritage as well as intellectual property must be shared with the communities and the public. The authenticity of cultural heritage, which has so much diversity with its values and meanings for different groups and communities, should be recognized and this knowledge should be equally redistributed to its owners and the general public. To illustrate these connections is an example from Burra in the mid-north of South Australia, with the story of Vincent Copley, who is indigenous and from the Ngadjuri lands. While his story below is about access and sharing knowledge, it is also very much related to human rights, social justice and ethics, because his grandfather's knowledge that was collected by an anthropologist was not accessible:

> My grandfather, Barney Warria, worked closely with the anthropologist Ronald Berndt when Berndt was a young man, about 18 years of age. After Berndt passed away in 1990, there was an embargo on his field notes for 30 years. We were moved off our lands in the late eighteenth and early nineteenth centuries, not long after British colonisers came to South Australia. We lost a lot of cultural knowledge. Native title came in and we needed access to Berndt's field notes to sort things out. There was some disagreement between Berndt and Tindale in terms of some of Tindale's genealogies, and we wanted to know whether our grandfather had been part of that. They did not want to give us access. It was a real battle. I couldn't understand it. Those notes are of conversations with my grandfather. I have a right to see what he said. (Smith et al. 2018, 9)

Article 5 of the 2001 Universal Declaration on Cultural Diversity[9] underlines the relationship of human rights, social justice and ethics:

> Cultural rights are an integral part of human rights, which are universal, indivisible and interdependent. The flourishing of creative diversity requires the full implementation of cultural rights ... All persons have therefore the right to express themselves and to create and disseminate their work in the language of their choice, and particularly in their mother tongue; all persons are entitled to quality education and training that fully respect their cultural identity; and all persons have the right to participate in the cultural life of their choice and conduct their own cultural practices, subject to respect for human rights and fundamental freedoms.

Considering heritage from an academic and professional perspective and contextualizing social justice in heritage studies, it needs to be as inclusive as possible and the redistribution of knowledge, recognition of all diversities and providing ground for learning all minority and marginalized groups have to be top priorities. In a museum context, inclusion is directly linked to social justice (Sandell and Nightingale 2012), demanding not only that the stories cultural institutions tell become reflective of a range of different experiences, but that members of marginalized groups themselves should be afforded both a greater say in shaping and increased access to institutional resources (Baird 2014). While heritage is seen as an ontology and narrative, and museums are representatives of these narratives, heritage sites and material culture of the past and present are significant for representation or, in other words, for the recognition of history, culture and heritage. It certainly plays a crucial role in the redistribution of knowledge that those objects store. Therefore, museums and heritage institutions sit in the centre of social justice, human rights and ethics. Museums and heritage organizations, as well as academics, need to reflect more effectively and be equal in the redistribution of heritage, which is possible in people-centred processes.

Although current trends in heritage management plans are participatory in many countries of Europe, the top-down approach is still common in many parts of the world, such as Brazil (Da Rocha 2020), Turkey (Apaydin 2020b) and many more. This approach excludes communities from managing their own heritage and prevents them getting an equal share from the knowledge production of those material cultures. Heritage management plans should be designed and applied in practice to acknowledge and recognize communities and heritage that they develop and to ensure the equal distribution of knowledge through heritage practices. Therefore, in the heritage context, first, social justice is the equal distribution of knowledge or intellectual property; second, the recognition of diversity that is ascribed to cultural, natural and intangible heritage; third, the encouragement and empowerment of communities to learn, construct and reconstruct, transform and develop new heritage through heritage institutions; and fourth, the provision of ground for people and communities to make decisions and manage their heritage and cultural institutions.

2

Oppression

With the introduction of the concept of neoliberalism, with its idea of the 'free market' and increased globalization (Harvey 2005), it was often argued that nation states began to decline and that the new global order dampened down nationalism (Winter 2015; Bulmer and Solomos 2012; Hardt and Negri 2001). However, in the last couple of decades, there has been one of the largest forced migrations since 2010, which has led to a new development in the West, particularly in Europe, whereby nationalism transformed into new form: 'right-wing populism' (Kaya 2019). This form of populism is based on propagating 'Europeanism' as an ideology, using history and the past (Hoffmann et al. 2021). This transformation from nationalism to right-wing populism has also been seen in Turkey since the Justice and Development Party (JDP) took power in 2002. Both nationalism, especially in the twentieth century, and populism in the twenty-first century created national narratives to impose their ideologies and political agendas, and key aspects of this included heritage and material culture (Atakuman 2008; Apaydin 2018c; Zencirci 2014) in Turkey as well as nations in Europe.

Although nationalism and populism are two different concepts, they often coexist and sustain authoritarian regimes in combination. In Turkey, nationalism has been used to support a political ideology, which is based on 'Turkishness' and the 'one nation, one state' concept, since 1923 when the Turkish Republic was established. In general, all political parties and Turkish elites, who had been in power up to the point when the JDP took power in 2002, focused on preserving the national narratives, centred around the notion of Turkishness, which were developed during the first two decades of the Turkish Republic (Ersanli 2003). In contrast, the JDP used populism as a tool to set the public against those Turkish elites who had been in power for almost eighty years. The JDP used populism as a 'political strategy', in contrast to 'political ideology', to create division among the people of Turkey and to take power. However, after being in power for over twenty years (2002–23), the JDP has created its own elites, who control and use all state communication tools, including schools and museums and other forms of learning spaces, to impose their own political agendas by developing populist and often ideological narratives. These narratives centre around creating a 'new Turkey', which is based on Islam and Ottomanism. As such, the use of populism as a political strategy eventually turned into a political ideology in Turkey. For instance, in line with the idea of the 'new Turkey', the JDP made major changes in the school curriculum, with religion and Ottoman history and values being allocated more prominence. The JDP also established new museums such as the Topkapi Palace Museum (Kinikoglu 2021) and the Panorama 1453 Historical Museum (Posocco 2018), which promote the JDP's ideology.

Within this ideological atmosphere, education is often used to promote a specific nationalist as well as ideological and populist narratives using heritage and to oppress the 'others', i.e. those not from the dominant groups. In countries such as Turkey where education is centrally controlled and managed, it is used as a tool to spread imaginary national narratives to support the government's own ideological discourses. In other words, both formal and informal education have become effective tools to oppress people whose ethnic backgrounds and/or religious beliefs and identities are not in line with Turkish national narratives. While this kind of oppression can be seen in school textbooks, which neglect the diverse histories and heritage of Turkey and impose Turkishness and the 'Turkish official ideology', it can also be seen in informal learning spaces such as museums and heritage sites, where displays and public interpretation panels do not reflect diversity (Apaydin 2022). For instance, although Armenians, Kurds and Greeks have lived in Turkey, represented by substantial populations, for a long time, their histories and heritage are not given the attention that they deserve. While this is linked to the human rights, as I discussed in the previous chapter, this also leads to injustices and becomes a form of oppression.

These forms of oppression are systematic and structural, particularly in nation states (Young 1990). In these countries, especially those with authoritarian regimes, oppression is embodied in different forms. Iris Marion Young (1990, 41) discusses the 'five faces of oppression' – exploitation, marginalization, powerlessness, cultural imperialism and violence – that have explicitly been implemented in Turkey's educational and cultural institutions, both before and during the JDP periods. Young further argues that, in these types of oppressive regimes, people are exploited through their labour and marginalized because of their belief systems and collective identities and, therefore, they become powerless and are prevented from using cultural and educational resources. For instance, the Kurdish and Alevi communities, whose identities and belief systems are different to the majority in Turkey (see Chapters 4 and 5) and thus do not fit within the official Turkish ideology and national narratives, have been excluded from all cultural and educational resources, particularly in the formal education context, which is structural in Turkey (and many other nation states (Apple 2004)). Further, Lee Anne Bell (2016) defines oppression as 'restrictive, pervasive, and cumulative; socially constructed, categorising, and group based; hierarchical, normalised and hegemonic; intersectional and internalised; and durable and mutable'. These features of oppression have been systematically implemented in Turkey for the last hundred years, thus affecting many generations of those minority groups, many of whom have lost their collective identities, sense of belonging and communities, and have been forced to accept official narratives that dictate an 'authorised heritage discourse'.

In this chapter, I will discuss how Turkey's nationalist approach to cultural heritage and material culture first developed and then turned into a tool to promote right-wing populism in the twenty-first century under an authoritarian government. I will then look at how nationalist and populist policies and ideologies were developed and spread through formal education to create the 'one nation, one history and one heritage' policy, which oppressed 'others' in favour of the 'imagined communities' (Anderson 1983). I will also discuss how ethnic and religious minority groups' right to learn and right to be recognized has been completely neglected and how their heritage has been erased or omitted in textbooks.

National narratives

In 2014, I was doing ethnographic fieldwork, looking at the heritage perception of local communities in Turkey. One of my case studies was a UNESCO World Heritage Site:[1] Hattusha, the capital of the Hittite Empire in the second millennium BC. The archaeological site of Hattusha affects much of the perception of history with its city remains, art, cuneiform writing, etc. It is also one of the first excavations of the Turkish Republic and the Turkish elite had a high regard for this site. It was argued that the Hittites were Turkic and built one of the first civilizations in Anatolia, and that, therefore, the Turks have the right of ownership over the land. The site, with its long heritage and high importance in Turkish history, played an important role in the identity construction in the national narratives and in the construction of nationalism in the early years of the Turkish Republic (Atakuman 2008). The site, its heritage and its uses were significant for Turkish nationalism. Along with other case studies in Turkey, I aimed to look at how local communities around Hattusha see the site's heritage and history. I wanted to see how they were connected to this heritage and whether they saw it as their own heritage, or if they saw it as a heritage at all. In other words, what was the importance of the site at a local level?

The site is right next to a town where the locals have lived for generations. On my first day, I visited the archaeological site. The remains and the landscape of the site were stunning (Figure 2.1). The rest of the day, I was walking in the town, visiting local shops and having tea with local inhabitants of the town to establish rapport between myself and community members. I set up interview dates and times with several people. On the second day, one of the archaeologists who worked on the site recommended that I see the site gates and reconstructed site walls in the early morning before sunrise. The following day, I got up before sunrise and walked up to the site, and was able to see the spectacle of two Hittite kings and a huge Turkish flag in the middle projected across the whole of the reconstructed city walls (Figure 2.2) through digital light installations, funded by the local governor. This demonstrates how the archaeological heritage here still plays a significant role in defining nationalism and Turkish ethnicity even

Figure 2.1 Overview of Hattusa Archaeological site. © Veysel Apaydin.

Figure 2.2 Reconstruction of Hittite city wall with Hittite kings and modern Turkish flag. © Veysel Apaydin.

though the argument that the Hittites were the first Turks was dropped from the national discourse decades ago for lack of proof.

After completing my fieldwork, I went to Ankara, the Turkish capital city. While I was sitting in front of the coach, the first thing that I noticed was the large Turkish flags waving on top of 50m high iron posts when we entered the city, and that all the government buildings also had large Turkish flags. Although this was a national day when all streets, houses and government buildings are adorned with flags and posters, even on an ordinary day, these flags can still be seen as national symbols. The scenes speak of the 'unbreachable coupling of nationalism, history and symbols' (Winter 2015). I considered that although globalization was on the rise and that the nationalism of the early Turkish Republic had been replaced with right-wing populism, hundreds of years of argument and use of nationalism meant that the past was still popular. The nationalist use of the past does not lose its popularity, as can be seen from many examples all around the world. The concepts of the past and heritage have often been used for the state's national interest because it is based on a certain ethnicity and identity; all states create their own 'imagined communities', which Anderson

(1983) emphasized are important for national narratives, even for the globalized world.

The world has witnessed a dramatic increase in globalization because of the impact of neoliberalism since the 1980s and surge in the use of digital technology in every part of our life. This has brought a high number of transnational interactions between countries, communities and groups in every part of the world (Hardt and Negri 2001; Urry 2003; Winter 2015). However, I argue that heritage and archaeology are one of these areas that prove nationalism is still on the rise in many parts of the world. For example, cultural heritage or material culture plays a great role in many conflicts today: groups in conflict claim their rights to own land by demonstrating and propagating material culture, including monuments and architectural heritage. This can be seen in many examples, for instance, the Cyprus conflict in the 1970s (Apaydin 2020b), the Bosnia and Kosovo conflict in the 1980s and 1990s (Walasek 2015), the recent Nagorno Karabakh conflict between the Armenians and Azeris and conflicts in Africa. Similarly, the idea and motivation behind the rise of right-wing populism and nationalism across Europe today is based on claiming a cultural heritage, or 'Europeanism' (Aykan 2019), which is often supported by populist approaches to any historical, social, economic and political issue. European Union Foreign Policy Chief Joseph Borrell recently stated that 'Europe is a garden ... most of the rest of the world is a jungle'. While the statement has many discourses that need to be examined, such as neo-colonialism, it also is strongly connected to a heritage linked with the reconstruction identity of Europeanism, placing it in the centre of inequality issues between the Global North and Global South.

The examples mentioned above show that while groups seek to exert power over other groups, in some cases they also destroy the other groups' symbols that are often tangible and monumental heritage. Every nation selects certain knowledge from the past to consolidate its hegemony and uses this knowledge for propagation of national narratives (see Anderson 1983). However, in most cases, we witness manipulation of history through material of the past (Eriksen 2010) to support the national interest. Hence, it is either a created or invented tradition (Hobsbawm and Ranger 1983). It is also used for creating single communities (Eriksen 2010) by eliminating the multicultural structure and material culture of 'others' of the lands.

The use of the material culture of the past and present for political purposes is not something new or unique to Turkey. It is one of the most common and effective ways of claiming ownership rights for specific lands, glorifying the nation's history, as well as oppressing minority groups, who are seen as a threat to national unities in many nation states. In particular, archaeological practices and the material culture of antiquities are seen as a resource for a mythological foundation to construct a modern nation (Winter 2015). There are many examples that illustrate the use of material culture for nationalism. Greece is an example of a state that has a long history in claiming the past of its lands, and making a connection with its national identity. Greeks see themselves as the heir of Hellenism and classical antiquities and argue that they are the processor of modern civilization and the foundation of European culture (Hamilakis 2007; Greenberg and Hamilakis 2021). Using Hellenism to claim the past and to being precoders of modern civilizations not only provided ground for national identity construction but also provided Greeks 'territorial and historical' continuity (Hamilakis 2007; Winter 2015). As Hamilakis emphasizes (2007, 79):

> It was the materiality of ancient sites, buildings, remnants, and artefacts, their physicality, visibility, tangible nature, and embodied presence, that provided the objective (in both senses of the word) reality of the nation. It was their sense of longevity, and their aura of authenticity that endowed them with enormous symbolic power.

In the case of Greece, the use of archaeological remains for constructing national identity goes back to the nineteenth century and continued through the twentieth century. Of course, archaeology and classical fields played a large role in this process (Trigger 2006; Kohl and Fawcett 1995; Diaz-Andreu and Champion 1996; Diaz-Andreu 1995, 2007; Meskell 1998; Winter 2015). With neoliberal policies, cultural resources have become something to consume and make profit from – or, in other words, they are marketized (Silberman 2007; Labrador and Silberman 2018). They have become a cultural product that can be consumed without acknowledging the value, authenticity and meanings (Apaydin 2016b). However, the use of material culture for consolidating specific ethnic groups' hegemony and to oppress others has never lost its importance. This can be illustrated by analysing many nation states' formal education systems, which are heavily dominated by national discourses. They are designed mostly on historical narratives (Gellner 1983; MacKenzie and Stone 1990) in order to create and consolidate the idea of 'one nation, one state'.

Developing national narratives through using the past and material culture has certainly been very effective in forming public perception. For instance, Sakellariadi (2011) conducted a large survey among local Greek communities who live near important archaeological remains. Many local community members consider that 'ancient monuments of the past for Greek national identity are significant' and they consider that 'Greek archaeology's national mission is to prove Greece's glorious past'. Many of them value archaeological remains in their relation to Greek national identity or history.

The UNESCO World Heritage Convention can also demonstrate the use and abuse of material culture by nation states. The UNESCO World Heritage Listing (WHL) has certain criteria in terms of value and meanings of the heritage sites that can be inscribed on the WHL.[2] However, many nation states abuse this international arena by either marketing heritage in order to bring more tourists to the country or claiming the past by putting national labels on the material culture (Meskell 2018). The Preah Vihear heritage site, which lies between Thailand and Cambodia, has been highly contested as both countries claim it as part of their past. The site was listed in Cambodia's UNESCO World Heritage List in 2008 and this led to high political tension between Cambodia and Thailand (Winter 2010, 2015; Silverman 2010). What I am trying to argue here is that an international organization, such as UNESCO, has been used by many nation states to prove their national identity and consolidate it by being named as the 'owner' of those heritage sites, which are then marketized. Meskell (2018) analyses the structure of the UNESCO World Heritage Convention and points out that most heritage sites that are listed as World Heritage, as in the case of Turkey, also serve to consolidate the national unity of those nation states (Meskell 2018). Along with Turkey and Greece, other countries such as India, Italy, Israel, Egypt, and many more have also used material culture or heritage to promote nationalism (Winter 2015).

Abuse of material culture to promote nationalism, use it to oppress others, erasing minorities, who are being considered a threat, purify lands to conserve hegemony of a single ethnic group, have a long history in Turkey. Therefore, it would be useful to briefly discuss and analyse the historical time framework and events that supported national narratives or national myths in Turkey in the creation of the 'one nation, one state' idea, in particular the last hundred years since the Turkish Republic was established.

As happened in many parts of the world at the end of the nineteenth century and beginning of the twentieth century, the Ottoman Empire, in its many constituent parts, witnessed the rise of nationalism. This political and ideological shift resulted in its collapse in 1923, with the establishment of the Turkish Republic. However, the plan of homogenization of Turkey was set out before the foundation of the Turkish state, during the 1910s with the rise of Turkish nationalists, the 'Young Turks' (Akçam 2004, 2012). The Ottoman Empire was going through very difficult times and losing its power. Within this politically complex period, nationalists planned and implemented resettlement and population movements of minority groups. The purification process was aimed at cleansing Turkey of non-Turkish-speaking minority groups (Akçam 2004). This mainly involved removing traces of ethnic minority groups, including Armenians, Greeks and Yazidis (see Akçam 2004; Akdar 2000) in order to create a nation state based on 'Turkishness' (Ersanli 2003) or, in other words, to create an 'imagined community' (Anderson 1983). Meanwhile, the main reason to purify and erase the material culture of those minority groups was to prove ownership rights to the lands and to develop a historical narrative that stated that 'these lands have always been Turkish'. The demographic structure of Turkey was completely changed between 1913 and 1918, and further in the 1920s as a result of these ethnic cleansing policies (see Hovannisian 1999b; Akçam 2012, 2004; Akdar 2000). One of the most traumatic events of this process was probably the Armenian genocide in 1915 when over a million Armenians were killed (Akçam 2004, 2012; Çetinoglu 2005).

The minorities I refer to here, in the context of Turkey, include both ethnic and religious groups, who are either recognized by law and not recognized as a minority by the state, who have dissimilar cultural values from the majority of the population in power and controlling state institutions. The United Nations Minorities Declaration in 1992, Article 1, defines minorities by their national/ethnic, religious, linguistic identity and cultural differences and emphasizes that each state must protect their existence.[3] The recognition of minorities under international law first began when the League of Nations, established after the First World War to resolve international disputes, adopted several minority treaties following the rise of nation states that were based on single ethnicity. Following the First World War, several months before Turkey was established officially, it signed the 1923 Treaty of Lausanne which in particular specified the legal status and protection of Jews, Armenians, Greeks and Christians in general, though other minorities such as Kurds, which is the largest minority in Turkey, were not granted legal status. The reason behind this was to extend ownership rights over territory and conserve the idea of Turkishness; in this way Kurdish people are counted as Turkish and even the significantly different aspects of their culture such as their language remain unrecognized.

Turkey as a country has been a historically ethnoculturally rich region; however, the number of those ethnic and religious groups is not known because of ethnic cleansing, assimilation and forced deportation policies in the past. Following the Treaty of Lausanne, minorities were grouped as non-Muslim, recognized by the state as Greeks, Armenians and Jews. Other non-Muslim minorities are not recognized by the state and have no legal status including Syrian-Orthodox, Chaldean Catholics, Assyrians, Arameans and Ezidis; and finally Muslim minorities exist such as the Kurds, Arabs, Roma, Caucasians, Zazzas and Alevis (Kizlikan-Kisacik 2013). Alevis consider themselves as a culturally different minority group rather than a religious minority, as their culture and belief system is completely different from the state practice of Islam (see Chapter 5). Yet the Turkish state considers them Muslim as part of their assimilation process. The number of minority groups without legal status is much higher than this, as many other culturally distinct groups exist in Turkey (see Karimova and Deverell 2001; MGIR 2007; Kizilkan-Kisacik 2013). They are mostly assimilated minorities including Circassians, Albanians, Pomaks, Laz, Slavs, Georgians, Azeris, Tatars and Ossetians (see Smith 2005). The discourses articulating recognition and misrecognition of minorities, their identity and heritage in Turkey are strongly linked to the development of a Turkish official ideology created in the first couple of decades of the Republic of Turkey.

The process of homogenizing the country continued in the first decades of the Republic with an attempt to erase the history of minorities and rewrite the official history of Turkey. In particular, between 1925 and 1939, research projects were carried out by many Turkish scholars as part of the newly established Turkish Institute of Anthropology. The results of the projects were published in the *Journal of the Turkish Review of Anthropology* (Maksudyan 2005). The research projects were not only used to develop a nationalist identity but served as part of developing racist discourses, as they argued that not all races are equal but are based on a racial hierarchy (Maksudyan 2005, 293). For instance, the first research project looked at the development of Armenian, Jewish, Greek and Turkish children from a physical anthropology perspective. Another project, the Istanbul Bone Collection, analysed Turkish 'race' by collecting bones from the Istanbul cemetery to expose Turkish race's characteristics (Maksudyan 2005, 294; Berkol et al. 1927, 1928). All these projects and publications, using anthropology, served to support the idea of superiority of the Turkish race, to consolidate Turkish national identity and develop a national myth against especially minority groups who were considered to be a threat to the Republic of Turkey.

The state did not only support anthropological research but also supported and funded research on Turkish history in order to find historical and archaeological evidence that supported the connection between modern Turks and the older civilizations of the Anatolian region. The aim of this research, including early archaeological excavations, was to claim ownership rights over the land (Atakuman 2008). In particular, the Armenians and Greeks were considered a large threat to Turkish nationalism because these two ethnic groups had at various points exercised historical control over Anatolia. Therefore, some of the research aimed to prove ownership of Turkish territories as against Armenians and Greeks, and to disenfranchise these populations living in Turkey (Üngör 2011).

It was no surprise that the new Turkish state attempted to use all the sciences to prove its rights of ownership over the lands of Turkey. This is also a good example of demonstrating how the sciences were used to serve nationalism in the early twentieth century. In the 1930s, two influential research congresses were organized to develop national narratives and rewrite Turkish history (Atakuman 2008), based on the concepts of Turkishness and Turkish nationalism. The first congress took place in 1932 and was organized as a rigorous scientific initiative open to all historians and academics who might have different views and arguments. However, the congress completely dismissed any different or counter ideas to the main agenda of the congress: to discover a relationship to the roots of Turks in the past, For instance, the main research aims of the congress were 'the definition of indigenous people of Anatolia; the first civilizations of Anatolia; how they settled and the role of Turkish people in creating world civilizations' (Atakuman 2008), the importance of Turkish language, and many more questions that related to glorifying the past of Turks (Ersanli 2003). In the meantime, the state supported and started the first archaeological excavations to find a link between prehistoric cultures and Turks.

These projects focused on Hittite archaeological sites, as they believed that Hittites had migrated from central Asia, as Turks, and settled in Anatolia. Likewise, archaeology was also a perfect tool to consolidate the newly established nation state through the development of myths on their history (Atakuman 2008). The Turkish elites and founders thought they could create these myths based on archaeological evidence that could date thousands of years back and link them to the Turkish people. The results of this archaeological research were discussed in the second Turkish History Congress in 1937, using 'archaeological evidence' to focus on the justification of ownership rights of the Turks over Anatolia.

The results of these congresses had a major impact on forming heritage policies in support of national narratives. However, the use of heritage that heavily focused on the Turkish past neglected completely other cultural elements, such as evidence of the pasts and heritages of minority groups. The reflection of writing in parallel to developing national narratives of Turkishness was clearly seen in the history books in the post-construction periods of the 1940s and 1950s. The history textbooks from this period focused only on the Turkish past and neglected the history and heritage of minorities (Güler-Biyikli and Aslan 2013).

This nationalist approach, based on 'one nation and one ethnicity' and constructed around Turkishness, continued until the 1980s in developing heritage policy as well as in the textbooks of schools. Together these formed an official heritage (Harrison 2013a) or 'authorised heritage discourse' of the country (Smith 2006), as is also seen in many other countries. The political turmoil in the country in the 1970s (Aydin and Taşkın 2014) ended with a military coup in 1980 and the militarized government introduced a new element: religion. After this, Turkish official ideology as well as heritage discourse turned towards 'Turkish-Islamic synthesis' (Zencirci 2014, 5). This new element became the official ideology of the Turkish state and formed the main basis for the authorized heritage discourse, from its foundation in the 1930s. Before the 1980s, religious elements were avoided in state institutions because Turkey was established on very strong secular values. However, the 1980 coup made religion part of the state ideology, and religion classes, designed to teach Islamic values, became compulsory in schools (Ersanli 2003). The introduction of Islamic values also heavily impacted history textbooks, which are used to teach cultural heritage to students until today (Bilmez et al. 2017).

I argued at the beginning of this chapter that the abuse of cultural heritage for developing national narratives and promoting national identity is very common and never lost its importance, even though we are witnessing the effects of globalization in every part of the world. However, what we see in the twenty-first century are other forms of the use of nationalism, which has adapted itself into right-wing populism, especially in Europe. This is also called 'national populism'. While the abuse of cultural heritage was based on the idea of developing and promoting cultural nationalism to claim the ownership rights to the land, right-wing populism has used cultural heritage, the past and the material culture of the past to promote 'anti-immigration', and 'nativism' (Kaya 2019). In other words, nationalism has transformed its forms and become more regional rather than national, as in the case of Europe.

Turkey is no different in its use and abuse of cultural heritage for nationalism and transforming nationalism into right-wing populism. According to the novelist Elif Shafak (2019), 'most of the conflicts which we are experiencing today within our societies are related to culture'. She argues that culture is often being neglected in political analyses and is used for the rise of populism, but that it can also help to stop the spread of it. Culture can certainly play an important role in stopping nationalism and populism but I argue that this is greatly dependent on more analyses of culture and cultural performances, which can help to build dialogues between different groups and increase learning capacities about other cultures and values.

On the contrary, in many parts of the world, cultural performance, which provides ground for developing tangible and intangible heritage, is restricted or totally forbidden (I delve more into this later in the book with case studies). This can especially be seen in authoritarian regimes that were very common following the Second World War and Cold War. With globalization and intense use of neoliberal policies (Brown 2019), this kind of authoritarianism also adapted itself into a new form and called 'competitive authoritarianism' (Levitsky and Way 2010). In a competitive authoritarian system, elections are still held and some democratic norms remain; however, the judiciary and the media are controlled by the ruling group, which also controls the resources of the country. This results in a restriction of human rights and freedom of expression alongside 'electoral manipulation, abuse of state resources, harassment and violence' (Levitsky and Way 2010, 3).

Since the JDP came to power in 2002, Turkey has been transformed into 'competitive authoritarianism', particularly within the last ten years. The use of national narratives to abuse governmental power has increased and has been used to oppress minority groups as well as diverse and opposition voices (Göçek 2018). Particularly in the first two decades of the twenty-first century, two different but highly linked policies shaped Turkish ideology and the authorized heritage discourse, although Turkish and Islamic aspects have predominantly continued.

Since the JDP, an Islamic-oriented party, came to power, dominant neoliberal policies have not only impacted every aspect of country and state institutions (Aydin and Taskin 2014; Bugra and Savaskan 2014) but also the use of neoliberalism-motivated authoritarianism (Brown 2019) in Turkey to 'consume' cultural resources. For instance, dam constructions in many parts of Turkey (but particularly in southeastern and eastern Turkey where the predominantly Kurdish population live) is erasing the landscapes and cultural, social and economic spaces where cultural activities have been performed, identities attached and memories developed.

The rampant neoliberal policies did not necessarily change the overall Turkish ideology, but they changed the understanding of the *value* of the past and its presentation through archaeology and heritage. Making a profit and acquiring capital have become more important than the authenticity of heritage sites (see Shoup 2006 for the dam construction in southeast Turkey; Apaydin 2016a). Archaeology and heritage also became a selling point; cultural resources were marketed and profits made through tourist attractions became important, rather than trying to understand the past and connecting its value with its communities. For instance, the number of inscriptions on the UNESCO World Heritage List demonstrates the idea of marketizing heritage, not only for Turkey but many other countries.

The JDP has also aimed to spread its own ideology and consolidate its power through using state institutions. This new ideology is dominated by constructed Ottoman–Islamic perspectives (Türeli 2014, 12) called 'new Ottomanism' or 'new Turkey' (yeni Türkiye) – for instance, investing more on Ottoman heritage (Türeli 2014; Zencirci 2014) and not recognizing heritage and material culture of minority groups, such as the Kurds and Alevis (see Chapter 5). In 2013, one of the largest environmental and political demonstrations took place in Turkey against the demolition of a city park to develop Ottoman barracks with a shopping mall in Istanbul (see Chapter 6). The case of demolishing Gezi Park and replacing it with Ottoman architecture and shopping malls also clearly demonstrates the new authorized heritage discourse of the state, which is based on an Islamic/Turkish and neoliberalist one.

The new heritage or national heritage discourse impacted heavily on heritage policies, to give more importance to Ottoman and Islamic-related heritage and material culture. That said, there have been some progressive developments regarding minority groups' heritage as well. In 2016, the capital city of the Armenian Kingdom from the medieval period was listed as a UNESCO World Heritage Site. Additionally, many archaeological sites, such as the unique Neolithic sites of Göbeklitepe and Çatalhöyük, were invested in and became UNESCO World Heritage Sites. However, none of this goes beyond the aim of attracting tourists to the country.

Using the ancient past and heritage and linking them with modern ethnicities to develop national narratives has been commonplace since the nineteenth century, when nationalism became more prominent across the world (Anderson 1983). Turkey is one of those countries that has created, reconstructed and manipulated history and material culture of the past to consolidate itself as a nation state. It has done so by developing discourses for every part of the daily, social, political and cultural life of the society which, as one can see everywhere, reminds the citizens of the Turkish national narratives. The Turkish authorized heritage discourse, which aims at linking the Turks to the land, glorifying its history, and creating national narratives through material culture, heavily impacted school textbooks and formed new generations of people with nationalist worldviews and heritage perceptions.

Education, textbooks and imagined community

Education shall be directed to the full development of the human personality and to the strengthening of respect for human rights and fundamental freedoms. It shall promote understanding, tolerance, and friendship among all nations, racial or religious groups, and shall further the activities of the UN for the maintenance of peace. (Universal Declaration of Human Rights, Article 26.2)[4]

Although the concept of right to education and right to learn was one of the core themes of the Universal Declaration of Human Rights in 1948 and many other international declarations emphasized the importance of this component for human rights, education has often been used to spread the ideologies of dominant groups and to oppress others (Apple 2004). The dissemination of history, the past and material culture of minority groups, who are often considered a threat to national unity and have the potential to disprove the national narratives of the dominant power, have often been either neglected or manipulated in the formal education of many countries (Stone and MacKenzie 1990). This is opposed to the Human Rights Declaration, which outlines that 'everybody has the right to learn the culture and their background and history'.

Turkey is one of those countries where the right to learn has been breached throughout its history, in particular its formal education that has been used to consolidate its own national narratives and myths based around Turkishness and later Islam. In order to analyse the impact of dominant national discourses, the use of nationalism and Turkish ideology in formal education in Turkey, I looked at recent history textbooks from 4th to 11th level that are managed and controlled centrally by the Turkish Ministry of Education. For textbooks, I looked at allocation of themes, particularly Turkish, Islamic and Ottoman history, archaeological past and the past of present-day minorities narrated to students and used in the curricula and textbooks.

I applied critical discourse analysis as 'language use in speech and writing is a form of social practice which implies a dialectical relationship between particular events and situations and social structures' (Fairclough and Wodak 1997, 258). Such writing is often used in textbooks, as texts are often written with implicit prejudiced utterances by the writers who use allusions (Fairclough and Wodak 1997, 266). In addition, I conducted surveys and semi-structured interviews in three communities located near to three UNESCO World Heritage Sites to see the impact of the ideological discourses in formal education. The three sites were: Çatalhöyük, a Neolithic period site surrounded by conservative communities; Ani, a mainly Medieval Armenian site surrounded by Turkish nationalists; and Hattusha, a Hittite Kingdom site surrounded by Turkish secular nationalists.

The textbooks from 4th to 11th levels are full of nationalist discourses and focus on historical events that are important for the unity of the Turkish state. Although history textbooks in schools present history-related subjects in detail and the time allocated is quite substantial, textbooks and curricula are dominated by intense national discourses, which emphasize the official ideology of the state. In all levels in the textbooks, Turkish nationalism is not only narrated in the texts but also in visuals including pictures, drawings and maps. For example, the Turkish flag can be seen in all textbooks; important figures from Turkish history including Atatürk and important heritage sites from the Ottoman, Islamic and Republican periods are often presented to students in order to support national narratives embedded in the texts. The general sections of curricula and textbooks are strictly controlled by the education ministry, which makes sure that all texts reflect the Turkish official historical perspective. The main reason for the strict central control of education is strongly related to conserving hegemony of the ideology of 'one nation, one ethnicity'.

The use of education in order to promote one's hegemony can be studied historically. Early philosophers, such as Plato, emphasized the importance of education for the state. Plato pointed out that the state could control every single individual and make them good citizens through the tool of education in order to secure the state's ideologies (Rusk 1965) and consolidate national narratives to continue their hegemonic powers. Similarly, Thomas Hobbes stated that in order to lead societies, states also needed to control every single action of the individuals and groups, therefore their thoughts and beliefs, as he argued: 'the act of humans are shaped by their thoughts, thus to lead to people, first, every single individuals' must be controlled' (Hobbes 1963, 181). Hegemonic power structures, which are on the rise all around the world and especially in Europe and Turkey (Brown 2019), think that they have the right to control and shape society; hence, through education and other forms of propagation and communication tools, they aim to control the thoughts and worldview of the public. This non-violent oppressive approach has been used as a tool in Turkey since the early years of the Republic.

For instance, the three elements, the Turkic culture in central Asia, Islam and the Ottoman Empire, were of utmost important during the construction of the Turkish nation state. These aspects were/are the main tenets of the official historical perspective of the modern Turkish state (Copeaux 1998a; Ersanlı 2003) and the identity of the Turkish state. However, since right-wing populist and Islamic-oriented government have come to power, what we have seen is more reflection and elaboration of the Ottoman Empire history because the current government has tried to shift the official ideology and authorized heritage discourse to a more Islamic and Ottoman orientation. This shift is also strongly reflected in history textbooks where cultural heritage is taught to students.

In all levels from 4th to 11th, the general sections from the textbooks were concentrated mostly on the importance of the history of the Republic of Turkey, particularly during the construction period in the 1920s and 1930s, the Ottoman past, the Islamic past and the Turkic past in central Asia. While the national past or official heritage is allocated the utmost importance in textbooks, prehistoric and ancient pasts are given very little space and minority groups' pasts are totally neglected. Minority communities, such as the Armenians, Greeks, Alevis and Kurdish, who have lived in Turkey for centuries, have developed memories that have been ascribed to intangible and tangible heritage and material culture, which are still visible and include monumental and architectural heritage. However, the exclusion of these pasts and their heritage in the textbooks demonstrates that the Turkish state aims to consolidate its official heritage discourses by neglecting these pasts. Neglecting particularly Armenian and Greek past and heritage is not something new. There is almost a century of history in which Armenians went through ethnic cleansing and the Greeks were subjected to expulsion from the country (Üngör 2010; Akdar 2000; Akçam 2004). The contestations of the lands between Turkey and Armenia and Turkey and Greece also have a long history (Bilmez et al. 2017; Copeaux 1998a). The embedded reason behind the neglect of the Greek past and heritage in textbooks is related to the early years of the twentieth century, when Turkey had a large Greek population, and then later, in the 1920s, when the Greeks claimed western Turkey during the war of Turkish independence. After Turkey declared its independence in 1923, a population exchange occurred between Turkey and Greece, whereby millions of Greeks and Turkish people migrated; before the exchange, many parts of Turkey were populated by Greek communities (Akdar 2000), especially in the western parts of Turkey where there are also ancient Greek remains and heritage.

While no curricula and textbooks mention the existence of the Greeks and their heritage, there is also a further manipulative approach. For instance, some parts of the social sciences and history textbooks introduce the prehistoric and ancient histories of Turkey. Although the texts mention the ancient Greek cities in western Turkey, such as Miletus and Ephesus, and historical figures such as Thales, Herodotus and Hippocrates as well as the gods and goddesses of Greek mythology, the Greeks are introduced as Ionians (see Nuri 2013, 92). In the history curricula and textbooks, an Ionian identity is reconstructed to manipulate the Greek identity and its past in Turkey, although the Ionians were also part of the Greek culture (Copeaux 1998b, 82). This type of manipulation and perception management is strongly linked to preserving national narratives and myths that were created on the idea that Turkey was always Turkish, therefore Turkey has the right to own its past as such.

Similarly, ownership rights of the land, which is an issue of conflict between the Turks and Kurds, is also an ongoing issue in the omission of Kurdish past and their heritage. In the Turkish formal education textbooks, most of the different identity and ethnic groups, and their heritage and pasts, are not recognized or allocated space. There are many discourses hidden in the denial of minority groups' rights, existence and material culture that symbolizes and represents their existence. This is strongly linked with 'the protection of traditional territories' (Langfield et al. 2010, 10). In the case of Turkey, the state does not want to lose its control over specific areas where the population is predominantly not Turkish through the recognition of the cultural rights of those groups. For instance, southeast and east Turkey, where the Kurdish population mainly live, is a good example to demonstrate this power and control relationship. Until two decades ago, the state 'assumed' that there were no 'Kurdish elements' in Turkish territory (Yegen 1999, 555). Since then, the method that the state uses to erase the Kurdish identity and their landscape, where identities and memories are developed and meanings are ascribed, have varied. For example, the dam building projects in many parts of the Kurdish region (Ronayne 2005, 2006) heavily impacted, and continues to impact, the local Kurdish population, who have been evicted from their homes and land. These are also the territories that serve as a resource and are strong representatives of sociocultural identities (Gilbert 2010, 31) and, for the heritage case, the landscape serves as 'heritage resources' (Harvey 2011). These are some of the main reasons that the material culture, heritage and the past of the Kurdish people and their landscape have often been neglected and not recognized in education at the institutional level.

This form of neglect – or, in other words, strong exclusion – further leads to oppression, as expressed in Young's (1990) 'marginalization' dimension of oppression. Young argues that marginalization is one of the most dangerous forms of oppression as it aims to exclude groups who share the same values and who are different from the majority of the social, economic and cultural lives and, of course, from their right to learn and their right to participate in cultural life. The complete omission of Kurdish history and heritage in textbooks, the Kurdish people's deprivation of learning about their own culture in the schooling process, marginalizes the Kurdish community in Turkey and additionally, they become 'powerless' as their labour and cultural production are exploited by the Turkish state (and have been for almost a century). While this type of neglect of a minority's past and heritage is oppressive and breaches their human rights, it is also strongly linked to the social justice dimensions of 'redistribution' and 'recognition', because inequality is deliberately developed for those who cannot access an equal share of education, particularly in terms of learning about their own past and heritage.

The injustice and inequality in education in terms of redistribution of knowledge and (mis)recognition of all backgrounds, groups and individuals of the society has a long history. In the nineteenth and early twentieth centuries, one of the most common education system was liberal education, which was thought to be a mirror of capitalism; it was constructed for specific purposes and mostly used to transfer the idea of capitalism to people (Apple 2009). In this unequal system, many groups of society are not able to reach and learn knowledge, and their culture and identities are not recognized by the state. In other words, the public is not provided sufficient resources and not encouraged to learn other cultural backgrounds and histories, which is completely opposite to the idea of social justice education that aims to challenge social, cultural and economic inequalities imposed on some groups and communities whose cultural differences are also not recognized (Adams and Bell 2016).

In Turkish history textbooks, along with the neglect of other cultures, more or less all levels of curricula and textbooks mostly focus on Turkish as well as Islamic aspects. The history of Islam and its diffusion across the world are discussed in detail, as is the history of Turks in terms of their historical development, migration from central Asia to other parts of the world such as Anatolia, central Europe and Siberia (see Okur et al. 2013; Turan et al. 2013). In the textbooks, the neglect is not only towards the past and heritage of minority groups but the neglect of early and ancient civilization can also be clearly seen.

While history of Turks and Islam are discussed well and are detailed in the textbooks and curricula, the archaeology of Turkey and nearby regions are much less covered. Thousands of years of ancient Anatolia and Mesopotamia are neglected. Tens of thousands of years of prehistory are introduced to the students in only two or three paragraphs. The world-renowned and famous Neolithic UNESCO World Heritage Site, Çatalhöyük, is explained and discussed superficially in the textbooks (Okur et al. 2013 to see how Çatalhöyük is narrated in textbooks). The life of the Neolithic Çatalhöyük people, with their unique egalitarian lifestyle, reflected through lack of property and equal food distribution (Apaydin 2022), are not even mentioned in the text. This is not only a simple neglect but the embedded discourse behind this is that the Çatalhöyük Neolithic lifestyle offers and demonstrates a different life to today's communities, which clearly contradicts the current government's very religious and conservative understanding of lifestyle that it has imposed for the last twenty years in Turkey. For instance, according to archaeological evidence, one of the most striking and interesting features of Çatalhöyük Neolithic society was a very egalitarian lifestyle (Hodder and Pels 2010). Decades of archaeological research at the site of Çatalhöyük has demonstrated that people lived a non-hierarchical lifestyle, had equal access to resources and had 'non-biological social bonds' that tied community members together. Very importantly, it was a non-violent society which shows a possibility of non-discriminative social structure (Brock 2019). As a result of this lack of information about prehistoric periods in the textbooks, individuals have grown up with very limited knowledge, and have been prevented from knowing about other cultures, and therefore developing historical empathy for the cultures that are not Turkish and Islamic.

While the Turkish history textbooks are problematic in terms of distribution of themes, which mostly focus on Turkish, Islamic and Ottoman periods, the education system itself is also problematic, as knowledge is only dictated to students rather than using constructivist learning approaches in the classroom. Learning is constructed through the person and therefore, they must be encouraged from an early age to learn self-development (Tobias 2009, 336). On the contrary, in the Turkish education system, students are considered as only knowledge receivers and are not expected to question the knowledge. Paul Freire (1970) critiqued this kind of education model, referring to it as a capitalist education system. In his classic book, *Pedagogy of the Oppressed*, he draws a clear picture of the capitalist education system by describing it as a banking approach to education (1970, 54). In this system, Freire argues that the relationship between the teacher and students in schools or in adult education is characterized by subject (teacher) and object (student). He emphasized that:

> the teacher teaches and the students are taught; the teacher knows everything and the students know nothing; the teacher thinks and the students are thought about; the teacher talks and the students listen. (1970, 54)

In Turkey, teachers go through a centralized training system and, most importantly, they have to follow the curriculum that has been provided by the Ministry of Education, which also has the authority of approving which textbooks can be taught at schools. Therefore, teachers in Turkey do not have much room to manoeuvre in order to overcome the issues developed through a centralized and hegemonic education system which does not only create inequality but also forces students to learn only national narratives. The one-sided education system prevents the 'right to learn' and equal distribution of knowledge and recognition of cultural differences. It imposes ideological knowledge that is manipulated and neglects 'other' histories. This can be seen, more or less, in all levels of schooling in Turkey. Although this kind of approach to education system is a 'non-violent' approach, it indirectly violates the 'right to learn' as well, as it powerfully reforms heritage perception and worldviews of the public in parallel to national and hegemonic discourses, as I demonstrate below through three local communities in Turkey.

In the case of Çatalhöyük, in south-central Turkey, many community members revealed their complete lack of information about Çatalhöyük and how their perception of heritage was shaped, in line with the official Turkish ideology, in which intense nationalist discourses are embedded, discourses that promote Turkish, Islamic and Ottoman heritage and history and neglect other cultures and material culture of the past. The following quotes are from qualitative interviews with local community members :

> the past and values of the Turks, Ottoman and Islam are very significant for us. If they did not fight for our lands and protect our identity and religion, we wouldn't be here now. However, archaeological sites such as Çatalhöyük are far from us because they are not from our past and culture.

> our own past began with the arrival of Islam and became very glorious with the success of the Turks and Ottomans … Çatalhöyük has no connection with Islamic periods; therefore, it does not have any importance for myself.

The views of these community members were similar to many others I interviewed in the region. The ideological aspects that were dictated through education can clearly be seen in these replies. Although Çatalhöyük is a UNESCO World Heritage Site with an international significance for the human past, they do not consider it as *their* heritage. The main reason for that is having intense educational discourses in the schooling process that either neglects other cultures or gives less importance to the ancient human past. Local community members interpret Çatalhöyük as something much less important than other tangible heritage that is linked to Turkish and Islamic history. The past is always about experience and learning from it and based on individual interpretation. This is based on evidence and resources that are provided through the schooling process, and most importantly, people have the right to learn that there is not one history but many. Jörn Rüsen (2007, 2) emphasizes:

> the past as a matter of experience and interpretation, offers a totally different impression of diversity and multifariousness. Difference in space and time is overwhelming. We experience a permanent change of views on the essential nature of what history is about. Accordingly, the representation of the past in the cultural orientation of human life reflects this difference and variety to such a degree that it is difficult to identify one specific form as essentially historical.

Cultural heritage and material culture are also very important aspects that provide ground for people who construct their identities with ascribed meanings and store cultural memories. While it is individual, it is also collective and serves community survival, as I discuss in later chapters of this book. Considering these two anecdotes of community members, they approach heritage from a very ideological and nationalist perspective as they were instructed to in the schooling process. The value of Çatalhöyük as a shared human past is not considered and it is excluded because is not from the Turkish, Islamic and Ottoman past. This kind of exclusion is common in many countries, where this type of systematic exercise can be seen to shape people's understanding of the past (Stone and MacKenzie 1990).

Participants' comments based on my interviews were also verified by my survey results that I conducted with sixty individuals who live near Çatalhöyük. I asked the question: 'Do you consider Çatalhöyük as part of your heritage?' The term heritage is a complex one and it is a complicated concept. Before starting to survey, I explained what heritage means to all participants. Only seven of the participants responded 'it is part of my heritage'; twenty-seven of the participants pointed that 'it is a heritage but not ours' and twenty-six participants said 'it is not heritage' (Apaydin 2016c). Most of the participants justified their responses by pointing out that Çatalhöyük has no connection with the Turkish, Islamic or

Ottoman periods, as these three elements dominate formal history education in Turkey. In contrast to not considering Çatalhöyük as heritage or as part of their heritage, most of the participants also gave examples, such as the Mevlana religious complex, which is in the city centre and seen as an important part of Islam, their history and heritage. Another interview participant pointed out what was his heritage and justified why the Mevlana complex has an importance as a heritage:

> We existed since the arrival of Islam, before Islam our existence could be questioned. Therefore, our history began with Islam. Anything that contradicts Islam we won't accept and anything that does not have any Islamic value has no importance for us. Yes, the past and the materials from the past are important for me, but these can only be the heritage that has Islamic values. For instance, Mevlana Celaleddin Rumi and his mausoleum are very significant for us. Therefore, we protect and preserve it; we go there very often to pray. It is important for us because it gives us spiritual support that is most important to our lives. Çatalhöyük is a different case. It is not from the Islamic period.

Considering the content of the history textbooks and curricula instructions, the above anecdote is completely parallel to history textbooks, which neglect other cultures and the heritage of others. Knowing and seeing, getting in direct contact as well as learning about things, in this case about other cultures, are significant for developing empathy and preventing prejudices for cultures and, therefore, can provide ground for peace building (Allport 1954).

While some of the histories of different identity groups are neglected in the curricula and textbooks, there are also strong discourses and manipulation about groups and historical events (see Başol et al. 2013; Turan et al. 2013). This particularly can be seen in the case of the Armenians who have been written about in the textbooks as the 'enemy', 'traitor', or an ethnic minority group who aimed to annex some parts of Turkey. This can also be seen in the visuals where Armenians are depicted with guns and presented as if they were all dangerous to the Turkish Republic. For instance, some sections of the 8th level classes are reserved for general social and political situations around Europe and Turkey in the twentieth century. The most striking is part of the last section named 'Threats to Turkey' and focused on the Armenians and the 1915 genocide (see Başol et al. 2013, 274 to see how Armenians are presented). While the text does not question the role of Turkish nationalism in the Armenian genocide, it tries to justify it by emphasizing that Armenians planned to annex the eastern territory of Turkey and therefore they were expelled from Turkey. As the text emphasizes:

Armenians were affected by nationalism and with the provocation of other countries Armenians rose up against the state ... as a result of this uprising the state had to make a decree about 'expulsion and re-settling for Armenians ...' (quoted in Başol et al. 2013, 207)

In the extract above, the 1915 Armenian genocide and cleansing is presented as a move that had to be made because of the incursions of the Armenians and to preserve the integrity of the Turkish state and territory. Although the text mentions the necessity of 'expulsion and resettling' of the Armenians, it does not mention the killing of one million Armenians (see Akçam 2004; Akdar 2000; Üngör 2011). Formal education has a role in forming worldview and in the development of consciousness of every individual. This is mainly because it has a formative role that enables individuals' socialization in society while it shapes and forms them, as Freud (1920) points out. This is the main reason that formal education in Turkey is designed to consolidate Turkish identity and an official history that is based on Turkishness and Islam. History textbooks and schooling have always been used for hate campaigns in undemocratic and authoritarian countries against certain groups to create otherness. For instance, one of the other textbook (see Turan et al. 2013, 188–9) emphasizes:

they [Armenians] claimed the east Anatolia to establish and Armenian state ... in many places, Armenians gangs murdered Turks and Muslims.

Given the fact that the schooling process is compulsory nationwide in Turkey, more or less the whole population of the next generation is educated with the language that imposes certain knowledge, discourses and hatred against certain identity and ethnic groups. Schooling serves not as places of education and learning, but rather as places where students develop unconscious bias against other cultures and identity groups. The impact of these intense discourses can be seen on community members who have biases against certain identity groups. For instance, to measure the impact of this type of dominant discourse that is used in history curricula, I carried out intensive ethnographic field work that included observation, participant observation and conducted interviews at the site of Ani, a UNESCO World Heritage Site located on the border of modern Turkey and Armenia, which I will discuss in more detail in the next chapter. The site contains mostly Armenian heritage but is surrounded mainly by Turkish communities who consider the Armenians as enemies who aimed to annex the lands of Turkey. For instance, the local community members pointed out in interviews:

Armenians always want to take our lands as happened in 1918. However, our grandfathers fought against them and died in order not to give away our lands ... the architectural buildings of Ani are mostly Turkish and Islamic, therefore, Ani is our heritage.

The Armenians aim to get strong in the region and take our lands. We would never allow such attempts in the region.

The first account of Turkish community members demonstrates how national narratives of Turkey were created and imposed in schools by using the word 'our land', which is often emphasized in the textbooks. The anecdote also reflects the intense impact of neglect of minority heritage in the textbooks and manipulation of history, but also how monumental or architectural heritage of Armenians is manipulated, as the community members describe it as Turkish and Islamic. Similarly, the second account also focuses on the threat of Armenians, as it is taught at schools.

The neglect of teaching other cultures and heritage, and the subjective and one-sided presentation of the past, deprives students from developing critical thinking and results in creating 'otherness' and hatred against certain groups and their heritage. Similar attitudes can also be seen in Armenian textbooks that present Turks as enemies (Bilmez et al. 2016). Therefore, it is not only an issue in Turkey, but also in many other nation states that are established on national narratives and nationalism based on one ethnic group that uses textbooks to shape public perception about historical facts.

In order to compare the impact of textbooks and school curricula, I also selected another UNESCO World Heritage Site, Hattusha, a capital of the Hittite Empire in the second millennium BC, and the modern community who live nearby. The general sociopolitical and cultural background of the communities around Hattusha (modern name Bogazköy) differs from the communities of Çatalhöyük and Ani in terms of understanding of the past as well as the approach to the material culture of the past. In contrast to Çatalhöyük and Ani, there are no political or ideological dynamics between the material culture of the site and communities. The main reason is that the Hittites were given a significant place during the first decades of the Turkish Republic and the construction of the Turkish official ideology and the rewriting of Turkish history in order to claim the ownership rights of the lands against Armenians and Greeks (Atakuman 2008). This narrative that was based on Hittites being Turkish was removed from Turkish official ideology and is no longer in textbooks and curricula. However, since the first decades of the Republic, the symbols of Hittites, such as the sun disk, have

Figure 2.3 Hittite Sun Disk in one of the biggest public squares in Ankara. © Veysel Apaydin.

been used as a symbol of many state institutions. Hittites and their symbols are still advertised well in many city squares. One example is the capital, where one of the biggest public squares has a Hittite sun disk statue (see Figure 2.3).

In contrast to modern communities of Çatalhöyük and Ani, the local members around the Hattusha site have a high awareness of the importance of the past, even though it is not linked to the Turkish authorized heritage discourse anymore. For instance, one local, who also worked at Hattusha as a labourer, points to his understanding of the past and Hittites and the site itself:

> the past could be anything that comes from the past for me. For instance, this could be the history of our ancestors such as the Turks, Ottoman and Hittites. We live in the capital of the Hittites; that is very significant for me, because it is a human history and I make connections between the Hittites and us in terms of lifestyle, such as houses, use of internal parts of the houses, or farming.

> our history is very important because if our ancestors had not fought against the enemy during the Independence War we would have been occupied by foreigners, therefore, our Turkish history is significant ... Hattusha is also very important for us, it is part of us.

my understanding of the past is anything that happened in the past . . . I think it is all our pasts . . . Turkish, Ottoman, Islamic and Hittites . . . looking at the structure of the houses in Hattusha, they are similar to our houses, their lifestyle was also similar, therefore, it is our past and is significant for us.

These accounts can be interpreted from three different significant points in terms of understanding and reflecting on the past and material culture and impact of state ideology and schooling process. First, as can be seen from these accounts, they do not differentiate one period of the past from another. The main factor influencing this understanding of the past, that makes the Hittites as well as the Turkish and Ottoman periods part of their own past, is the effect of state ideology and its official historical perspective that recognizes only the Turkish and Ottoman past. The interview accounts above come from different age groups and generations: the first interview participant is forty-seven, the second is seventy-six and the third is twenty years old. Therefore, almost three generations think and make similar points while they are interpreting the understanding of the past and material culture.

As I discussed above, students in Turkey are indoctrinated with Turkish ideology in formal education. It is important to point out that history and religion classes are compulsory during primary and secondary school education in Turkey. Considering that the years between the ages of six and fifteen are the most significant part in terms of shaping worldviews and forming people's behavioural and cognitive structure, it is no surprise that most of the public, as can be seen from the extracts of interviews, have internalized intense nationalist discourses about the past and heritage because of eleven years of compulsory formal education dominated by nationalist discourses. One of the academics specializing in education, who is also a secondary school teacher, points out the importance of subjects and time that impact on students:

intensive teaching about the subjects of Turkish, Ottoman and Islamic values, lasts almost eleven years, with the result that children have a strong Turkish and Islamic perspective which affects the worldview of the children.

The strict and authoritarian system also puts teachers under pressure and prevents them from teaching or promoting any other subjects. The same secondary school teacher emphasizes that:

We can't promote subjects such as art and history or cultural heritage [about other cultures] because we are under too much pressure from the government inspectors . . . If we do anything that contradicts the state or current government ideology we may face charges.

The intense ideologies that are implemented through all state institutions, particularly through education, shape people's belief systems. In Turkey, as in many other authoritarian nation states, education as an institution becomes a hegemonic tool to serve the dominant group, as in the case of JDP, which aimed at shaping people's belief systems, telling them what to think and how to act in order to support its own ideological discourses and keep in power. Most people in Turkey and other authoritarian countries, who go through this form of ideological education process for years, become passive citizens and do not question the selected knowledge they are taught in the classroom. This was clearly reflected in the comments of the interview participants who all interpreted the past, heritage and material culture in parallel to state ideology; therefore, this intense ideological education system is an effective tool. This is the main reason that particularly authoritarian regimes pay extra attention to education and the design of the curriculum, and to centrally training teachers to support their ideologies. This is not only important for those authoritarian regimes from the perspective of politics but also it is important culturally and economically. The British sociologist, Raymond Williams (1973, 1976, 204–5), in his discussion of hegemony, points out why education is so important for control and its link to hegemony:

> The educational institutions are usually the main agencies of transmission of an effective dominant culture, and this is now a major economic as well as cultural activity; indeed, it is both in the same moment. Moreover, at a philosophical level, at the true level of theory and at the level of the history of various practices, there is a process which I call the selective tradition: that which, within the terms of an effective dominant culture, is always passed off as 'the tradition', the significant past. But always the selectivity is the point; the way in which from a whole possible area of past and present, certain meanings and practices are chosen for emphasis, certain other meanings and practices are neglected and excluded. Even more crucially, some of these meanings are reinterpreted, diluted, or put into forms which support or at least do not contradict other elements within the effective dominant culture.

Since the JDP took power, particularly in the last decade, Turkey has attempted to go through ideological transformation. During this transformation, the JDP created its own dominant culture and group, and through this also redesigned the education system and curricula, from primary to secondary schools. This redesign of the curricula did not just exclude the past and heritage of diverse groups but also, in some cases, imposed specific knowledge, values and new meanings to maintain their economic, social and political power, as Raymond Williams emphasizes – for instance, allocating more time to the Islamic past and Islamic practice. The attitude of the state towards non-Turkish, Islamic and Ottoman has changed in some occasions and this is also links to the current government's perspective that aims to make more profit out of material culture, as in the case of Ani and Çatalhöyük. The attitude of state with the new ideology, which is based on Ottoman and Islamic and is called 'new Turkey', has changed. Turkey's authorized heritage discourse or official heritage ideology has been also switched to more Islamic (see Zencirci 2014; Apaydin 2022), along with neoliberal and authoritarian approaches, which I delve into more in Chapters 4, 5 and 6.

3

Abuses and Uses

The idea for this book can be traced back to my first fieldwork, almost thirteen years ago, at Ani in east Turkey. The site has stunning medieval monumental heritage, which was built during the Armenian Kingdom in the tenth and eleventh centuries AD. Armenians in particular attached great meaning and value to it and through it developed collective memories. Therefore, the site has become very important for constructing their sense of belonging and identity. The site is also very significant for Armenians from a religious point of view. It has significant religious architectural heritage, including churches such as the great cathedral and Holy Apostles church at Ani.

One of the most significant characteristics of Ani is an accumulation of memory by different claimants which demonstrates its continuous use across the history. For most of the tenth and eleventh centuries AD, the site was occupied and ruled by the Armenian Kingdom and was subsequently conquered by the Seljuk Empire, which also built some notable monuments. The site has numerous Byzantine, Islamic, Arabic, Persian and Georgian archaeological remains. However, it remains famous for its Medieval Armenian architectural heritage, especially its churches (Cowe 2001; Akçayöz et al. 2007; Figure 3.1). Following a large earthquake in the thirteenth century, the site was abandoned, but communities continue to live in and around its environs.

The site never lost its importance for Armenians because it represents their identity, their sense of belonging and tangible heritage imbued with memories (Watenpaugh 2014). On the other hand, the site is also significant for the Turks, who see the conquest of the site by the Seljuks in 1041 as the beginning of the arrival of Turks to Anatolia. The site illustrates how heritage can also be very contentious: both the Armenians and the Turks claim it as their heritage and, from an official perspective, neither recognize the other's past and heritage.

The heritage site of Ani and the surrounding area were off limits until 2006. The main reason was that the region was highly contested between Turkey and Armenia. Additionally, the border between the two countries lies right next to

Ani (Figure 3.2). More recently, the site was inscribed as a World Heritage Site by UNESCO in 2016 and the Turkish government increased access to the site and helped fund the conservation and restoration of some of Ani's monuments. However, as in many parts of the world, the UNESCO WHS inscriptions have become prestigious and are used to attract tourists rather than to aid in understanding and conceptualizing the importance of the heritage for the past, present and future (Meskell 2018). Until 2015, when Ani became a UNESCO World Heritage Site, the city's Armenian past was not recognized and usually neglected. Even Ani's entrance board said nothing about Armenians (Figure 3.3; the photo was taken before Ani became a UNESCO World Heritage Site). This is fairly similar to the Armenian state perspective that considers Ani as only Armenian and does not recognize the other histories of the site (Apaydin 2018c; Bilmez et al. 2017). Both countries use the heritage site as a tool to consolidate national unity and to promote nationalism. As part of this approach, authenticity of the material culture, values and communities is neglected. In the case of Turkey, the inscription to UNESCO can primarily be seen as a means to increase profit through tourism at Ani, as well as other World Heritage Sites, through the

Figure 3.1 Overview of Ani with its landscape and monuments. © Veysel Apaydin.

Figure 3.2 Arpacay River. The border between the two countries lies right next to Ani (left side is Turkey, including Ani, and right side is Armenia). © Veysel Apaydin.

neoliberal policies that marketize cultural heritage in Turkey and elsewhere (Apaydin 2016a; Resco 2016).

In her book, *Uses of Heritage*, Smith (2006) discusses the different uses of heritage (see also Apaydin 2018c) by different claimants, but she also demonstrates how authorized heritage discourse is developed by the ruling powers or elites of society. As I discussed in the previous chapter, the Turkish authorized heritage discourse is based on Turkish ideology, which officially recognizes any heritage that is related to the Turkish and Islamic past, and which is imposed effectively and widely in formal education. In addition, the prehistoric past, which has no connection to modern identity groups, is nevertheless used as part of neoliberal development to bring tourists to the country, which has become very common all around the world (Zhu 2021). However, in cases such as Ani, specific heritage, particularly monumental heritage, are strong reflections of past cultural participation and performances, which are the bases of cultural orientations of modern groups. Especially from the point of cultural or collective memory (Halbwachs 1950), Ani, with its monuments and as a memory store, is significant for Armenians and for Turks who both claim the site's heritage and the region's ownership rights.

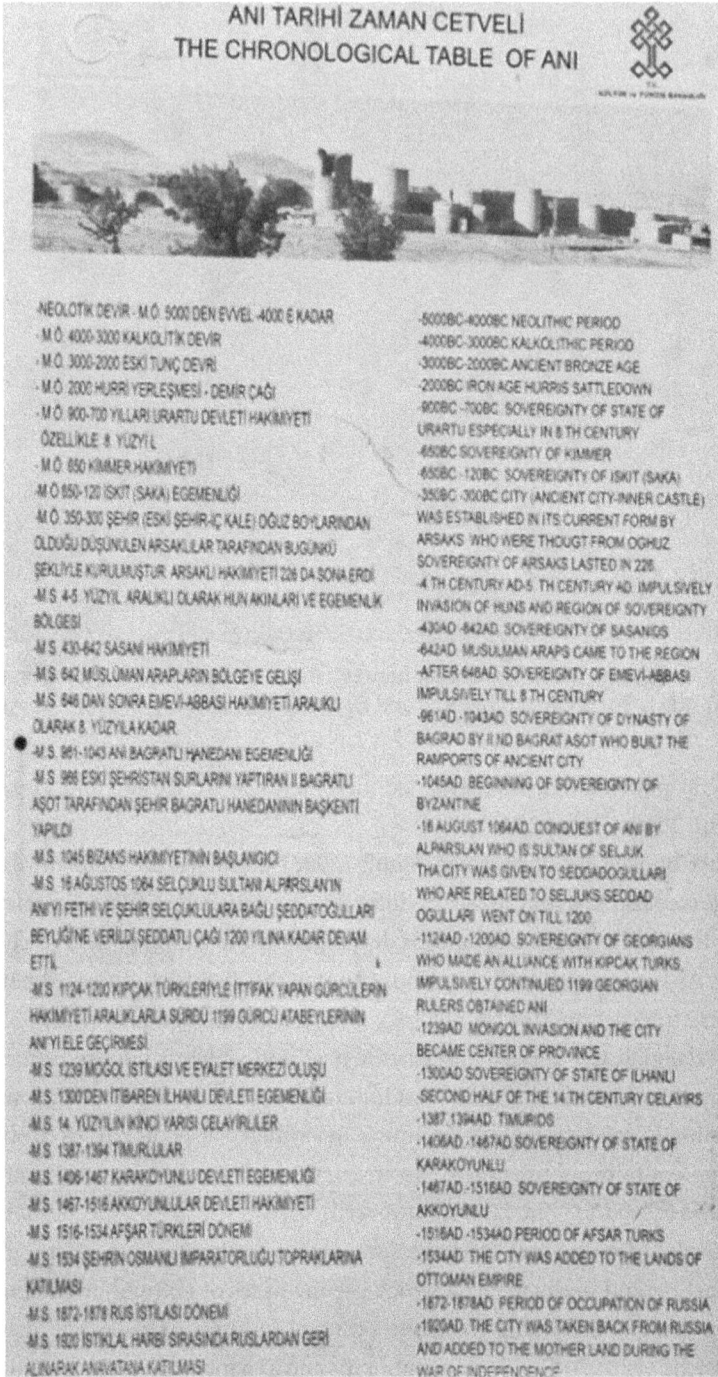

Figure 3.3 Ani's entrance board (the photo was taken before Ani became a UNESCO World Heritage Site).

Contestation, architecture and memory

When I first arrived in Kars, the closest city centre to Ani, I was able to sense the tension, because Ani and Kars are in the border region with the Armenian state, therefore nationalists and the state attribute extra importance to this region. I was also able to see how the city was very multicultural, which is reflected in the monumental heritage all around the city of Kars (Akçayöz et al. 2007), a forty-five-minute drive to the west from Ani. As part of my anthropological approach, I aimed to observe local communities' social, cultural and economic life right next to the heritage site. I wanted to see their relationship to this monumental site with its well-preserved churches and other religious buildings dating from Armenian Christianity periods, and I wanted see how local life is conducted in the middle of a contested site that is also on a border that has been disputed since the 1915 Armenian genocide. Also, I sought to find answers to the questions: 'What is heritage from indigenous perspective?' 'What does Ani mean for local people?' 'What is the heritage of Ani?' and 'What are the local level politics and interpretations of Ani and Armenian heritage?' I managed to interview many local members of the village aged between twenty and forty, as well as older generations in their seventies and eighties who gave more historical overviews about Ani and the village. In addition to interviews and ethnographic fieldwork at Ani, in the city of Kars I managed to interview locals as well as Armenians who were visiting Ani from abroad, to find out their views about Ani in contemporary politics.

Although I went to Ani for fieldwork many times from 2010 onwards, my first arrival was in the 2010 summer season. The rest of Turkey was experiencing high temperatures, but the region of Kars, where Ani is located, was much cooler because it lies on the high steppes, with an altitude of 3,000m above sea level. I was amazed at the landscape as well as the structure and colour of the buildings in the city centre. The buildings are constructed using a black stone, which is very characteristic of buildings in the region (Figure 3.4). The city centre is small, with the current population consisting mostly of ethnic Turks, Kurds and Azerbaijanis. It used to be very multicultural, with Armenians, Georgians, Yezidis, Assyrians, Malakans and many other identity groups (Akçayöz et al. 2007). Ani, with its monumentality, landscape and geographical location, has played an important role in cultural interaction throughout the centuries. All of these cultures, including the Turks and Armenians, left traces in the region.

Figure 3.4 Black stone buildings in the city centre. © Veysel Apaydin.

However, since the early twentieth century, because of nationalist policies and increased nationalism, most of this multiculturalism has been erased, as I discussed in the previous chapter. Most of those ethnic groups' architectural heritage is still standing and preserved, although they have been converted into either official buildings or churches, later converted to mosques (Figure 3.5).

The city of Kars itself was very interesting, though I was very much looking forward to going to see the Medieval Armenian site of Ani. There was no public transport for people to get to the UNESCO World Heritage Site, which surprised me, so I had to hire a taxi. The drive there was amazing: the landscape is beautiful all the way to the Arpaçay river, a natural border, where Ani is located. While we were travelling along the plain of the high steppes, the driver pointed to Ani, whose massive architectural structure could be seen from miles away. Getting closer to the city walls from the west, massive Turkish flags were waving on the city walls (Figure 3.6). This hinted at ownership issues and at how Turkey wanted to demonstrate its presence on monumental heritage and make people think that the site is Turkish. We passed through the gates to get into the site, which used to have a population of more than 100,000 during the Armenian Kingdom

Figure 3.5 Apostolic church in the city centre, converted to mosque. © Veysel Apaydin.

period and was key for the Silk Road trade. Lord Kinross (1954, 69) describes the landscape and the city in a novel way:

> To the south, on Turkish earth, the phantom dome of Mt. Ararat emerged for a moment from the distant haze, like a giant sentinel ... then slowly vanished. We seemed to be heading straight for Russia with no obstacle between, when there was a slight, sudden fall in the ground – and a cleft opened ahead of us. I caught my breath with surprise and even the captain exclaimed 'oh.' For on the brink of it, set alone in the midst of the infinite rolling down land, were the great brown walls and towers of a ruined city. This was Ani ... I walked through the double city gateway, past the stone relief of a lion beneath a carved Armenian inscription, to be confronted on the inner wall by an ancient symbol of eternity – a crooked cross, inlaid in black stone. Around me, scattered over a wide expanse were the architectural shapes, the cones and drums and blind arcades of a civilization utterly unfamiliar. It was an architecture with a mystery of its own, a promise of new aesthetic experience to be slowly absorbed and digested.

I was enchanted first by the great and unique architecture of the cathedrals, which are still standing despite the massive earthquakes and human destruction

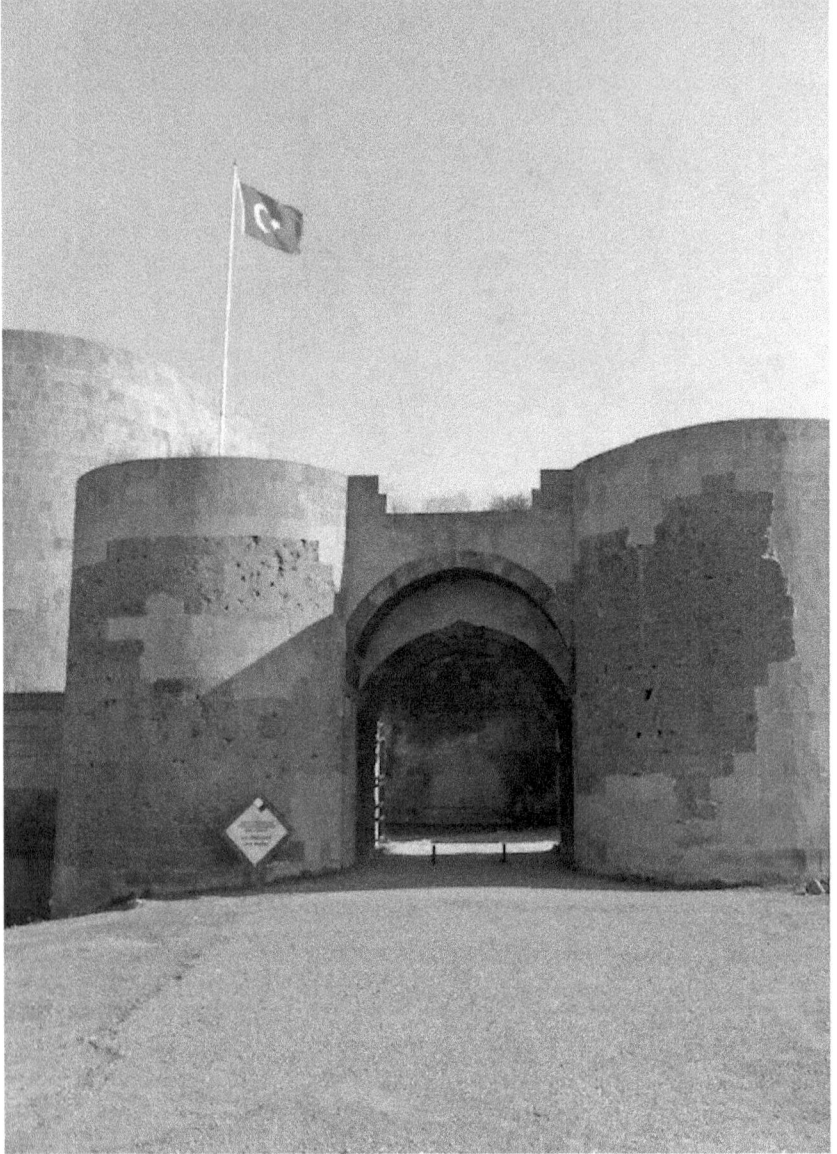

Figure 3.6 Entrance of Ani with its city wall and Turkish flag. © Veysel Apaydin.

in the past (Figure 3.7). I walked towards the hillside where the Arpaçay river flows incredibly strong, then I decided to go down to the river where the riverbanks are fenced, marking the border between Turkey and Armenia. I could see the Armenian soldiers who were watching the Turkish side from towers. I walked down particularly to see the Silk Road bridge (Figure 3.8). Right on the

Figure 3.7 The great Cathedral at Ani. © Veysel Apaydin.

border, I rested for a couple of minutes and listened to the sound of the river and looked at the Armenian side and then looked back at the Turkish side. I thought about how borders are artificial and divisive, separating people from each other and from their heritage. Borders also represent a 'border line of identities' (Donnan and Wilson 1999), particularly for nation states where one ethnic group dominates, oppresses or denies the existence of other ethnic and cultural identities, those that they consider as existential threats to their national unity.

Any form of heritage is significant for the collective identity of groups and communities (Howard and Graham 2016). However, tangible remains of the past, particularly monumental heritage, are often used to present groups' and communities' links to the landscape or natural environment to which they have had generations of connections. They also operate as a means of memory storage and for shaping identities. Of course, any form of heritage can be said to act as a symbol of identities and to have importance for a sense of group and community. However, why I am particularly pointing to monumental or architectural heritage is that it embodies the power of meanings and knowledge that are ascribed by groups and communities more precisely. It is more visible compared

Figure 3.8 Silk Road bridge on the Arpaçay River. © Veysel Apaydin.

to other forms of heritage (Vale 2008) as it reminds others about the existence of certain groups. Throughout history, from prehistoric times to the present, this is the main reason that monumental or architectural heritage is often the first target (Sommer 2017; Apaydin 2020a). The case of the Yugoslavian war, where both sides targeted religious places, is an example (see Bevan 2016; Walasek 2015). Even in times of peace, there are examples, such as when churches are converted to mosques or vice versa, as happened to the churches in Kars.

Architectural or monumental heritage sites are not only significant for their visibility but they are also strong memory places where certain groups develop their collective memory. This is strongly linked to performance and experience and active engagement of individuals and groups in the past (Ricoeur 1999, 2004). However, memory is also an active engagement in the present (Nora 1989) that is used for different purposes. In the case of Ani, cultural memory is significant for the Armenians because for them, it provides a sense of belonging and consolidates a collective identity. As well, the material culture of the site offers them forms of emotional connection. This is mainly because Ani is a living 'archaeological record' for Armenians that represents feelings and attachment

(Perry 2019). Ani is also significant for the Turks, but from a more nationalist and political perspective: its history is reconstructed and used for discourses of the Turkish nation state. Both nation states attach great significance and meaning to Ani as a monumental site and landscape. For the Armenians, this is because they built most of the site's monumental heritage a millennium ago; for the Turks, it marks the period when they arrived almost a millennium ago.

The site and landscape of Ani, because of their collective representations for both countries, clearly represent that memory, particularly cultural or collective memory, is an ongoing process – a concept that was defined by Maurice Halbwachs in his pioneering work, *La Mémoire collective* (1950). However, the main difference between the Armenians and the Turks is that Ani represents remembrance as a performative agent for Armenians rather than forgetting, which is another concept of memory (Erll and Rigney 2009). This is in contrast to the Turks who consider Ani significant, based on a singular event: the arrival of Turks to Anatolia. In other words, Ani becomes important for Turks as a history that is reconstructed, but Ani is a living memory (Nora 1989, 2) for many Armenians, especially those who lived in Turkey.

The monumental aspect of the site, which stores the cultural memory and preserves the collective identity of Armenians, becomes more important from the beginning of the twentieth century onwards. Since the increase of nationalism in the early twentieth century in the Ottoman Empire, nationalists took power and began to eliminate non-Turkish cultural aspects of the country. The Armenians were perhaps most affected by this nationalist purification process. The year 1915 marks the Armenian Genocide in which millions of Armenians were forced to leave the country and hundreds of thousands were killed (Akçam 2004). Today, most Armenian populations live in diaspora across Europe and America. Around 100,000 live in Turkey as a recognized minority group. As such, Ani, and many other monuments and cultural landscapes where Armenians lived before the ethnic cleansing, became more important for Armenians who were socially and culturally dispersed and faced losing their cultural memory.

Of course, as cultural heritage, memory is a process that is developed, constructed, reconstructed and deconstructed through time and space (Holtorf 2018). In many cases, as in heritage and culture, memory is also usually resilient and people tend to develop new memories through interaction with new environments, communities and spaces (Mohamed and Holtorf 2017). However, traumatic events, such as genocide and ethnic cleansing, lead to generations of remembered traumas, and people often look at back to the past to heal themselves – or, in other words, they often tend to search for a connection with their memories in homelands as a part of the relationship between collective identity and homes (Clifford 1994). This is a relationship between the past and present, time and place that is socially constructed and affects generations. Armenians who visit Ani and other cultural and historical places in Turkey related to their cultural memory and their past strongly demonstrate this relationship between the past, present and future. The complex relationship between the past and the present for different cultural groups, who interpret the material culture from different perspectives, can also make these lands and heritage contested.

The strong and powerful representation of tangible heritage is one of the main reasons that Turkey's authorized heritage discourse neglects the Armenian past from public institutions, such as the Turkish education system, as I discussed in the previous chapter. Nation states are constructed under certain perceptions and supported by mass communications, such as educational institutions (Gellner 1983), and the concepts of the past and heritage are used in the interests of the nation state (Anderson 1983). Or the heritage is neglected and left to decay, as in the case of most ethnic groups' heritage in states like Turkey that deconstruct and reconstruct the meaning and value of heritage.

Of course, heritage is a process (Smith 2006) and this means that its meaning and values may change over time (Ashworth, Graham and Tunbridge 2007; Apaydin 2018c), or new meanings, values and memories can be added to specific heritage and interpreted from a variety of perspectives (Harvey 2001). However, the questions are, should this be initiated from the bottom up with a democratic approach by local communities or stakeholders through preserving previous heritage and transforming it for the future? Or should it be through a top-down and authoritarian approach by undemocratic nation states, who neglect the rights of other groups who attach values and meanings and develop memories that are significant for their sense of belonging and cultural identity? Making heritage accessible and decision-making processes democratic would render the changing process more ethical and prevent the violation of the rights of people (Silverman and Ruggles 2007; Logan 2012). In other words, this process should be initiated by communities who have a relationship with that specific heritage (Apaydin 2020a). This is also strongly linked to the 'representation' dimension of social justice (Fraser 2009), as I discussed in Chapter 1, that aims to make the decision-making process as democratic as possible by being inclusive and making decisions in parallel with people's needs and priorities as well as their own interpretations. From the 'representation' perspective of social justice, who gets precedence in the case of Ani must be local communities who have lived there for generations and developed memories and a sense of belonging, as well as Armenians whose identity, memory and sense of belonging are similarly attached to the site.

The exclusion of local communities and stakeholders from the decision-making process has been important for the Turkish state in terms of conserving its official ideology and authorized heritage discourse. This is mainly because excluding communities and stakeholders, who could bring out multicultural sides of Ani, allows the state to present a singular version of heritage which aligns with its ideology. The misrecognition of the site's material culture is not only a breach of human rights, but it is also opposed to the 'recognition' dimension of social justice that emphasizes the importance of recognizing multiculturality, different identities and backgrounds. The case of Ani demonstrates the state's ideological and nationalist discourses, which have played a large role in deconstructing and reconstructing meanings and values (Smith 2006, 2010, 2012) that are implemented top-down, excluding local community members and other stakeholders such as Armenians.

Ani has unique monuments that have played a large role in the politics of Turkey in the past and today as well as in the politics of the Armenians in Armenia and the global diaspora (Watenpaugh 2014). Most Armenians consider the region to be part of Armenia and, in fact, call it 'West Armenia'. Attempts at claiming heritage are very common all around the world (Tunbridge and Ashworth 1995; Lowenthal 1996; Smith 2006; Ashworth, Graham, and Tunbridge 2007; Silverman 2010) and these are, of course, linked to asserting power and used to construct identities both as dominant ethnic groups or elites and in contestation or opposition to them (Silverman 2010).

Tension and division

In contemporary politics, Ani is often at the centre of national tensions and illustrates how heritage can lead to division between communities, as we see with many heritage sites around the world (McDowell 2016). However, Ani was also historically a significant place where contention and conflict between kingdoms was not uncommon. It was a strategic trading centre, located on the Silk Road, and thus a battleground between empires, such as the Armenian Kingdom, and the Byzantine, Seljuk and Georgian civilizations (Apaydin 2018c). All of these cultures and civilizations left traces, making Ani multicultural alongside its Armenian monumental heritage (Akçayöz et al. 2007). However, tensions and divisions between Turkey and the Armenians in relation to Ani only date back to the first quarter of the twentieth century.

In the past, Ani's cathedrals and churches were very significant for Armenian Christians, standing as places of pilgrimage; in the early twentieth century regular tours were organized to Ani (Watenpaugh 2014). The site is also now significant for Turkish nationalists because it marks the location of the arrival of ethnic Turks to modern Turkey, when the Seljuk Empire conquered the city in 1064. This is one of the reasons that the Turkish state promotes and emphasizes Seljuk heritage in state institutions, particularly in the education system. This arrival status of Turks to modern Turkey is also one of the other reasons that nationalists use the site as a tool to promote nationalism and Turkishness. For instance, in 2010, ultra-nationalists carried out a large rally in Ani and organized a prayer in the great Cathedral of Ani to commemorate the Seljuk victory in the eleventh century (BBC 2010), illustrating how cultural heritage can complicate and intensify political tensions between groups and can be a reason for conflict.

Because of nationalist propaganda, the promotion of Turkishness only, the authorized heritage discourse that is dominated by Turkish and Islamic perspectives (Zencirci 2014), and the neglect of other minority identities in school textbooks, younger generations in Turkey also grow up without any awareness of other cultures and their associated past and heritage (Güler-Biyikli and Aslan 2013; Apaydin 2016c). Additionally, there is the impact of formal education that not only neglects the past and material culture of minorities but also uses discriminatory discourses against the Armenians, portraying them as an enemy (Bilmez et al. 2017). This heavy nationalist propaganda impacts on communities' perceptions of heritage and is a dominant cause of 'othering'. The heavy anti-Armenian discourse, which has been supported, backed and promoted by state institutions for over one hundred years, leads to local people developing biases and prejudices against Armenians and their heritage. Most of the ethnically Turkish local community members in the region, in Ani province, do not recognize the existence of Armenians or their heritage and past in the region.

The accounts of my interviewees in and around Ani clearly indicate how state manipulation of the past and nationalist pressure is strong, and how generations of this strong and effective perception management have been successful in influencing people's views about the past as well as the future of the region. For instance, some people of Turkish ethnicity, including locals of Ani and Kars, do not recognize that Armenians ever occupied the region, nor do they accept Armenians' claims to Ani's monumental heritage. Rather they emphasize 'how these lands have always been Turkish and Islamic', arguing that 'all the monumental heritage from Ani is Turkish and Islamic'. Although physical evidence indicates the long-time existence of Armenians in the region, interview participants only recognize the official history or, in other words, the authorized heritage discourse of the Turkish state, which has been implemented in every part of educational and social life. This kind of understanding and interpretation of the past is also a result of present social and political requirements (Eriksen 2010): Turkey claims ownership of the lands, arguing that this territory has always been Turkish. A similar phenomenon can also be observed in the Armenian state official view, which also claims these lands as theirs (see Bilmez 2017).

Comparable attitudes and approaches are common across the world (Kohl and Fawcett 1995; Meskell 1998; Silverman 2010), and there are many cases demonstrating lack of recognition and acceptance of the links of certain identity groups to the past. This is obviously part of the political exercise of hegemonic power that controls nation states, where specific material culture linked to specific ethnic groups is seen as a threat to national unity. Appadurai (1991) calls it a contradiction of nationality and locality. In the past, there was even an attempt to completely eliminate Ani's monumental heritage. At the end of the Ottoman Empire, the period when nationalism was on the rise and nationalists took power in the Ottoman Empire, one of the main generals of the Turkish army was ordered to demolish the monuments of Ani. The main reason for the order was that Ani represented Armenian identity and Armenians' existence in these lands. His reply to the Turkish ministry, which had demanded that Ani be demolished, is recorded:

> There is no possibility of demolishing Ani. Its city walls are as big as Istanbul's city walls and it contains many churches … if we demolish them it would increase the tension of [the] Armenian community in the region. (Karabekir 1988, 924)

Although the heritage of Ani was not destroyed at that time, many cultural heritage sites and monuments of the Armenians and other minority groups, and indeed anything unrelated to the authorized heritage discourse of the Turkish state, disappeared over time because of neglect (Bevan 2016). This type of neglect is not necessarily due to ignorance, but is often a deliberate action that is part of nationalist heritage policies. In the case of Ani, such action began following the collapse of the Ottoman Empire and continued throughout the establishment of the Republic of Turkey and into the present day. For instance, changing the non-Turkish place names to Turkish names, or not allocating space in textbooks to covering the heritage and past of minority groups (Gül-Biyikli and Aslan 2013), or not allocating any space in museums for the cultural objects of minority groups, all demonstrate political acts underlying the neglect of the heritage and the past of minorities. Instead, the state applies its education and museums services to protect national unity and the national narrative, furthering the Turkish heritage discourse. This is something that Anderson (1983) describes as the 'imagined community', which needs constant protection through intervention and promotion by nationalists. Today, many Turkish local communities in the Ani region, who were raised under strong nationalist policies and education, interpret the heritage of Ani from a strong nationalist perspective:

> Ani is important for us and it is my [our] past because the monuments and architecture, which contain much Turkish architecture, of the city, were built in the reign of sultan Alparslan who conquered Anatolia in 1071 and afterwards by Turks ... there is not such a past and history of Armenians in the region ... Ani and the region have always been Turkish and Islamic.

> What I [we] know about the past of this region is that it was always Turkish, only the Russians occupied it for several years in the past but we [Turks] took our lands back again.

> The Armenian inscriptions were made during the Russian invasion ... Armenians came here to take over our lands together with the Russians during the war.

These anecdotes from Turkish local community members clearly illustrate how heritage and material culture can be interpreted through the lens of politics, as Smith (2006, 2010, 2012) has demonstrated through many case studies. This kind of interpretation and lack of acknowledgement of certain pasts and heritage is partly a consequence of a one-sided educational system in which selective knowledge, created by society's elite, is imposed (see Bilmez et al. 2017) through state power. Such commentaries also demonstrate how the values and meanings of cultural heritage and material culture can be deconstructed and reconstructed through nationalist heritage discourse.

For instance, one of the anecdotes above reinterprets and revalues Ani in parallel with official heritage discourse created by the elites of Turkey. Turkey is not the only country which revalues and redefines heritage; such acts are evident throughout history, as can be seen in the case of the Yugoslavian and then Kosovo war (Herscher 2010; Bevan 2016; Walasek 2017). As I pointed out earlier in this chapter, Ani is located on the border between Turkey and Armenia and there has been a long history of conflict. Therefore, Ani also represents the borderline of state identity (Donnan and Wilson 1999). Such identity shaped demographic changes following the Armenian genocide and cleansing in 1915: most places that were left by Armenians were repopulated by Kurds, Turks and Azerbaijanis through state intervention (Üngör 2011).

The neglect of specific ethnic and identity groups' heritage is not only limited to Ani; it can also be seen in the city centre, where Armenian houses are totally neglected to the point where they are left to ruin or demolished through the gentrification process. Orhan Pamuk (2004), a Nobel prize winner, exposes the multicultural past of Kars, including the past of Armenians, in his famous novel *Snow*, which can be seen from the remains of houses or churches in Kars. During my second ethnographic work period at Kars, I walked through the streets that

Figure 3.9 Traditional Armenian black stone house in the city centre. © Veysel Apaydin.

are located away from the city centre: traditional Armenian stone houses can still be seen in many parts on those streets (Figure 3.9), although most of them have been demolished or reduced to ruins. The nationalist and dominant neoliberal policies, particularly since the right-wing populist JDP took power, have shown a more effective and destructive impact on the Armenian past and heritage in the city.

Most of the Armenian names, along with other non-Turkish names, have been replaced (Tunçel 2000). This is also the case for the Kurdish region of Turkey, where Kurdish place names were replaced with Turkish names. One of my interview participants, who used to work in the city council and lived all his live in Kars, points out:

> as a person who has lived here for all my life, the state has always been careful and sensitive about anything related to Armenians as this can be seen in place names. Although it is known that there is a strong Armenian history in the region, you cannot even see one single Armenian name . . . they were all replaced with Turkish as part of the assimilation process.

Since the beginning of and during the rise of nationalism, particularly throughout the end of the nineteenth century and beginning of the twentieth century, when nation states became very common, creating myths and glorifying nations' history also become very popular in many parts of the world. Most nation states made connections with older civilizations to claim ownership rights of territory, particularly against minority ethnic groups who were considered to be a threat to national unity (Kohl and Fawcett 1995; Meskell 1998). Within this nationalist phenomenon, archaeology and heritage became very important to prove ownership rights for particular groups who considered material culture as key assets for national narratives and identity making.

While this neglect of Ani's past and heritage was very significant for developing national narratives to preserve the unity of the Turkish nation state, Ani was also used for alternative narratives, including the collective identity of Armenians. Armenian nationalism is no exception (Rutland 1994) and is similar to other nationalisms. It is based on a single ethnic group and based on myths and imagination, creating Armenian national narratives to create unity. These national narratives are similar to Turkish and other nation state examples, developed here by the Armenian elite as part of their official history and authorized heritage discourse. However, Armenian nationalism is bound up in two different forms: first, through nationalism that is developed and based on the Armenian Republic and especially constructed and formed by the Armenian church (Apostolic church), which has great influence in Armenia; and second, through diaspora nationalism, which was developed by Armenians who live in different parts of the world (Guroian 1994 for more on diaspora nationalism) and whose roots tie back to Turkey where ethnic cleansing and genocide took place in 1915 (see Akçam 2004).

Another significant difference between these nationalisms is that sites such as Ani and other historical sites and monuments are significant for the diaspora Armenians for a sense of belonging and sense of place. Even though these Armenians were born and have lived in other parts of the world for generations, most of them still have great emotional attachments to these lands in Turkey, as some of those Armenians who visited Ani pointed out. However, because Armenia is a nation state, nationalism takes more strict, heavy and systematic forms here, as it does in Turkey. For instance, there is a similar abuse of the past and heritage and material culture in the development of the national narrative and myth. Moreover, the active reconstructing of values and meanings can be seen in the Armenian education system as well (Bilmez et al. 2017).

For example, Armenian school textbooks contain discriminatory language against Turks, and Turks are usually presented in narratives as the enemy. The textbooks contain narratives that glorify the Armenian past, and Armenians themselves, through text, images and maps, and emphasize how Armenians are a unique nation that is proud of its ancient heritage (Bilmez et al. 2017, 51). Because Ani contains great architectural examples of Armenian churches, symbolizes Armenian identity and stores memories for Armenians, it is given special attention and importance by the Armenian state and nationalists who consider it as one of its key assets for its national identity (Watenpaugh 2014). For instance, the great cathedral at Ani, which was built during the eleventh century, is very important for Christian Armenians because it is one of the earliest cathedrals.

Similar to how Turkish nationalists abuse Ani, the monuments and material culture, as well as the past of Ani, are very often abused by Armenian nationalists, who use it as a tool to promote nationalism and claim ownership rights over the region. To exemplify, to commemorate the 1050th anniversary of Ani, many exhibitions and events were carried out in 2011 across the world that emphasized the importance of Ani for Armenians and their identity construction. The exhibition 'Ani: Capital of Armenia – 1050' was held at the History Museum of Armenia in Yerevan and subsequently travelled to many other countries.

Likewise, the systematic perception management of the public in Turkey, abuse of heritage and the past for consolidating and promoting national narratives in education and other forms of public events are also heavily forming the public's perception of Armenians. Because of its significance for memory, identity and sense of belonging, the monumental site of Ani receives thousands of Armenian visitors annually, particularly from the diaspora. This also correlates to the argument that diaspora nationalism is based on a thread of assimilation and elimination, as Gellner (1983) emphasizes. Many diaspora Armenians and Armenians living in Istanbul who visit the site point out the importance of Ani for their heritage:

> although I was born and grew up in France . . . the real home is here for me.

> Ani is important for us, it represents our culture and our existence in these lands . . . however, as long as it is protected and access is possible, I don't mind who owns it . . . it had many civilisations such as e.g., Armenians and Turks.

At the beginning of the twentieth century, the last census of the empire demonstrated that almost a third of the Ottoman population was Armenian and Greek. Today, there are around 70,000 Armenians, mostly living in Istanbul where Armenian architecture can still be seen, particularly in central Istanbul. While Armenians who live in Turkey are less affected by Armenian nationalism than those in Armenia or diaspora Armenians, the material culture of the Armenian past is still symbolically important for their collective identity. While they point out their feelings about their vanishing heritage, they also articulate their feelings about how institutional and systematic discrimination have made them the 'other':

> although we are originally from these lands we have been made 'other' and our cultural heritage in many parts of Turkey has been erased.

> Ani has great potential to open up dialogue and build a sustainable future as long as its multicultural past is recognised by both sides.

Ani certainly has a tremendous multicultural past, which also illustrates how memories can be built and constructed on top of each other. As such, it could be a symbol and tool for dialogue and peace between the two nation states. Although in the past, there was an attempt to break the barrier between the nations and establish a dialogue, it was unsuccessful because of Turkish nationalist propaganda. More than a decade ago, as part of a campaign of the former mayor of Kars and local NGOs, and with the support of academics and artists, a 35m high 'statue of humanity' was erected in the city of Kars to initiate and symbolize peace between Turkey and Armenia. However, ultra-nationalist organizations, such as the 'Grey Wolves' and other associations, including the governor of the state, began to campaign against it, and not long after the statue was built, the Turkish government ordered it to be demolished because of the nationalistic activities of these individuals and organizations. The policy of erasing the past and associated heritage was not only about destruction or neglect but it was also, in this case, more systematic.

Heritage is highly related to social and political issues and I consider heritage as beyond the material culture of the past because it constructs and forms the future of societies, as well as their social and political structures. However, when discussing the importance of Ani for contested heritage, national narratives, increasing tension and dividing groups, we also need to consider what is the meaning of the cultural heritage and material culture for local communities and how do they engage and value it through daily interactions?

Locality and values

At the beginning of the twentieth century, following the genocide and ethnic cleansing of Armenians across Turkey, Turkish nationalists, who were in power, carried out a massive demographic change in many parts of the country (Akdar 2000; Üngör 2011). The demographic change can be seen clearly in east Turkey where the Armenian population was high at one time. The region of Ani and Kars is key here: the places where Armenians used to live, including homes and lands, were populated by Kurdish or Turkish origin communities. The occupants of Ocakli village, right next to Ani, who describe themselves as of Turkish origin, point out that their great grandparents were repopulated to this region from other parts of Turkey. They used to live in the caves of Ani before the village was established. During my ethnographic fieldwork, I managed to meet most of the community members who had been living there for generations by that time.

One morning during the hot summer, I woke very early to catch the sunrise over Ani. Most of the villagers were also up and were taking their animals for grazing (Figure 3.10). Most of the time, they take their animals to the edge of the Arpaçay river, which is also the natural border between Turkey and Armenia. The villagers do not have many places for grazing here: one side is a military area, the other side is a closed border. After spending a few hours there, I walked back to the village to talk to community members. On the hill, I saw a very big Turkish shepherd dog, which suddenly disappeared. I was curious where the dog had gone. I walked over and found a big cave with many galleries, which was right next to Ani and a modern village (Figure 3.11). At the same time, the owner of the dog and the cave showed up and wanted to show me the whole cave. It was amazing because it had a living area, a stone oven, rooms for animals and people. He said:

> We used to live in this cave for a long time. I remember that we used to bake bread in this oven ... the cave kept us very warm during winter and it made it very cool during the summer ... until the 1950s, we used to live in the caves of Ani ... it was our home.

The commentary exposes how memory has been developed in relation to this place and how meaning may differ at a local level, highlighting a 'sense of place' for community members. The aforementioned anecdote of the local resident also demonstrates that living in and next to a heritage site and using its landscape for decades leads to forming a personal and communal relationship to which they ascribed and attached values, meanings (Ashworth and Graham 2005; Waterton 2005; Smith 2006; Smith and Waterton 2009) and memories that are not related to nationalist discourses.

In contrast to the abuse of heritage to create division and increase tension between communities, heritage also has different meanings, representations and

Figure 3.10 Animal grazing in Ani. © Veysel Apaydin.

Figure 3.11 A reconstructed natural cave. It used to be a home for villagers. © Veysel Apaydin.

values for local people in their social and daily lives. In other words, heritage represents different values and meanings at the grassroots level (Waterton 2005; Smith 2006; Smith and Waterton 2009). It also represents plurality (Ashworth, Graham, and Tunbridge 2007) because its relevance and uses vary for every individual who develops a different level of relationship with the heritage in everyday life (Smith 2006; Smith and Akagawa 2009). Emma Waterton (2005) clearly demonstrates, with her case study in the UK – the Hareshaw Linn community project in Bellingham, Northumberland – how values and meanings at a community level can be substantially different from those imposed through a top-down, approach. A similar case study in the North Pennines in northern England demonstrates the different meanings and values of heritage as place at the local level versus those developed at a national level power (Hawke 2012). These heritage phenomena provide different senses of place for people (Tunbridge and Ashworth 1995; Davis 1999; Graham, Ashworth, and Tunbridge 2000; Ashworth and Graham 2005; Atkinson 2007; Crooke 2008; Schofield and Szymanzki 2011; Convery, Corsane, and Davis 2012; Hawke 2012).

Ani as a site and landscape is one of the best examples of such a local level relationship with the site. Most of the community members of the modern villages point out that the landscape, and Ani itself with its monuments, take a great and important place in their daily life, resulting in related individual and group memories. Memory has always been embedded in the contested political relationship between the past and present (Hodgkin and Radstone 2003), used as a tool for ownership and contestation of landscapes. However, as in the Ani case, the concept of memory also has different meanings and importance developed through individual relationships with the material culture, landscape and nature. I was able to to see such relationships every day during my participatory observation over years of ethnographic fieldwork at Ani.

As I walked in the ruins and standing monuments and churches of Ani, the first thing I noticed was the writings and drawings on the stones of monuments and ruins, mostly done by local children. Many archaeologists and heritage specialists could interpret such interventions as forms of vandalizing heritage, but for me these are graffiti that are made naturally as part of attaching new values and ascribing meanings to the historic monuments: they are part of the layering of memory. 'Sense of place' is developed over time via the interactions of individuals and groups with the place and the landscape. However, the period of childhood is more important than any other period in one's lifetime as it so deeply shapes our personalities and views (Smith 2013, 115). More or less every individual who lives in the modern village has memories of the site of Ani and its monuments, particularly from their childhood, as many villagers describe:

> every monument and building of Ani is important for me, as we used to play and had a picnic with friends and family long ago.

> It encompasses all my childhood memories. Since early age, my friends and I used to play and spend time in Ani.

While local children and youth from modern villages use Ani as a playground, they also leave tangible traces of their interactions with the monuments and material culture of Ani. My argument is that this is not the destruction or vandalizing of heritage but rather the layering of memories on top of old ones, reconstructing and transforming tangible heritage for the future. This is not political reconstruction or, in other words, top-down reconstruction, but very bottom-up and natural reconstruction of heritage that has meanings for local people. This is also a very significant example of why cultural heritage sites that are falling into ruin should be reused to transform heritage into something new.

Transformation

In her book *Curated Decay*, DeSilvey (2017) demonstrates the public benefit of reusing heritage sites or ruins. Of course, there are great benefits of reusing heritage and spaces for local community members. However, what is more important here is the process, and whether it is done bottom-up through local communities who are able to take initiative over such transformation or top-down through national-level management that may neglect the local value and meaning of heritage and its associated landscape. Since Ani has become a UNESCO World Heritage Site and a new site management plan has been developed, villagers cannot access or use the site monuments and its landscape as they did in the past. During my ethnographic fieldwork, most of the community members pointed out how their daily life became quite difficult after they were cut off from the site. The site and its landscape, which is several times bigger than the current village and its landscape, is now fenced off and therefore local people cannot interact with it as they did before. This is very significant for local communities, as emphasized by Smith (2006) and Waterton (2005). Heritage and landscapes have great meaning for local communities who engage with them daily and they are a part of the ongoing long-term process of meaning making.

The top-down management approach, which completely neglects local views and needs, has acted as a tool to change the relationship between locals and the heritage site because it plays a significant role in reconstructing local community members' sense of place. Protection and preservation should be led by local people, as they are the natural guardians of cultural heritage sites (Pearson and Sullivan 1995), even if their roles have been neglected in the current management plans of many UNESCO heritage sites and others around the world. The neglect of local people in such management plans demonstrates that imposing meanings and values that were originally formed through 'western elites' (Smith 2006, 11) is still common in many parts of the world.

As I pointed out previously, the current community in the modern village was repopulated in the early twentieth century, when they were living in the caves of Ani. In the 1950s, the central government allocated a space right next to the heritage site where they established a village. I visited most of the houses of the village (Figure 3.12). Houses were made of mud bricks and stones. However, what surprised me while I was visiting the village houses is that most of the stones were transferred from the monuments of the heritage site of Ani, as many Armenian inscriptions on stones were partly visible. Villagers also confirmed

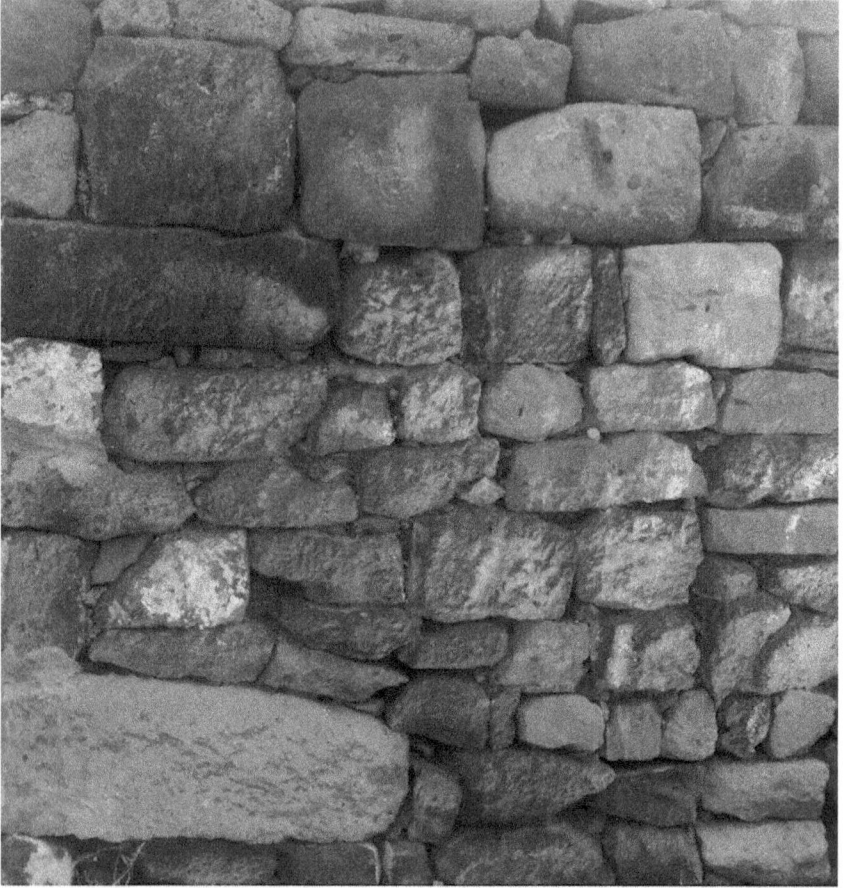

Figure 3.12 Modern village house wall. Stones were taken from Ani's monuments.
© Veysel Apaydin.

that their grandparents carried those stones from the ruins of Ani. This example demonstrates and reflects on Holtorf's (2018) point: it is not necessarily destruction but a natural process of reconstruction, which is sometimes inevitable and unavoidable as present requirements shape the use of heritage. The villagers' needs and current daily requirements forced them to build houses by using the original stones of Ani. Here transformation has happened and sometimes must happen via using and developing with the surrounding material culture.

Ani, with its stunning monumental heritage and landscape as well as accumulated memories for centuries, offers an example of how material culture can be rejected and abused to consolidate and promote nationalism and oppress the 'other' whose rights, which are ascribed to that material culture, have been breached. Secondly, it shows how cultural space, including its associated material culture, may be developed, reconstructed and transformed – as well as destroyed – in ways that have different significance, meanings, uses and values for different groups, each of whom have varied links with and agendas for the cultural heritage.

The case of Ani clearly demonstrates that cultural heritage, its management and practice, is highly linked to human rights and social justice. The past of certain groups' identities is undermined and neglected, and those groups are prevented from learning about their own history and heritage. At Ani, the past and heritage of the Armenians is not recognized and the knowledge of those material cultures is not equally distributed to the public as part of the 'redistribution' dimension of social justice. As in the case of Ani, heritage and its management as practised today are often used to reassert the legitimacy and reinforce the power of hegemonic entities rather than paying attention to the 'representation' dimension of social justice where people have a voice and say in the decision-making processes.

However, while the example of Ani demonstrates the link between human rights and social justice and its breach through abusing heritage for political purposes for nationalist discourses, it can also demonstrate varied meanings and values for people's daily lives. Though the evidence of 'hegemonic' or 'authorized' heritage discourses can be seen to operate fairly universally, values and meanings of heritage can be different at the local level because of the relationship of locals, who are culturally different from communities in other parts of the world, and the use of such heritage resources in their daily lives.

As I have tried to demonstrate with the case of Ani, every individual and group varies with their social, cultural and economic backgrounds, which in turn form and shape their needs. Such diversity has great impact in terms of how heritage can be used as a resource for the local population. Smith (2006) clearly exemplifies the difference between authorized heritage discourse and a local community's sense of heritage in Castleford in the United Kingdom. The town of Castleford represents a significant history of industrial heritage, as it was one of the mining towns in England. With its Roman period history, it is often regarded as quite significant in British national identity making and is used as part of the authorized heritage discourse (Smith 2006). In contrast, Smith (2006) points out that the alternative use of heritage and memories that are constructed between place and locals as a result of daily relationships are often neglected. Similarly, Ani as a heritage site, a built environment and landscape embodies meaning and value in opposition to the nationalist positions and authorized heritage discourse, but it also highlights the inherent contest and contradictory nature of heritage. This includes its importance for cultural rights and social justice, particularly where historic ownership of sites is contested (see also Apaydin 2018c for more discussion about Ani, its heritage and communities).

4

Conflict

In my work as an archaeologist and heritage specialist as part of the Ilisu Dam project, I travelled to southeast Turkey many times. The region is the most unstable area of Turkey because of over forty years of continuous conflict between the Turkish state and Kurdistan Workers' Party that aims to establish autonomy in the Kurdish region of Turkey (Watts 2010). The Kurdistan Workers' Party was established in 1978 and has been in conflict ever since with the Turkish state (Barkey and Fuller 1998). Since then, restrictions, exclusions and breaches of human rights against the Kurdish community have been systematically implemented and have continued to increase (Bozarslan 1996, 2008). The conflict is ongoing, with several previous moments of ceasefire and peace negotiations that in the long term were unsuccessful (Savran 2020; Yegen 2015). The devastating impact of decades of conflict has, without doubt, affected almost all communities in the region (Göç-Der 2022). Tens of thousands of people have lost their lives, hundreds of thousands have been displaced to the big cities or resettled (Jongerden 2007; Gambetti and Jongerden 2015). These have been traumatic experiences for the people of the region. They have lost their lands, their farms and the places where they used to practise those cultural activities that bound them together.

Decades of conflict have created extremely high levels of tension in the region as well as high levels of anxiety for the people who were living in these conditions of conflict. The tension is visible everywhere: from heavy military presence in both cities and rural areas, checkpoints, to fighter jets and military helicopters constantly flying overhead, to organized protests by Kurdish people against the restrictions of their cultural rights which usually end up in clashes with security forces (Watts 2010; Gourdillo 2014). Such tensions can especially be seen in big cities such as Diyarbakir, a stronghold of the Kurdish struggle and the People's Democratic Party (hereafter HDP, which is a pro-Kurdish party in the Turkish Parliament). Diyarbakir is considered as a foremost centre of Kurdish heritage and identity, as well as a capital (Gambetti 2009). It is also known for its active social and cultural life (e.g. coffee shops and bars) as well as its multicultural heritage stemming from the joint influence of Kurdish, Armenian, Yazidi and many other ethnic groups.

During my many visits to Diyarbakir, I had the opportunity to talk to locals and NGO representatives and obtained a deeper knowledge about the role of Diyarbakir and Sur for the cultural life and heritage of the Kurdish people, as well as their views about the Ilisu Dam project. These conversations helped to expose the experiences of conflict that have affected local people's social, cultural, tangible and intangible heritage. Although the conflict had mainly taken place in the rural areas of the region, in 2015, the city of Diyarbakir witnessed a dramatic development that affected one of the largest and most historical towns of Diyarbakir, Sur (which is also part of the UNESCO World Heritage Site Diyarbakir Fortress and Hevsel Gardens Landscape,[1] Figure 4.1). The Kurdistan Workers' Party declared self-autonomy in Sur as well as in other towns in southeast Turkey (Saadi 2021), and this development led to months of conflict between Kurdish militias and Turkish armed forces, which responded very strongly to this move, resulting in the destruction of the majority of the town.

Figure 4.1 UNESCO World Heritage Site Diyarbakir Fortress and Hevsel Gardens. © Ibrahim Yakut/Anadolu Agency/Getty Images.

Destruction and discourse

The destruction of monumental and architectural heritage, as a tool, is used by many authoritarian regimes and sectarian groups to wipe out the existential symbols of a specific identity or ethnic group. This destruction comes in many forms, including the assimilation of those who develop distinct memories and tangible and intangible heritage, the neglect of a specific heritage, or the specific destruction of symbols that represent a particular identity as part of a non-violence approach (as discussed in Chapter 2). However, armed conflict, or forms of direct violence, is perhaps the most destructive method, as is well documented and can be traced back to the prehistoric times (Sommer 2017); it is an effective method of eliminating, dispersing and dismantling groups and communities. The aim, purpose or goal is the same in both earlier periods and modern times, as heritage represents people who ascribe meanings and develop values with material culture, although the tools and capacity of destruction have changed with the development of technology. An example is the recent destruction of monumental and architectural heritage (houses, religious buildings, ancient monuments) in the last couple of decades during the Bosnia and Kosovo wars and in Iraq (Herscher 2010; Walasek 2015; Stone and Farchakh Bajjaly 2008). Many parts of the world still witness the destruction of heritage through different methods, as in the case of Ukraine.[2] Cities have been levelled, landscapes and forests are being burnt and transformed, objects and material culture are being looted, as Robert Bevan points out in his book, *The Destruction of Memory: Architecture at War* (2016):

> The levelling of buildings and cities has always been an inevitable part of conducting hostilities and has worsened as weaponry has become heavier and more destructive, from the slings and arrows of the past to the daisycutters of today. Continents rather than cities can be devastated. This damage may be the direct result of military manoeuvres to gain territory or root out a foe, or a desire to wipe out the enemy's capacity to fight. The division of the spoils also plays a part. But there has always been another war against architecture going on – the destruction of the cultural artefacts of an enemy people or nation as a means of dominating, terrorizing, dividing or eradicating it altogether. (Bevan 2016, 17–18)

Particularly, monumental or architectural heritage is of the utmost importance for both groups in conflict because they are strong symbols of cultural and collective identities and memory stores and therefore they provide the ground for a group to exist and keep their sense of belonging as a community (Vale

2008) (as I demonstrated in the case of Ani in the previous chapter). This representation of monumental and architectural heritage also makes it a target at the same time for the opposing group. Therefore, heritage is a positive representation for one group and a negative one for the other. This paradox of opposed values is one of the most complex ontologies of heritage, which is usually considered to be a positive asset from one perspective.

The last forty years of armed conflict between the Turkish armed forces and Kurdistan Workers' Party, which aimed to establish autonomous areas in southeast and east Turkey, is perhaps one of the best examples to demonstrate one of the most complex ontologies and discourses of heritage. While heritage and material culture are imbued with positivity for Kurdish people, it is also considered a threat and/or negative to the national unity of Turkey, which is established on a strong one nation, one ethnicity with its ideology centred around Turkishness (Ersanli 2003). As part of the heritage process, Kurdish people have used the landscape and nature to develop tangible and intangible heritage and have created monumental heritage and architecture to maintain their sense of place and belonging and to consolidate their collective identity as a community. This heritage-building process of the Kurdish community was a threat for Turkey and Turkish nationalists because the Turkish official ideology did not recognize any ethnic groups outside of the Turks and their heritage. Without doubt, the situation between the Kurdish people and their (mis) recognition by Turkey is more historically complex and has deeper origins (Jongerden 2007; also see McDowall 2000). However, as Fraser (1998) demonstrates, the importance of recognition is significant in the concept of social justice. Similar misrecognition and abuse of heritage in order to claim ownership rights of the lands can be seen in the case of the Turks and Armenians and disputes of ownership rights between Armenia and Azerbaijan over Nagorna Karabakh (Van Heese 2018) and many other examples.

The use of material culture to prove ownership rights and establish autonomy in the Kurdish region by the Kurdistan Workers' Party was seen as a great threat to its autonomy and a challenge against its power by the Turkish state. However, fighting to control power and implement hegemony by both sides has led to incredible losses, from human lives to heritage and the environment in the region. During the forty years of conflict, material culture has been destroyed, defenders of human rights became targets,[3] and, perhaps most importantly, hundreds of thousands of people have been displaced in the predominantly Kurdish region of Turkey (Jongerden 2007; OHCHR 2017). Additionally, in the past, the natural environment was destroyed through, for example, systematic forest burning (Van Etten et al. 2008). This form of direct violence not only has an impact upon local people, who use the natural environment to develop tangible and intangible heritage, but also a greater environmental impact on biodiversity and climate, which has a long-term impact regionally and globally.

The inner city of Diyarbakir, part of the UNESCO World Heritage Site and very densely populated by Kurdish people, was one of the towns that was declared to be autonomous by the Kurdish militias. Sur or Suriçi (the inner city) is located on the Upper Tigris river, which is part of the 'Fertile Crescent'. The fortified city of Diyarbakir surrounds the heavily populated town of Sur/Suriçi (Figure 4.2). The town and surrounding landscape's history goes back to ancient periods, with archaeology from the Hellenistic, Roman, Byzantine, Islamic and Ottoman, Turkish and Armenian periods, as detailed by the UNESCO World Heritage Nomination process.[4] The site has been continuously occupied to the present, which also makes it a great case to demonstrate the accumulation of memories that have historically developed by different cultural communities. However, the city of Diyarbakir and the inner city of Sur were both significant for Kurdish people who developed memories, attached meanings and constructed their cultural and collective identities on these landscapes (Gambetti 2009; Saadi 2021).

Figure 4.2 Overview of Sur citadel and modern town. © Travel Photography/Istock by Getty Images.

The inner city within the walls of Sur had preserved its architectural and monumental heritage relatively well up until 2015 when the conflict began, and right after its inscription on the UNESCO World Heritage list. However, the UNESCO World Heritage Convention did not even reflect on the destruction of the inner city during the conflict, even though it was heavily critiqued by the media (France24 2016). The main reason for that is UNESCO, as a global organization, has a complex structure that is managed by the member states (Meskell 2018). Therefore, the state's interests reflect heavily on the decision making of the World Heritage listing. Most of the inscriptions by each state, such as the case of the Diyarbakir Fortress and Hevsel Gardens Cultural Landscape, do not go beyond the aim of international recognition and bringing economic benefit, and the states' national and ideological interests play a more important role in inscribing for World Heritage Sites during the selection process (Meskell 2014, 2018).

On many occasions, international and national organizations and NGOs criticized the heavy-handed reaction of Turkey from an international human rights and property law perspective, because the conflict led to great architectural damage and destruction of churches, mosques and homes. Among the architectural and monumental heritage, Kursunlu Mosque, the Surp Giragos Armenian church and the city walls, which were listed as part of the UNESCO World Heritage Site, were heavily damaged (Soyukaya 2017; Figure 4.3). The

Figure 4.3 Damage on the Surp (Saint) Giragos Armenian Church following the conflict. © Ilyas Akengin/AFP via Getty Images.

majority of the inner city was levelled and the rest of the neighbourhoods of Sur were left empty and stayed under curfew for years (Amnesty International 2016).

The damage to properties of the inner city, houses and heritage was greater after the end of the conflict (OHCHR 2017). Half of the inner city was wiped out and locals were displaced (Soyukaya 2017). People who had lived in the inner city completely lost access to their own neighbourhoods and participating in cultural and public events was banned. Following the conflict, although access was granted for some locals who lived in the inner city, they could not do so because of the heavy destruction – some 70 per cent of buildings in the inner city were destroyed by shelling (OHCHR 2017 for detailed report and Soyukaya 2017). The scale of the damage and destruction, in particular for architectural heritage, demonstrates the embedded discourses of conflict, because architecture is a strong representational aspect for identity and memory. In the Sur case, it represents the memory and the past of minority groups and Kurdish heritage. Similarly, wiping out the inner city also shows why 'space' is important for heritage making (Harvey 2007; Lefebvre 1991) because it plays a significant role as a resource (Apaydin 2020b) for preserving the collective identity of a local community.

The case of the Sur conflict is important for two reasons. First, it demonstrates how space, both built and monumental heritage, can lead to destructive armed conflict between powers who are fighting over ownership rights to claim lands; and second, how the conflict over heritage leads to forced displacement of communities, who lose their space to perform social and cultural activities. The spaces people use to perform cultural and social activities to make heritage is important, from the point of social organization and production (Lefebvre 1991).

In the case of southeast Turkey, particularly between July 2015 and December 2016, breaches were made in terms of the 'right to live': the destruction and expropriation of property, which includes housing and lands, access to health, access to justice, right to liberty, as well as participating in public activities, as detailed by the OHCHR (2017), Amnesty International (2016) and Human Rights Watch (2015) reports. The OHCHR report points out that when the committee visited the region, it was not able to access places, particularly Sur, the town of Diyarbakir, where the conflict took place. Therefore, the committee had to use alternative methods to gather information, including satellite imagery to see the destruction, interviews with the victims and people who were displaced, and the information provided by the Turkish government (similar to the Amnesty International Report).

Restriction and exclusion

During the forty-year conflict between Turkey and the Kurdistan Workers' Party, there have been heavy clashes and intermittent peace processes, especially since the JDP came to power in 2002. In contrast to the previous conflicts that usually took place in rural areas of southeast Turkey, conflict was brought into the inner cities (Amnesty International 2016). The Kurdistan Workers' Party, in contrast to its earlier strategies, began to declare self-autonomy in Kurdish areas. The declaration of self-autonomies simultaneously in many areas of the Kurdish region was heavily resisted by the Turkish military (Human Rights Watch 2015). The inner city of Sur witnessed the heaviest clashes and destruction during the armed conflict. Following this unexpected development, Turkish authorities began imposing indefinite twenty-four-hour curfews and the Turkish army used heavy artillery and tanks against the Kurdish militias (OHCHR 2017).

In contrast to this ongoing destructive conflict, at the local level, the Kurdish people have shown great resilience and persistence in their attempts to keep conserving and building their heritage. This is positive that the destruction motivated them to rebuild their heritage and their sense of community. However, this attempt has been seen negatively by the Turkish state, which has taken extreme measures to prevent the Kurdish community from building new heritage by restricting local access to lands and spaces, which were the resources for heritage making (see Amnesty International 2016). This conflict and the measures that the Turkish government took no doubt had a great impact on the people of the region. Their basic human rights were breached, as detailed by the Office of the United Nations High Commissioner for Human Rights (OHCHR 2017). The OHCHR compiled a detailed file on breaches of human rights, including restrictions on access to homes and the landscape lasting months and in some areas years, such as Sur.

Performing cultural activities as part of developing heritage is a basic human right that has been breached across the world (Silverman and Ruggles 2007, 2011; Logan 2010). In the past, Kurdish people have had many restrictions imposed on them, from speaking the Kurdish language freely to celebrating cultural events such as Newroz, which is a celebration through festivals of the Kurdish New Year coming with the welcoming of Spring. Although Newroz is celebrated in many countries in the Middle East and central Asia, since the 1990s it has become a symbol of Kurdish resistance and freedom in Turkey. As a cultural activity and performance, it has played a significant role in preserving Kurdish identity. Because of this, the Turkish state has often tried to restrict or ban it (Özbudun 2012; Aydin 2013). Although restriction of this type of Kurdish cultural activity was common in Turkey, the recent conflict in Sur has demonstrated another type of human rights breach.

The inner city, as a space, has been a resource for different cultures throughout history and today. Space is always a resource for heritage making and it takes generations, as people attach meanings and develop memories within a particular space; this also creates the 'sense of place' for local communities (Ashworth and Graham 2005; Smith 2006; Convery, Corsane, and Davis 2012 for more about how communities develop sense of place). The importance of Sur and the surrounded landscape, including Hevsel Gardens, for heritage making was also emphasized in the nomination file of UNESCO WHL inscription:

> This landscape is what makes the city of Diyarbakir outstanding as it has been the lifeline of this city over millennia. Some of the crops may have changed but most of the crops and the trees are what have always been cultivated in this region. Furthermore, many features of the intangible heritage of the city are linked to this landscape as well [such as that related to pigeon breeding].[5]

Therefore, a specific space plays a significant role in creating a sense of place that provides belonging for communities. The communities of Sur were displaced during the conflict and had no opportunity to go back to use the space, landscape and resume heritage making or develop memories.

The entire conflict and the consequences of it were breaches of international human rights conventions, which are tightly linked to cultural heritage and performing cultural activities and participation. First, freedom of movement (Article 12) of the International Covenant on Civil and Political Rights (ICCPR[6]) was breached because people were forced to leave and access to return home was restricted. Article 17 of the ICCPR[7] states that people's homes, families and privacy should be protected. However, most of the houses were destroyed and people's family lives and privacy were breached. Some of those cases were taken to the European Court of Human Rights, which found breaches of many articles, especially of those related to destruction and inhumane treatment (see Articles 3 and 4 of European Convention on Human Rights and Fundamental Freedoms[8]) as well as forced evictions and displacement.

After the conflict ended, restrictions of entry to Sur continued for everyone for a while. Amnesty International managed to conduct detailed ethnographic research in Diyarbakir about the conflict of Sur and its destructive impact on communities. The research involved discussions with displaced families, NGOs and the authorities as well as ethnographic fieldwork. One of the Sur residents described the panic and the beginning of the conflict:

> the announcement from the main street, they said that for our safety we should leave our houses. Now everyone was calling each other saying 'they are telling us to leave'. By the time we got out on the street many people had already left, we went left, then we went right, trying to avoid the clashes. (Amnesty International 2016, 13)

Amnesty International (2016) reports that following the start of conflict, a curfew was declared in the town and many families' access to very basic needs, such as food and water, became impossible. Although the people of Sur were very keen to stay in the town, they had to leave for many reasons, including safety and food and water restrictions, as the report indicates, based on the accounts of Sur residents. People did not want to leave because it was their space and landscapes, natural environments and built heritage, such as houses, and these are resources for people as well and are physical symbols of the senses of community and belonging, both of which have great importance for mental health and well-being. A conflict that leads to displacement has an immediate impact on these. As in the case of Sur, people lost their resources for heritage making and had to move elsewhere (Amnesty International 2016; OHCHR 2017). The forced displacement and the loss of the ability to practise their heritage leads to a long-term impact, as people are traumatized (Thomas and Thomas, 2004). An extensive study conducted on individuals forcibly displaced clearly shows long-term impacts, including post-traumatic stress disorder (PTSD) and other psychological issues (Mels et al. 2010). Mels et al. (2010, 7) also point out 'the notion that discontinuation of existing stressors – such as socio-economic hardship and social exclusion – can be considered an important starting point for healing'.

The loss of space, in the case of Sur, was not only about losing homes but also losing the economic resources that most community members relied on for their income. Further, the forced displacement also dispersed the community across the big city of Diyarbakir and community members lost contact with each other. Therefore, the long-term impact of the Sur conflict on people is much greater than just the destruction of the material culture; the impact of the conflict also prevents the making of new heritage and creates a discontinuity for the accumulation of memory, which embodies heritage and material culture.

The impact of forced displacement through conflict can be seen not only in the material culture but also in the making and preserving of intangible heritage.

Research from different societies across the world shows how both tangible and intangible heritage have strong associations with landscape and community space (Ruggles and Silverman 2009), where knowledge is produced, values are attached and meanings are made (Armstrong-Fumero and Gutierrez 2017). In heritage studies, many scholars usually focus on the material traces of production, how to preserve this heritage and its links to human rights. Material culture and use of space have been well researched from social, political and economic perspectives and their importance exposed in heritage studies and other social sciences, especially from the point of social organization (Harvey 2007; Lefebre 1991). However, the intangible dimension and the importance of space, landscape and the natural environment are often neglected. Space, human actions and the social organization of space are also significantly linked to intangibility and the intangible production of heritage, such as the development of collective memory (Nora 1989; Hanks 1990), as well as other forms of intangible heritage (storytelling, traditional dance and songs that all play a role in the sense of belonging and sense of place). The discontinuity between space and human action because of access restriction or forced displacement, therefore, has a negative impact on intangible heritage making and preservation.

The UNESCO (2017) report on 'Intangible Cultural Heritage of Displaced Syrians' clearly demonstrates the connection between and the impact of displacement on intangible heritage. Many displaced intangible cultural heritage performers cannot find events or places to perform or teach dancing, songs or stories because communities have been dispersed and this has significance for the identity of Syrian people. In addition, other forms of intangible cultural practices, such as food preparation, have been altered by the conflict and been affected greatly by the displacement as local people had to move to other countries. Many local cuisines, based on local produce and recipes, were transformed in the displacement (see UNESCO 2017).

Intangible heritage has strong connections with resources as well as people, particularly in regions such as southeast Turkey where most of the population is Kurdish and oral tradition has a strong impact on identity (Allison 1996; Kreyenbroek and Allison 1996; Apaydin and Hassett 2019). However, due to the conflict and displacement, songs, dances and other forms of intangible heritage cannot be performed because of the destruction of the sense of place and community and people cannot develop new forms of intangible heritage and transform them for future generations. Diyarbakir, as a whole, has great importance for Kurdish people who developed their identity and sense of community intensively throughout the history of this city. The city itself represents the identity of Kurdish people, with its monumental heritage, landscape and nature, which all played a significant role in the development and preservation of their intangible heritage, including food, songs and dances. Sur, as the inner city of Diyarbakir, was even more important with its multicultural representation of monumental and intangible heritage, therefore again being a resource for Kurdish identity in modern times. For example, traditional song making and singing, called 'Dengbeji', and 'Dengbej', an artist who sings, were very common in Diyarbakir and Sur. Dengbej centres in Kurdish oral folk tradition and the songs are mostly related to social and political issues (see next chapter) which was practised often in Sur and Diyarbakir. These important components of Kurdish cultural identity were even listed in the UNESCO WHL nomination file.[9] However, breaches of human rights through conflict and forced eviction of local people from the inner city put this important intangible heritage in danger of extinction.

Routine, expected processes of change in cultural heritage include construction, reconstruction, transformation and destruction as parts of the process (Holtorf 2018). However, this process is only natural as long as it happens from the bottom up. What I mean by this is that people themselves should be able to lead this process by referring to the representative dimension of social justice, rather than it being the result of war, conflict or sectarian violence, or authoritarian and undemocratic state policies. In the latter cases, it leads to displacement and trauma, where people are unable to develop heritage for generations. Here, it is also significant to point out the role and aim of critical heritage. As I discussed in Chapter 1, critical heritage is not only about material culture but it is also about people who construct, reconstruct and transform, as well as protect, that heritage. During the conflict, half a million people were forcibly displaced in southeast Turkey, and 40,000 people were forced to leave Sur, their homes and their representation of their sense of place and belonging as a community. Most of the people from Sur who were displaced have not been able to go back to their homes because the town was almost completely levelled and access was restricted for a long time (Amnesty International 2016; Soyukaya 2017).

Critical heritage scholars have a significant role in these highly unethical, social and economic situations to reflect on injustices, which have a great impact on tangible and intangible heritage, by bringing out and exposing the locality of this heritage as well as exposing the truth. Material culture as developed by humans is significant because it represents identities and values of people and acts as storage for memories and knowledge. As heritage scholars, people are our resources: we collect data from them and study the heritage they develop. People must be given utmost importance in these highly traumatic circumstances and it is also important to expose the situation with its dynamics and critically question the impact of these developments from an anthropological perspective.

Heritage is a process and this process can only be progressive when people have sufficient resources, such as lands and homes. Holtorf (2015) argues that destruction is also a process that can lead to opportunities, such as new heritage development. This may well be true sometimes. However, it is problematic when we consider displaced people, particularly people who lost their homes and lands (Chatterjee et al. 2020). The case of Armenian ethnic cleansing in 1915 and onwards is a good example, demonstrating that forced displacement and the destruction of heritage can prevent communities from creating new heritage and memories. Millions of Armenians were forced to leave Turkey a century ago, but this still has a huge impact on the Armenian diaspora (see Chapter 3). Similarly, during the 1990s, many Kurdish villagers were evicted and forced to leave the cities (Muller 1996) and they are still having traumatic experiences.

The case of Sur is a recent example that shows how rights of people have been breached twice in terms of a heritage context. First, the people of Sur were forced to leave their homes and landscape, when these were destroyed. Second, their access to the town has been restricted subsequently, despite it being their right to return to the homes and landscape where they can perform cultural activities. International human rights law, to which Turkey is also a signatory, clearly indicates that displaced people need to be protected. However, most of the people from Sur who were displaced are not being supported by the state (Amnesty International 2016; OHCRH 2016), neither in returning home nor in being given new homes. The immediate effect of this and subsequent long-term trauma and losing their sense of belonging and community is expressed by this Sur resident who was displaced:

> Our extended family of about 500 people all lived in the same district of Sur, we saw and talked to each other every day on the street. Now we are spread across the whole of Diyarbakir and only speak on the phone. (Amnesty International 2016, 25)

State policies against Kurdish identity, which has been in existence for almost a hundred years, does not recognize the past, heritage or identities of the Kurdish people (Yegen 1999, 2007; see also Özbudun 2012 about discourses of misrecognition of other identity groups in Turkey) and this is the main driver behind the heavy destruction which took place in Sur. A second, and also very significant, reason is that neoliberal policies, which became more intense in the last couple of decades after the JDP assumed power, have led to the transformation of landscapes and the rivers and natural areas in the rural and urban regions of Turkey – in other words, a destructive transformation process and gentrification. This leads to further questions: What does neoliberalism have to do with the heavy destruction of the UNESCO World Heritage Site of Sur? What are the links between neoliberalism, populism and heritage destruction in the case of Sur? How is the destruction of Sur related to social (in)justice?

Authoritarianism and neoliberalism

In her recent book, *In the Ruins of Neoliberalism* (2019), political theorist Wendy Brown discusses 'neoliberal rationality' and argues how it provided the groundwork for 'antidemocratic forces', how neoliberalism has affected social and political structures, and often dismantled them, providing the groundwork for the rise of antidemocratic politics. The embedded discourses behind neoliberalism are more than about a 'free market'; they have created undemocratic, antidemocratic, totalitarian regimes in many parts of the world. Since the beginnings of the imposition of neoliberal policies, the world has changed in many ways and this has had a significant impact on social and political structures (Harvey 2005). The last couple of decades have seen a great increase in right-wing populism, which was caused by neoliberal policies that have motivated undemocratic and authoritarian regimes, as Brown (2019) discusses in her book. Turkey is one of those countries that was heavily affected by the impact of neoliberalism that led to the authoritarian establishment.

The rule of neoliberal undemocratic powers in Turkey is not that different than in other parts of the world. Under the rules of the JDP, Turkey underwent a fairly fast and destructive transformation. The state became authoritarian first and thereafter the ongoing practice of neoliberalism also changed the term 'authoritarianism' in the last couple of decades with the rise of right-wing populism in Turkey. This new form of authoritarianism is described as a system that still has some democratic norms (for example, elections are still held) but power – including state institutions, the judiciary and the media – is controlled by the ruling group and very often the rights of people are breached and the freedom of expression and access to performing cultural activities are limited, as in the case of southeast Turkey (Levitsky and Way 2010).

In the last two decades, the JDP increasingly used public spaces, where people perform cultural activities and participate in events, and natural resources to make more profit and grow the country's economy (Bugra and Savaskan 2014). The neoliberal and authoritarian right-wing populist policies have been applied heavily in many parts of the country. This can be seen in the cities, with large gentrification projects, as in the case of Istanbul (Aksoy 2012); the construction of one of the world's largest airports in northern Istanbul that destroyed millions of trees in the northern forest (Bianet 2019); and in the rural areas with large dam construction projects, especially in southeast and east Turkey (see Chapter 5). While these large developments are erasing the landscapes and cultural, social and economic spaces of people, these developments also 'dismantle society' and destroy the flora and fauna of the regions, as I discuss in the next chapter.

The conflict and the destruction at Sur were a great opportunity for the JDP, which considers the natural and built environments, as well as urban spaces, as resources to increase profit (Göçek 2018) while using neoliberal policies along with a right-wing populist approach. While the conflict led to destruction and displacement, it has also given the JDP a great opportunity to apply its neoliberal policies in order to wipe out the meanings, values and memories of the old Sur by constructing a new town with luxury houses and reconstructing a new identity at Sur (see Figure 4.4).

Figure 4.4 Construction of New Sur following the conflict. © Ilyas Akengin/AFP via Getty Images.

Although the conflict itself led to cultural property in Sur being heavily damaged, the aim and plan of reconstruction through rebuilding was even more destructive. During and following the conflict, homes were levelled by bulldozers (Amnesty International 2016; OHCHR 2017) in order to develop a new town and erase the memory and identity of the Kurdish people. The destruction and damage were so great (Soyukaya 2017) that it was impossible to restore the city and so the only option was to rebuild it. This gave the government an ideal opportunity to gentrify the whole town, change its demography, erase the identity of Kurds, and to develop a new identity in parallel to its own ideology.

The new construction at Sur was also in violation of Turkey's own law on the Conservation of Cultural Assets. The Conservation of Cultural Assets law clearly emphasizes that any building that is in danger of collapsing should be reviewed by the technical team and professionals and the demolition of the building must have permission from the Conservation Council for Cultural Assets and the local municipality. However, neither professionals nor experts reviewed any buildings to be demolished, nor was permission granted from the council and municipality (Soyukaya 2017). Nevin Soyukaya, who is a local archaeologist in Diyarbakir and a former head of the UNESCO World Heritage Site, points out in her observation of Sur (2017, 3):

> Without any design of surveys, restoration and restitution plans for the affected registered buildings, the remaining qualitative building elements have been excavated with heavy equipment and dumped outside of Suriçi [inner city] by personnel who have no expertise on this subject.

After the end of the conflict and the levelling of most of Sur, the Turkish government immediately began to build new luxury houses. In the period of demolition and the construction of the 'new Sur', all stakeholders, from individual local people to the local municipality, were completely excluded. Instead, a top-down decision-making process was carried out in order to make as much profit as possible and at the same time to change the identity and the history of Sur. The exclusion of local people from the rebuilding of the town leads to a new heritage being made in parallel to JDP's ideology of a 'New Turkey'. What the discourse of the conflict and the dominant neoliberal policy of the Turkish government clearly illustrate in the case of Sur is that the new heritage practices are 'socially powerful' (May 2019, 72) and will create 'different forms of realities and different futures' (Harrison 2015, 24). A combination of heavy right-wing nationalist populism and neoliberalism led the JDP to make authoritarian decisions in order to make profit and to protect and promote its ideological agenda by wiping out a whole town, rebuilding it and changing its demographic structure. The displaced locals of Sur will not able to return their home and instead have been dispersed to other parts of the region. The new houses have replaced what used to be the heart of Kurdish identity and multicultural heritage of the city.

5

Slow Violence

In this chapter, I will discuss the impact of two dam projects in southeast and eastern Turkey. The construction of dams transformed the landscape and natural environment which acted as a focus of cultural and social meaning for two minority communities in Turkey. In what follows, I demonstrate the crucial role of this landscape, as part of the natural heritage, in playing a significant role for a sense of place and belonging for these communities.

This significance of landscape for identity formation and maintenance is particularly true for minority groups, who are not always recognized in terms of their identity, values and cultural backgrounds by the authoritarian regimes. In the case of the Turkish government, the JDP used neoliberal policies under the auspices of 'economic development' to make a profit and show the power exercised by the nation state against minorities (I demonstrate this below with dam projects in southeast Turkey). Against this background, natural heritage, including the landscape and rivers, flora and fauna, acts as a resource that local people have the right to manage and to use to construct identities, develop memories and transform for future generations. In heritage studies, natural heritage is usually considered separately from cultural heritage. However, it can also act as a resource for both tangible and intangible cultural heritage. Lowenthal (2006, 1) emphasizes its importance:

> natural heritage comprises the lands and seas we inhabit and exploit, the soils and plants and animals that constitute the world's ecosystems, the water we drink, the very air we breathe.

As Lowenthal points out, the natural environment is vitally important for climate, ecology and biodiversity, and I argue it is a resource for people both for survival and for developing heritage and memories to consolidate a sense of community and place. However, although the natural environment plays such a crucial role, we are seeing great threats to this important aspect of people's lives. As well as broader threats caused by climate change and habitat destruction, large-scale infrastructure projects are leading to the destruction of these resources and I focus on this in considering the impact of large-scale dam building. The impact of these construction projects causes the destruction of natural and built environments, which in turn heavily impacts on the use of these resources. Further, these construction projects lead to the forced displacement of people and restrict them from using resources where communities had previously carried out cultural activities and performances.

The reason for my choice of title of this chapter – 'Slow Violence' – is twofold. First, the violence of large-scale dam construction itself happens slowly in terms of its impact on heritage, landscape and nature and, secondly, its impact is rapid on people who are being socially dismantled, dispersed and ultimately devastated. This is caused by these large infrastructure projects, particularly dam building projects in rural areas across the world (Nixon 2011; Schoub 2006; Ronayne 2006; Rocha 2020; King 2020). Rob Nixon's (2011) concept of 'slow violence' reflects these contradictions in time and space, and it creates both provocation and destruction effects on environment:

> By slow violence I mean a violence that occurs gradually and out of sight, a violence of delayed destruction that is dispersed across time and space, an attritional violence that is typically not viewed as violence at all. Violence is customarily conceived as an event or action that is immediate in time, explosive and spectacular in space, erupting into instant sensational visibility. (Nixon 2011, 2)

Nixon's reflection mainly focuses on the Global North's toxicity in the Global South. This colonial approach to the Global South shows its impact in the long term in terms of accelerating climate change and deteriorating landscapes, nature and well-being of people. Similarly, in this chapter, in the cases presented here, the violence that is experienced by the people takes place over years in terms of the impact of the slow violence on the climate and biodiversity of nature and landscape which people use as a resource.

The violence I discuss through case studies in this chapter is not through war, conflict and sectarianism; it is instead violence inflicted under the promise of 'economic development' plans that are politically and ideologically motivated (Brown 2019). I argue that extreme neoliberal policies have become a kind of violence under these economic development projects in undemocratic countries, as in the case of Turkey. This link to large-scale infrastructural development is especially more visible in the regions of the world that are populated by minority and indigenous groups who have been treated unequally in terms of the 'redistribution' of wealth and resources, 'recognition' of their rights, as well as exclusion of these groups from the decision-making process – as opposed to the 'representation' dimension of social justice which aims to bring voices of people into the decision-making process as part of democratic and people-centred approach.

Through certain forms of neoliberal development, violence can appear indirect in taking nature and landscape as commodities that can be consumed in order to make a profit and accelerating violence and destruction in the long term. As I discussed at the beginning of this book, critical heritage is highly social, political and economic and creates many narratives, not only for those people whose sense of place and belonging depend on the use of natural resources but also in terms of serious consequences for climate and biodiversity. Therefore, we need to engage with this type of 'slow violence' and its effect on heritage more effectively by developing critical methods that can be beneficial for people and have impact in terms of preserving the climate and natural resources. We need to consider this type of visible violence as a global issue because the changing climate and nature are global matters. This is certainly a challenge for critical heritage scholars. Harrison (2016, 165) emphasizes:

> one of the central challenges for archaeology [and heritage studies] over the coming decades will be to find a way to engage with emerging, contemporary, sociomaterial and, hence, with issues of both contemporary and future ecological, social, political, and economic concern.

Slow violence is also highly associated with the colonial approach that sees the Global South as a resource that can be consumed to make the Global North richer. While this has a huge impact on the wealth redistribution concept of social justice, it also increases inequality and poverty because people of the Global South lose their resources and do not get an equal share. This type of slow violence, the stripping of natural resources, does not only happen in terms of the Global North's impact on the South, but also happens in countries that are undemocratic or authoritarian, as in the case of Turkey.

As noted above, this particular form of slow violence in the name of development often occurs in the lands of indigenous and local minorities in so-called settler societies – for example, the opening of indigenous Australian lands to mining, the construction of oil pipelines on tribal lands in North Dakota in the United States (Estes 2019) and Canada, the exploitation of the Argentine Chaco for agribusiness (Gordillo 2014) and destruction of the Amazonian indigenous landscape through dam building in Brazil (Rocha 2020). In Turkey, similar projects negatively impact upon areas where predominantly Kurdish and Alevi people live (Göçek 2018). These are just some examples that demonstrate how ruling elites, in parallel to state ideologies and under the guise of 'economic development', are exploiting the landscape and natural resources to make a profit and erase minority and indigenous people's identities and memory resources. This is one of the main reasons that I argue we need to engage more effectively in this form of violence, because the consequences of these slow-violence actions affect the world as a whole in terms of increasing injustice, poverty, changing climate and deteriorating biodiversity, thus preventing the right to perform cultural activities, maintain and develop heritage, both 'cultural' and 'natural'. For example, the case of the systematic deforestation of Amazonia in Brazil has not only had an impact on the indigenous people of those lands but is also contributing to accelerated climate change (Stall et al. 2020; Swann et al. 2015). This is a global problem. Dam construction projects can have similarly significant effects given their influence on climate change and water scarcity on a regional level (Graf 1999). As David Harvey (2011, 2) states:

> particularly at the global level, some sort of enclosure is often the best way to preserve valued commons. It will take a draconian act of enclosure in Amazonia, for example, to protect both biodiversity and the cultures of indigenous populations as part of our global natural and cultural commons.

In the heritage context, the landscape needs to be considered more seriously and more often for heritage making as part of protecting rights of people. This includes all its resources (natural, agricultural/managed, pastoral), its biodiversity and its human and non-human inhabitants. It is the common good of all humanity and therefore also needs to be considered from a human right as well as a social justice perspective.

More recently, the concept of the common good has been studied as part of landscape studies, which has emphasized its importance for human and non-human participants of the ecosystem. Although the common good or landscape has been the centre for the survival of many indigenous communities all around the world for thousands of years. Robin Wall Kimmerer (2003, 2013, 2021), a Native American scholar well known for her work on the importance of biodiversity, ecosystems and landscapes, demonstrates the interrelationship between biodiversity and landscapes, their importance for heritage making and preserving heritage and what land means in indigenous cultures. She lists a number of aspects of land: 'land as residence of non-human relatives; land as sustainer; land as identity; land as home; land as enspirited; land as connection;

land as source of knowledge; land as moral responsibility and land as healer' (Kimmerer 2016, 8:37). The main reasons that land holds so many characteristics and so much power is that it does not only offer resources, such as water, pasture and minerals, and provide shelter to 'non-human relatives', but land also provides for and enables people to make heritage, and to develop and conserve identities and memories, all of which bind people together.

Landscapes are generally considered as part of the common good as they represent and play a role as resources for people and 'sustainable development of societies and ecological issues' (Menatti 2017, 649). Therefore, the management of these lands, from the bottom up, by local people is very important. In other words, the 'representation' dimension of social justice gets even more vital in terms of managing landscapes. However, bottom-up management has been undermined, especially in authoritarian states that consume the resources of the landscape in order to make a profit and erase the resources of the minority groups and indigenous people, whose values do not fit with the dominant or ruling group. The top-down and consumerist approach in those authoritarian states leads to debates around landscapes and rights. In what follows I explore this relationship between landscape and rights and how this can be contextualized in the framework of heritage.

Cultural landscape

In the social sciences and humanities, most research that is related to cultural studies indicates that 'culture' is not easily defined because it is a very abstract concept. One of the main reasons for this is that culture is developed through the interaction of people and nature and this relationship is different everywhere. Neither nature nor people produce culture by themselves, but nature is used as a resource for developing culture (Lowenthal 2006). Landscape is a significant part of nature, but also it is culturally constructed and extensively used by people as a space to produce culture, and 'active agent for people's needs' (Mitchell 2003b, 93, 2003a). This is also not about using landscape only for cultural production but how landscape is used as a space where people develop and transform memories and heritage (Lefebvre 1991; Harvey 2007; Apaydin 2020b; King 2020). Therefore, production becomes a value and significant aspect for cultural orientation and highly attached to the landscape, which creates a physical space for people over time (see King and Nic Eoin 2014) – becoming a 'cultural landscape' and 'cultural right' for people who use it as a space.

The strong interlinkage between landscape, ecology, biodiversity and people also demonstrates that nature and culture cannot be separated from each other. Bruno Latour (1993), in his book *We Have Never Been Modern*, argues that the nature and culture divide is a European Enlightenment separation that was constructed in order to justify the domination of nature; however, throughout history, humans have always relied on agents of nature, including the 'non-human relatives'. Unfortunately, in the Anthropocene Age, people ignore the role of these agents of nature for sustaining the planet. There are many anthropological studies demonstrating that nature and culture have always been strongly intertwined in 'non-modern societies'. Phillipe Descola (2013), in his book *Beyond Nature and Culture*, demonstrates this by analysing the lives and relationships of indigenous communities in Amazonia with nature. Descola calls non-human participants of the 'wild space', the forest, 'natural beings' and the indigenous people have strong relationships with these natural beings. For instance, Descola (2013, 6) states that 'for the women, their plants are blood relatives; for the men animals are relatives by marriage: the natural beings that become real social partners'. Ignoring nature and natural beings as 'social partners' brings not only the destruction of the environments, landscapes and biodiversity and the deterioration of the climate regime, but also diminishes the importance of the role of natural beings in conserving a sense of place for many communities. The only way to restore this broken relationship or overcome the divide between nature and culture and human and non-human participants is through what Latour (1993, 2004b) calls an 'expanded democracy', where all species and their voices and rights are represented equally.

Understanding the landscape as a space, home and resource to all natural beings, including human and non-human participants, and Latour's idea 'expanded democracy' is one way of protecting and preserving the environment against human-led destruction. The idea of protecting and conserving landscapes in particular is embodied in UNESCO's approach. In 1992, the UNESCO World Heritage Convention (WHC) recognized landscapes as cultural resources that needed protection. This was a significant move to protect landscapes that have importance for climate, biodiversity and people. Article 1 of the WHC clearly states that landscapes represent the 'combined works of nature and of man'. Furthermore, the WHC elaborates on the protection and importance of cultural landscapes:

> They are illustrative of the evolution of human society and settlement over time, under the influence of the physical constraints and/or opportunities presented by

their natural environment and of successive social, economic and cultural forces, both external and internal. The term 'cultural landscape' embraces a diversity of manifestations of the interaction between humankind and its natural environment … Protection of cultural landscapes can contribute to modern techniques of sustainable land-use and can maintain or enhance natural values in the landscape. The continued existence of traditional forms of land-use supports biological diversity in many regions of the world. The protection of traditional cultural landscapes is therefore helpful in maintaining biological diversity.[1]

As an international legal instrument, UNESCO WHC signatories have the responsibility to protect cultural landscapes and their inhabitants, and landscapes, because they are a part of nature, should not be considered separately, as one produces the other for cultural activities and heritage making (Taylor and Lennon 2011). The European Landscape Convention[2] further details and elaborates on how to conceptualize landscapes:

an area as perceived by people, whose character is the result of the action and interaction of natural and/or human factors.

This is one of the main links between landscape, heritage and rights: people use the landscape for their cultural activities and this is strictly protected and clearly emphasized in the Universal Declaration of Human Rights, as I discussed in Chapter 1. This link is also supported by the European Landscape Convention[3] (Council of Europe 2000), which states:

a common heritage with an important role in the cultural ecological, environmental and social fields … contributing to human well-being and consolidation of the European identity … the quality and diversity of the European landscape constitutes a common resource.

Further, as part of the European Landscape Convention, the Évora Declaration[4] (2011) makes an important point by emphasizing the significance of landscape as memory storage and the making of the sense of place and belonging for communities. The 2012 UNESCO meeting on the 'International Protection of Landscapes' resulted in the Florence Declaration on Landscape,[5] which states that the 'right to landscape is a human necessity'. (see Menatti 2017 for more discussion). The statements by UNESCO and the Council of Europe particularly emphasize the links between nature and people – how people use the landscape and what they use it for. This is significant because landscape is a resource and heritage in itself for people; it is also important for biodiversity and ecology. The use of the term 'resource' here refers to the cultural rights, which are also protected under the Human Rights Declaration. Landscapes and rights have strong links, as attested by both UNESCO and the Council of Europe.

However, despite their many strengths, all these declarations and conventions could further emphasize the multicultural characteristics of landscapes (Menatti 2017) where diverse groups attach meanings and develop values – or, in other words, 'recognition' dimension of social justice, which has been often neglected. This lacuna has had a particularly negative impact for minority groups who are, in some cases, already oppressed by the dominant powers and whose rights and access to the landscape and to conducting and participating in cultural activities through the use of that landscape have been restricted (see next section for Kurdish case). For those groups who use the landscape for the survival of their community and for their sense of community, the landscape becomes more important because it is the resource for identity construction, as stated in the European Landscape Convention. In those countries that signed these conventions, these rights are often breached in rural areas where the natural environment and landscape had been relatively free from marketization and neoliberal development policies, until the dam building projects. These dam construction projects have breached the 'rights to landscape' for many local communities and minority groups all around the world. Turkey is one of those nation states that has used dam constructions systematically to make money and subjugate minority groups.

Since the Turkish nation state was established in 1923, it aimed to consolidate the idea of 'one nation, one history' through all state institutions and spread the idea of Turkishness and, later, religious values through education, as I discussed in Chapter 2. This process greatly neglected and erased the memories and heritage of minority groups, particularly the Armenians, Kurdish and Alevis. Constant forced displacements also became a tool for the ruling elite in Turkey to consolidate its ideology, as in the case of Kurdish communities. This constant displacement, mainly because of the dam projects, interrupts memory and heritage making and therefore consolidating collective identity of minority groups. Creating a situation of constant interruptions further prevents minority groups from consolidating and transforming their identities against the dominant and oppressive groups.

Dams

The construction of 'megadams' became particularly more common in the twentieth century with the development of new technologies and increased demands for electricity and water as populations and industries grew. However, this development brought its own destructive consequences. What we have seen in the twentieth and twenty-first centuries is that dam developments across the world transformed the landscapes and impacted the natural environment. This phenomenon is mainly linked first to 'modern capitalism' (Harvey 2005) and its insatiable appetite for resources to consume, and secondly, and most importantly, to the nation-building process, which accelerated in the twentieth century. Monuments, large urban constructions and megadams became key symbols of the nation states (Kaika 2006; Neimark 2013; O'Lear et al. 2018).

Particularly in the twentieth and twenty-first centuries, we have witnessed about how nationalism and the nation state use different tools to develop their 'imagined communities'. Anderson (1983) discusses how and why nation states want to create their own imagined communities. The nation state uses a variety of tools to create its own imaginary communities and consolidate itself. This can be through developing advanced cities and megabuildings, which can be symbols of the nation. Another way is to build megadams to prove to other countries how economically and technologically developed it is. The Aswan Dam in Egypt (Hassan 2007), dams in China, the GAP project in east Turkey (Shoup 2006) and dam projects in the United States (Nixon 2011; Estes 2019) and Africa (King 2020) are some examples initiated under the idea of the 'nation's economic development'. However, many of these dams have had a destructive impact on the material culture of the past, the environment and local communities and indigenous people. In the case of Egypt, large monuments from the Egyptian pharaonic period were moved to other places (Hassan 2007 for more about Aswan Dam and rescue efforts) and indigenous people – nomads – in Nubia were displaced, while in the United States the cultural landscapes of indigenous communities were erased (Estes 2019).

With the introduction of neoliberalism, the idea of building a nation and consolidating it combined well with the idea of economic development. This idea has pushed many undemocratic nation states to use the natural resources and environment more effectively in order to make more profit in a very top-down fashion, excluding local communities from the decision-making processes. The justification of economic development has been abused in many parts of the world and provided the groundwork for many nation states to become more undemocratic and more authoritarian, using the natural resources of minority groups to enrich themselves and erasing the history of minorities who were deemed to be a threat to the imaginary community of that nation state in the process.

Turkey has been in the forefront in the construction of megadams in order to consolidate itself as a nation state under the idea of 'economic development'. The DSI[6] (State Water Institution) states that hundreds of dams were built across Turkey; these were mostly constructed through the top-down approach without consultation of the local people, who were then either displaced or lost their lands as a consequence. Particularly during the late twentieth and early twenty-first centuries, Turkey went through a great transformation, with its leaders ensuring that its state ideology used every state institution to create a modern, strong and one-nation state. However, much of this modernization – notably, the megadams – took place in areas of 'contested spaces and lands', and this is process is still ongoing in much of east and southeast Turkey, as I will show later.

In his *The Making of Modern Turkey* (2011), Ugur Üngör discusses how Turkish institutions provided the basis for the Turkish ideology in the name of 'modernization' and economic development during the twentieth century. The consumption of lands and resources, especially in areas predominantly occupied by minority people in Turkey, has increased dramatically under the rule of the JDP over the last ten years (Göçek 2018). Environmental assessment and protection rules have been amended to make neoliberal development more practical and faster. The embedded discourse for deliberately selecting these contested lands is based on their ownership rights, especially in relation to the Armenians in the early twentieth century and the Kurds in the twentieth and twenty-first centuries (Üngör 2011; Apaydin 2018c). While the 'one nation state' aims to erase the cultural landscapes of minorities, which are seen as a threat to Turkish ideology, through the construction of dams, the state also aims to show itself as a power in the region and remind those minority groups that they have to live under the idea of imagined community or the one nation state.

Dismantling and displacing

I consider heritage more about the people themselves who construct, deconstruct and transform heritage from the bottom-up perspective, and who use the landscape and natural resources for cultural performance, production, participation and heritage making, which also makes a sense of place and community. The concept of community is very complex and it is not easy to define, because it varies from one group and place to another. This is one of the main reasons that the heritage of communities can only be conceptualized and understood with reference to their locality and with local values that emerged there, rather than on the basis of an abstract notion of 'universal value'. Having said that, it should be remembered that what is common for all communities is that it is the *place* they inhabit where they have interactions, build experiences and learn from one another. Cohen (1985, 15) points out: 'it is where one learns and continues to practice how to be social: and transforms these experiences to next generations by using the same resources.' These resources have vital importance for those communities whose lands and natural resources are under threat.

The case studies of this chapter, the Botan and Munzur valleys, are important cases with which to demonstrate that landscape and environment are very significant elements in terms of the formulation and maintenance of cultural practices, performance and participation to develop heritage and values. Both valleys have hosted unrecognized Alevi and Kurdish minority communities who developed memories and values, ascribed meanings and constructed their identities for generations as a result of the landscape and natural characteristics of these areas. Both Alevi and Kurdish *halklari* (communities) are self-recognized collective groups, whose values and memories are different from the majority in Turkey. In both of the case studies, developing memories and value and meaning making are strongly bounded within an 'emotional geography', a geography that embodies both home and part of their cultural identity. People of these lands engage with this geography from an emotional perspective because the 'value' of these lands is personal as part of their cultural identity. This is strongly linked to concepts of 'affect' as people engage with these landscapes from physical and social perspective because it is important for them (Smith 2020, 68) on a personal as well as a community level. Kearney (2009, 3) defines 'emotional geography' (see also Davidson et al. 2005), based on her work with Yanyuwa indigenous communities in Australia:

> an emotional geography concerns the social and sensory relations that define homelands. Patterns in human engagement have an effect on place, the individual and group. The experiential process of cultural habitus, that ultimately shape cultural identity, are dominant in shaping emotional encounters.

Therefore, the landscape, rivers, mountains and nature as a whole are significant for the Kurdish and Alevi communities of Botan and Munzur valleys. In other words, the landscape of these regions represents their collective identity that links heritage and politics (Smith 2020). From an authoritarian nation state perspective (i.e. that of the Turkish state and ruling party), this form of emotional geography can be considered as a threat to national unity, as these landscapes are the resources for minority groups' cultural identity that is seen as in opposition to a dominant notion of a singular Turkish nationhood.

The Kurds and Alevis are minorities whose identity constructions are not parallel to Turkish ideology, which is based on Turkishness and Islamic values. Kurdish communities value Islam but want to be recognized by their Kurdish identity and take part in cultural activities and express themselves freely (Van Bruinessen 1989, 1994, 1995, 1996; Yegen 2007; Gambetti 2009; Gambetti and Jongerden 2015). In contrast, Alevi communities (particularly Kurdish Alevis in Dersim (Tunceli)), whose values and identity construction are distinct from Islam and have different spiritual values (see Deniz 2012; Aydin 2020 for more on Alevi identity), and who have been oppressed since the Ottoman period want to be recognized by their own cultural values as part of their cultural right. This is one of the main reasons that Turkey has used the idea of 'economic development' in these regions, especially Alevi communities in Dersim, to disperse and dismantle these communities – they are thought to be a threat to the ideology of the state, unity and the 'one nation state' idea based on Turkish ethnicity and Islam.

Botan Valley and Ilisu Dam

> once this dam is completed, us, as a community, won't exist anymore. I won't be able to interact with my lands and community members and won't be able to teach my children and grandchildren how to farm. (villager commentary in Botan Valley; Figure 5.1)

The Ilisu Dam project has a long planning and construction history and is well known as a point of dispute through global and national campaigns carried out to stop its construction (Dissard 2021; see Figure 5.2 for completed Ilisu Dam). The Ilisu Dam-impacted area covers part of four cities, which have rich archaeological remains along with a multicultural history from Armenian to Kurdish, Turkish to Yezidi, as well as from Christianity to Islam. All these culturally and ethnically varied identity groups had constructed and reconstructed a great material culture over centuries here by using the landscape that they occupied.

In the beginning of the Ilisu Dam construction in 2006, it was supported by an international consortium, which included countries such as Austria, Germany, Italy, Japan, Switzerland and others that guaranteed hundreds of millions of dollars for the construction (Ronayne 2005). The dam is located on the Tigris river, 65km upstream from the Syrian and Iraqi borders. This sheer size sparked local and international campaigns because the entire landscape would be wiped out under the plans, changing ecosystems and flooding towns and villages (Kitchen and Ronayne 2002). It also led to international disputes because the Tigris river also supplies water to the neighbouring countries, Syria and Iraq. Because of the international pressure and campaigns, the outside, international support was cut; however, Turkey declared that it could build the controversial dam with its own resources.

In 2012, I arrived in the city of Siirt to work as part of an ongoing Ilisu Dam archaeological rescue project. This was the second year I came to the city to work as a heritage researcher and archaeologist, through which in the following years I continued to work in the region. However, this was the first year that I was able to work at the archaeological site of Çattepe, which is located right on the confluence of the Botan and Tigris rivers (Figure 5.3). I was extremely excited because we had not been able to access the site and the region the year before due to heavy conflict between the Kurdistan Workers' Party and the Turkish armed forces. However, my excitement turned into anxiety while we were driving through high mountains on top of the Botan Valley and were passed by military vehicles and almost empty villages on the way to the site. As we neared Çattepe, which could be seen from a very distant hill (Figure 5.4), a very different beautiful landscape of the site emerged, surrounded by the Botan and Tigris rivers.

The archaeological site of Çattepe is itself very interesting in terms of demonstrating how memory accumulates through time and space through its occupation by different cultural groups over millennia and how it became heritage for the modern communities who have participated in cultural activities and performed heritage over generations. The site's history goes back to prehistoric times, fourth millennium BC, and it eventually became a *höyük* (archaeological hill or tell), with different cultural layers left by different communities in the past. Çattepe was particularly significant during the Roman period and used as a small port where goods were transported from northern Mesopotamia to the south, all the way to the Basra Gulf via the Tigris river (Saglamtimur 2014, 2015). While the site itself is important from an archaeological perspective, it is also significant for the local Kurdish community members, who built a village on top of the archaeological site.

I walked through the site and got to know the locals and the landscape. While archaeologists were working in very hot weather, around 100 local community members were also hired to work as labour to rescue archaeological artefacts. Despite the beautiful landscape and river, seeing some modern houses

Figure 5.1 The point where the Tigris and Botan rivers merge at the edge of Çattepe site. © Veysel Apaydin.

Figure 5.2 Çattepe archaeological site. © Veysel Apaydin.

Figure 5.3 Çattepe and landscape with Tigris river. Archaeologists are digging archaeological remains. © Veysel Apaydin.

Figure 5.4 Çattepe Höyük and modern houses that were left to decay following dam construction and conflicts in the region. © Veysel Apaydin.

demolished or in ruins got my attention (Figure 5.5). Some of the workers pointed out that these were the houses that were left from the 1990s conflict and some of the houses were also left because of the Ilisu Dam project. One of the locals said:

> This was [indicates a house on the site] my family's house. I was born here. However, 15 years ago we moved to another village. These farms [next to the site] are ours but the state bought them as part of a dam project and we didn't have a chance to keep but to sell them as they are about flooded.

I walked between the houses and went into one of them, which was relatively new compared to the others. According to one of the workers, the house had not been inhabited for several years, though it still had some furnishings, including chairs, tables, curtains and portraits of villagers. Although the house was left by its owners who had moved to Siirt, it still demonstrated its long history and memories through the objects that were left behind. The same site worker, who was born and lived in the village, took me down the hill to show me the primary school where he and other children of the village used to attend. This small building still had a couple of classrooms left standing, with graffiti that the students left – traces of the memories of childhoods of those who studied there.

While speaking to one of the other local workers, he gestured to his current village, a twenty-minute walk away on the skirt of a hill. He told me that his grandparents used to live in the village of Çattepe, where they were also buried. The archaeological site of Çattepe, along with its village, also contains a village graveyard where locals have buried their community members for generations. Graves are usually considered by local communities as part of their sense of place because they are symbols and links to those lands that they have lived in (see Byrne 2008). I continued to walk with the same local man around the ruins of houses and he showed me the house where his grandparents lived. The house was more or less levelled. He showed me the farming lands that his family owned, which were bought by the state under the law of nationalization as part of the dam project. He pointed out that his family owned these lands and farmed for generations, grew corn, barley, wheat and other kinds of grain that they used to export to the city and that acted as staple ingredients for their families and villages. He stated that:

> we are villagers who are experienced in farming and animal grazing ... first my family was evicted from the village of Çattepe and therefore we were displaced and had to move to another village. Now, we are facing a second wave of eviction and displacement because of the Ilisu Dam.

The above account shows the importance of landscape from an affect and emotional perspective, as this villager and his family had engaged with this landscape on a personal and family level, as well as from a socioeconomic perspective, as the landscape is also significant for their livelihoods. In this part of the Turkey, more or less everyone's life centres around farming and animal grazing. Most villagers get up early in the morning and begin by taking their animals to pasture and then go to work on their farms. Therefore, sociocultural dynamics are also being formed around these activities in this region. This also demonstrates the links between emotional and political geographies (Kearney 2009) as similar to 'emotio-spatial hermeneutic', which argues that in order to understand emotions, the particular context that refers to space needs to be considered in its own right (Davidson and Milligan 2004; Kearney 2009). Therefore, the value and meanings of this landscape are completely different for local people here than those developing the dam, ascribing different meanings linked to cultural and social activities that shaped their cultural identity.

In one anecdote, the same villager referred to the brutal 1990s conflict between the Kurdistan Workers' Party and the Turkish armed forces. The cost of conflict was high for communities and the environment, with many villagers losing their villages and with them, their access to the landscape and natural environment and required to resettle in other parts of the region (Jongerden 2007). Many villagers were forced to leave their villages in this region and Çattepe, with the villager's parents included in those who had to move out their homes, gardens and farms. Following this original forced resettlement, the Ilisu Dam led to further displacement and the destruction of the landscape on which they relied for their survival as well as the communities to which they belong. Landscapes, space or any place provide resources for people who create memories and heritage through social interactions (Harvey 2009; Lefebvre 1991), cultural activities and participations in cultural performances. It is a space where social actions take place. However, as many of them were dispersed and resettled in other parts of the region, they had been cut off from their own landscape – or, in other words, from their own 'emotional geography', where they developed memories and constructed cultural identity through social and cultural interactions. For this reason, any attempts to sustain or relocate meaning making and developing memory and value may not be straightforward for those displaced people. They are emotionally attached to those lands as well as ethnically bounded together and their survival as a community depends on a sense of belonging, as in the case of Kurdish people who have continuously faced forced displacement either through dam projects or armed conflicts (OHCHR

Figure 5.5 Modern houses on top of Çattepe archaeological site. © Veysel Apaydin.

2017; Amnesty International 2016; Gambetti and Jongerden 2011; Ronayne 2005; Shoup 2006). In a similar example, Halilovich (2013) discusses how, in the case of the Bosnian ethnic cleansing between 1992 and 1995, many people who were displaced forcefully and survived the ethnic cleansing have post-traumatic stress disorder (PTSD) issues. He shows how forced displacement makes it harder for people to develop new memories and new sense of communities. It is very possible the same thing will happen to these communities because of their displacement due to the Ilisu Dam.

For the last hundred years, since the establishment of the nation state of Turkey, the Kurdish identity has never been officially recognized and, one way or another, through conflicts (Jongerden 2007, 2010; Van Bruinessen 1995) and dam projects (Ronayne 2005, 2006), they have faced constant displacements. Between the 1960s and 1970s, the GAP project in southeastern Anatolia encompassed many dams covering huge landscapes and even separating cities from each other (Shoup 2006) and had an enormous impact on the Kurdish sense of community and identity as well as the natural environment and the landscape that played a main role in the development of their cultural values. This constant forced displacement not only leads to traumas but also to the interruption of memory and heritage making, because displaced communities lose their resources (Summerfield 2000; Thomas and Thomas, 2004; Mels et al. 2010), such as in the case of Kurdish local communities in the Botan Valley. I do not suggest here that people who are displaced cannot develop heritage and memories with new resources; however, I do argue that this would take generations. Therefore, the concept of 'forgetting' (see Erll and Nunning 2008) is not a simple process for displaced people who tend to 'remember' memories and develop material culture that is linked to their past life experiences rather than begin to make new lives and new heritage and memory making (Chatterjee et al. 2020). In the previous chapter, I attempted to illustrate the importance of access to sites and landscapes to Kurdish community members, in terms of their collective identity and cultural memory. Their values have been developed through their interactions with the landscape, sites and material culture. For instance, towns and cities, such as Sur and Diyarbakir in southeastern Turkey, play a large and important role in Kurdish identity construction (Gambetti 2009; Gambetti and Jongerden 2011; see Chapter 4).

A week after arriving in Çattepe we drove through the Botan River and Valley to one of the small remote towns outside Siirt, on the top of the mountain, to visit locals who witnessed and were affected by dam construction and conflicts. The road was very remote and quiet and not many vehicles could be seen besides the military vehicles and bases on the top of the hills. After listening to the locals' stories and memories of the region and the valley, we drove back to Siirt. We passed through houses and villages that were burnt and forcibly abandoned during the conflict of the 1990s. Coming down the mountain to the river, fruit and vegetable gardens, and many natural drinkable water springs could be seen. As we drove towards the river bridge over Botan River, a very old Kurdish woman and her granddaughter, with traditional (very colourful) clothing, waved at us to stop. We let them into the car because they needed a lift to the city where they had moved to and currently lived. It is a one-hour drive from there to the city centre and no public transport exists. I asked the old woman where they wanted to go and what they were doing here. She didn't respond. After a moment, her granddaughter pointed out that she didn't speak Turkish, only Kurdish. Her granddaughter translated our questions and she responded:

> we come here every day to check our fruit and vegetable gardens. We used to live here in a nearby village but moved to the city. I have to come and look after our garden as this is our only income and food ... there is no public transport between the city and here so I sometimes walk hours to get and go back to the city.

She was not only the one who was still trying to keep her garden alive; there were many others in the same position who live far away and come to their gardens during the day if and when they were allowed to come and if there were no restrictions, as many other locals told me. Her point also demonstrates that the people of the region have few economic options beyond growing and selling fruit and vegetables, with this providing their only income to survive, since grazing had also become difficult because of security reasons. After an hour's drive, we arrived in the city centre and her neighbourhood, which was the poorest part of the city – incredibly densely built and impoverished. Most people who were displaced through the dam projects and conflicts had moved to this neighbourhood and other parts of the city. Siirt has constantly received local refugees from nearby areas such as Botan Valley. People who were forced to leave their lands tried to bring as many of their belongings as possible with them, including some animals which can be seen in many parts of the city. The commentary of the local Kurdish women clearly reflected the brutal impact of the dam's displacement and how the landscape and resources so significant for people's sense of belonging and place as well as economies are affected by its construction. Even though the elderly woman had managed to go back to her garden, she had totally lost access to her village and home as well as to her own community. One of the other Kurdish local community members, who had been a politician in the past, stated:

> even though access has always been restricted to the Botan Valley because of the conflict, in the last several decades, the progress and to protect dam construction made it even more difficult.

Restricting access to the landscape or natural environment, where people take part in cultural activities and perform heritage, is contrary to human rights; as stated above, access to these places is protected by human rights decrees and other international declarations and conventions, such as the UNESCO declarations (Olwig 2011; Silverman Ruggles 2007) that were signed by Turkey. However, as I discussed earlier, international organizations such as UNESCO are combined and managed by states, some of which do not follow the regulations. Turkey is one of those countries: it often restricts access to lands and natural environment so the people are also excluded from using their lands and from any sort of activities. Of course, Turkey is not the only country that restricts access to landscape and cultural activities and the ideological attempts to restrict access and exclusion can be seen in many parts of the world. This kind of exclusion is usually perpetrated on ethnic grounds (Silverman and Ruggles 2007). For example, in Mexico and

Honduras, often Maya origin ethnic groups are excluded from accessing their ancestors' sites (Clifford 1997; Mortensen 2006; Silverman and Ruggles 2007). In another colonial example, in Zimbabwe the black majority of the population were not able to access their heritage and their past, which were not recognized. The main reason was that the majority of black people's cultural heritage was representative of their identity, which did not fit in with the nationalist and racist government ideology in place until the 1980s (MacKenzie and Stone 1990; Silverman and Ruggles 2007). Monuments and architectural heritage are great symbols of nation states (especially the ones whose ideology is based on a single ethnic group and nationalism) and these are used to remind citizens that every citizen is under the control of and ruled by the state. Silverman and Ruggles (2007, 10) point out that in the case of Great Zimbabwe, material forms are used as a symbol for building its 'imagined community known as the nation', with the post-colonial state taking its name from the site itself.

There are many other examples where the dominant ideology considers specific ethnic groups as a threat to it and its official ideology and authorized heritage discourse, and as a consequence does not recognize those groups whose cultural heritage is not parallel to this official ideology. These kinds of destructive and assimilative methods are usually combined with restrictions on access and exclusion to prevent those groups from producing and transforming new heritage and performing the one they have already developed, with the aim of making these groups forget their heritage. However, it is frequently the case that this kind of negativity or attempted negation of indigenous or minority heritage is also usually confronted by a strong persistence and resistance from the minority group (also see Chapter 6); in some cases, this can result in violence. I do not argue here that the state-built dams have the direct aim of destroying the Kurdish identity, and the State Water Agency states that the functional reason for dams is to increase irrigation for farming in the region. However, this argument is very much a top-down process and many villagers in the region stated they had already been able to farm through traditional irrigation systems, using rivers and streams such as the Botan and Tigris (Dîcle). Although dams in the Kurdish region may have functional reasons, it is obvious that Kurdish rights were ignored and not considered in the decision-making processes. The consequences of the dam building led to a breach of Kurdish rights, one of many breaches the Kurdish communities experience in everyday life (Hemmerechts et al. 2017).

The dam projects are obviously considered as a threat and 'negativity to the Kurdish identity which is not recognised by the Turkish state. Because of this, Kurdish people have shown great resistance and persistence which became a heritage culture for Kurdish communities in the last several decades. Nevertheless, the loss and traumas have led Kurdish communities to disperse into small cities of southeast Turkey as well as big cities such as Istanbul and Izmir in the west of the country, which widely impacted the making and preserving of tangible and intangible heritage.

The Botan Valley is not only significant for tangible heritage making but also it is very crucial for the local Kurdish people, who used it intensely for intangible heritage making as part of their identity and cultural production. In 2006, Turkey became a signatory of UNESCO's Convention for the Safeguarding of the Intangible Cultural Heritage (ICH),[7] which lists and registers intangible heritage all around the world. However, in practice, as in the case of the Ilisu Dam, protection and preservation of elements of intangible heritage of the Kurds were widely neglected and undermined. As I discussed earlier, UNESCO is managed by states parties that aim to promote first their own national interest before the protection of the authenticity of heritage for all groups. As in the case of ICH, state parties, particularly undemocratic and authoritarian regimes like Turkey, have abused the ICH to assimilate heritage narratives of minority groups and promote a nationalist heritage (Logan 2010).

While the manipulation and assimilation of intangible aspects of minorities continue at a national level through neglect and undermining Kurdish identity, building dams are seen as a more effective method to erase the tangible and intangible heritage of minorities. The main reason for this is that it can be more easily justified under the idea of 'economic development' and the true motivations of ethnic nationalism can be concealed. The impact of this type of large construction seems to increase particularly in places where oral tradition is common, as in the case of Botan Valley – for instance, producing songs that are related to the natural heritage of the valley (mountains, rivers and whole landscape). Here, in Botan Valley, because of the conflict and dam projects that led to displacement, traditional song making has been greatly impacted. For example, the traditional culture of 'dengebeji' has been endangered.

The term 'dengebej' refers to the artist who makes and sings songs without instruments and is very important in Kurdish literature and poetry. It is an oral cultural practice that contains history and knowledge (Schäfers 2015, 2023). With the displacement, most of the dengebeji artists have also been dispersed to other parts of Turkey where they can no longer produce songs and sing because this is a cultural practice that needs resources and audiences. One of the last generations of dengebeji artists, who still lives in Botan Valley and is also affected by the Ilisu Dam project, points out:

> I learnt how to be dengebej in my village from old community members. It is a
> cultural production that's based on our history, social and political struggle that
> Kurdish people went through for generations as well as the songs talks about our
> nature, mountain, river ... but I won't be able to pass this skill into next
> generations ... It is a dying Kurdish art.

The commentary of the Kurdish villager explicitly points out that the megadam
does not only erase the tangible heritage but also the intangible in the long term,
especially in places where oral tradition is more dominant than other forms of
cultural orientation. Therefore, the importance of engaging with emotional
geography (Kearney 2009) becomes even more important for Kurdish people
who make cultural meanings in these lands, with those cultural meanings a set
of knowledge and skills that need to be transferred from one generation to
another to survive. When I first listened to a couple of songs from this dengebeji
artist in Kurdish, I was able to recognize some words such as mountain and river
names or historical events that either negatively or positively have had impact on
Kurdish identity. This made me think that dengebeji is beyond singing songs but
it is also oral and intangible storage of cultural memory of Kurdish people whose
emotions and feeling are represented.

Kurdish culture has been transferred from one to another through storytelling
and songs and other forms of intangible practices (Schäfers 2015). However,
this form of intangible heritage needs resources to survive. These resources, for
Kurdish people and many other cases, are community and the natural
environment that people use intensively throughout their life. As in the case of
Kurdish community members from the Botan Valley, this may not be possible
because they need the natural environment as a resource (landscape, mountain,
river, valley) to practise the intangible heritage. One of the villagers, who also
worked at the archaeological rescue excavation, points out the importance of the
Botan and Tigris rivers for oral history and intangible heritage:

> I learned from my grandfathers that the site Çattepe was built by different
> cultures in the past and these rivers were used for transporting goods from the
> city of Diyarbakir to here and all the way south. I remember that we used to
> make traditional river boats (*kelek*) to pass these rivers and transport goods.
> These rivers are in our songs and stories that we tell our children.

The comment of the villager reflects on historical use for transportation of the
Tigris river, which flows from Turkey to Syria then Iraq and all the way to the
Persian Gulf (1,750km long). The villager also emphasizes one of the intangible
heritages that has been endangered because of dams and conflicts that have led

to forced migration. *Kelek* (a form of river boat) were used for a very long time in the region as a common transport for goods, animals and people (Saglamtimur 2015). The use of these boats requires skills which are also taught as part of oral tradition passed from one generation to another. Today, in the region, there are not many people left who have the skills to make *Kelek*. This is not only the case for the forms of oral intangible heritage but also other forms of intangible heritage, such as local food that depends heavily on specific environments to be grown.

The Botan Valley, with its ecological structure, is also home to local flora (see Doga 2016 for all Ilisu Dam-impacted areas) that is often used by villagers as ingredients for their local cuisine. One of the villagers whom I met during the archaeological excavations invited me for lunch with his family who lived in a nearby village, ten minutes' drive from Çattepe. I was surprised to see very different local leaves, which I had not seen before, that were used as part of the traditional food making. He pointed out that:

> Most of these leaves grow up by themselves without any agricultural intervention. They are totally organic and very unique to this region. When the season of leaves comes we just go and pick them up and use them.

The villager pointed out that while the local flora is part of their nature and used in daily life it also represents the value and cultural characteristics of the local people. The Convention for the Safeguarding of Intangible Cultural Heritage (ICH) recognizes food as part of intangible heritage, with the link between food and identity acting as a significant element of the cultural values of certain groups who transform values and identities constantly (Labadi 2013). Food is also significant as a representation of culture and symbol of recognition as it demonstrates cultural diversities. However, food heritage can also become highly politicized and is often used as a nationalist instrument, particularly for the idea of ownership rights. This is one of the reasons why nation states are competing with each other to register specific foods under their nation, using UNESCO or other international institutions (Demossier 2016). As such, while food becomes a commodity it also serves as part of nationalism (Mack and Surina 2005) under the idea of imagined community.

Food as a symbol is significant for national identities as it is also used to consolidate the dominant group's ideology. In other words, food has always been central in politics and state politics (Amir 2015). While food is important for a sense of belonging and the identity construction of communities, it can also draw boundaries, dividing different ethnic groups, as well as demonstrate the existence of multicultural ethnic and identity groups (Barth 1969; Appadurai 1988; Gabbacia 1998; Brulotte et al. 2016). However, in most cases, different cultural, ethnic and identity groups' food is registered under a singular national identity, as in the case of India, in order to unify Indians under a national identity and neglect other groups (Appadurai 1988). As in the case of Turkey, there is no registration of Kurdish cuisine and it is not recognized as part of the Kurdish identity; this is also the case for the Kurdish language, which is also not recognized by the state (Schäfers 2015) and not taught in schools as part of the assimilation process that I laid out in Chapter 2. Food is another significant aspect in the sense of belonging for communities and for identity construction in the face of nationalistic uses and appropriation, because recipes pass through experiencing and learning from one generation to another. Building a megadam that affects the landscape and nature has inarguable impacts on the local cuisine, which is developed and transformed by local communities over time and becomes part of the community identity. One of the local Kurdish community members showed me a selection of local mezes and pointed out:

> Most of these mezes are unique to this region and passed from my parents and they learnt from their parents ... there are no recipes for these mezes. It is all in our memories.

The same community member, who lives in the centre of Siirt, also reflected on the displacement. He emphasized that local Kurdish cuisine is highly dependent on the combination of local plants, vegetables and the way they are cooked in the stone ovens outside the houses in the villages. Because of the dam construction that led to displacement, with people moving to cities, there will not be much traditional practice of cooking in the cities.

Similar devastating consequences, which have great effects on natural heritage or landscape which are the resources for local flora and fauna, could also be seen in the historical town, Hasankeyf, located on the shore of the Tigris river in the city of Batman, a place that is also heavily affected by the Ilisu Dam. Hasankeyf was one of the oldest settlements in the region, occupied for over 12,000 years and continuously up until the flood reached the settlement in late 2019 (Figure 5.6 and 5.7). It contains thousands of caves, tombs and churches and archaeological remains from almost all periods. The material culture and intangible heritage that developed over years also demonstrates how memories can be accumulated and this can reflect on the landscape, nature as well as the material culture. One of the other significant characteristics of Hasankeyf is that it also represents the multicultural history of the region. From ancient

Mesopotamia to Byzantium and the Ottoman Empire to Arabs and Kurds, local people have developed cultural memory and heritage and attached meanings to those material cultures and developed values, which effectively provide ground for their identity construction.

Until the completion of the Ilisu Dam the town had 6,500 inhabitants, who had been there for generations and whose sense of belonging is strongly attached to this historic town, landscape and the river (the Tigris). Since 2006, when the Ilisu Dam project started, they had been campaigning with many national and international organizations and NGOs to stop the ongoing construction of the project that would displace them (Dissard 2021). The Turkish government had built a 'new Hasankeyf' for local residents of 700 households, which did not meet the needs of the local population of Hasankeyf, and which was located 3km away from historical Hasankeyf (see Figure 5.8 – this shows 'new Hasankeyf' and the flood after the dam began to hold water). One of the main arguments of locals was that new Hasankeyf could not meet their daily requirements as they mostly farmed and grazed animals. According to the Doga Dernegi (an NGO), which carried out a survey among the local population, 68 per cent wanted to stay in the historic town, as they emphasized that 'their history, heritage, past and the graves of their relatives are here'.[8] Most of the local people from the historic town pointed out that they were not really consulted and included in the decision-making process when the construction decision was made. I discussed the importance and value of representation dimension of social justice in the decision-making process, in particular, in situations that affect people's lives, culture, and cultural activity. As with the region of Çattepe, local people's voices were not considered and taken into account on either building the dam or moving Hasankeyf to a new place where local people's lives and culture will be transformed through a top-down approach to development.

From the beginning, the dam projects had always been controversial. Local and international campaigns were carried out to stop the dam and save Hasankeyf. The World Archaeological Congress made a statement (Ronayne 2006) to stop the destructive process of the dam project and campaigners wanted Hasankeyf to be inscribed on the UNESCO World Heritage list so it could be protected from flooding. However, the Turkish Ministry of Culture did not put Hasankeyf on their agenda to submit as a World Heritage Site to UNESCO even though it had all the criteria that UNESCO defines in its guideline.[9] At the end of 2019, the Ilisu Dam was completed and began flooding the area (see Figure 5.9), which left the historic city of Hasankeyf and its 12,000 years of history and its multicultural

Figure 5.6 Hasankeyf overall view before the dam. © Veysel Apaydin.

Figure 5.7 Hasankeyf's monuments and the landscape before the dam. © Veysel Apaydin.

Figure 5.8 New Hasankeyf in the background of the photo and water flood after the dam began to hold water on the Tigris river. © Philipp Brezhnoy/Istock by Getty Images.

Figure 5.9 Change of landscape after dam construction. Old Hasankeyf is no longer visible. © Philipp Brezhnoy/Istock by Getty Images.

past underwater. Some of the big monuments, such as Tomb and Mosque, were removed before the flood and relocated near the town.

The destructive impact of the Ilisu Dam is not only on people and material culture but it can also heavily be seen on biodiversity and non-human participants of Hasankeyf. The impact of dams in terms of the environment that forms the basis for cultural practices and developing cultural knowledge (King and Nic Eoin 2014) is greater and its impact is 'slow', but it affects generations of people as well as the climate and biodiversity of the environment. Although the impact of climate change (Graf 1999) will be seen more clearly in the long term, it has already threatened the inhabitants of the Tigris river. The report of the environmental impact assessment by Doga Dernegi (NGO) discusses the unique biodiversity of the Ilisu impact area, hosting, for instance, Bonnelli's eagle, Griffon vulture, Egyptian vulture, lesser kestrel, partridge and many more, which have already lost their breeding grounds following the completion of the dam.

Hasankeyf, as a historic and modern city, which was valued and which had meaning ascribed to it and the surrounding landscape by local communities for hundreds of years, is a good example for demonstrating that heritage has a strong link with rights, ethics and social justice. First, building dams and flooding a landscape that has been home to thousands of people who did not give permission is a breach of international human rights and all other conventions.[10] The basic human right of the people of Hasankeyf to perform and develop their cultural activity was breached and they were forced to leave the place where they had developed values, memories and constructed their identities.

Second, the archaeological rescue projects focused only on the material culture of the past, but the people who maintained and developed those material cultures were neglected. Furthermore, the contemporary social and political relevance of the sites were never explored by archaeologists or heritage specialists, which directly links to the (un)ethical approach and (mis)recognition concept of social justice that I discussed above. For instance, the museum that was established in the nearby city of Batman only focuses on the objects that have been excavated from the site, but the social, cultural and political contexts of those objects are widely neglected. Third, from the social justice perspective – considering the redistribution and recognition dimensions that I discussed in Chapter 1 – while the people of Hasankeyf were excluded from the decision-making process (Aykan 2018) of the dam construction, their values, memories, identities that are linked to the landscape of Hasankeyf are not recognized. This is more to do with the ideology of the state that does not recognize minority identity and locality in order to consolidate its own dominance.

The breach of rights of the people of Hasankeyf, the neglect of social, political and cultural contexts by professionals and the state, unequal redistribution and the lack of recognition of heritage is strongly linked to the authorized heritage discourse (Smith 2006) of the Turkish Republic. The case of Hasankeyf is not something unique to Turkey, but this combination of authoritarian and neoliberal policies that violate rights and exclude local communities from the decision-making process occurs all around the world (Silverman and Ruggles 2007; Langfield, Logan and Craith 2010; Blake 2011; Logan 2014; Ekern et al. 2015). What also should be considered in the case of Hasankeyf is that it also represents the multicultural past where material culture and memory were developed and identities were constructed (Rowlands 2004; Brown 2005; Smith 2006; Ashworth, Graham, and Tunbridge 2007; Graham and Howard 2008), and that provides a valuable opportunity with which to reflect on how cultural heritage can play a role in sustainability and peace processes and can start a dialogue between communities. However, the completion of the Ilisu Dam project in southeast Turkey led to the displacement of locals, mainly Kurdish, and destroyed the history of humanity from 12,000 B C to the modern period.

The construction of the Ilisu Dam has certainly demonstrated the power of the nation state. Ethnic and identity groups, which were seen as a threat to national unity, were assimilated through the consequences of the dam created; their history, material culture, intangible heritage and memories were erased through the guise of 'economic development'. The destructive impact has already been felt since its completion at the end of 2019. The immediate impact of the dam was seen as the landscape, nature, houses, farming fields were flooded; most of the villagers from the flooded areas have moved to cities; rivers have become lakes; the region's biodiversity has deteriorated. As in the case of Botan Valley, the destructive impact of dams is used by the state to abuse the cultural and natural resources of minority groups. Below, I will discuss in more detail the significance of natural heritage for identity making and sense of community, and resistance of the Alevi minority group. Munzur Valley and the authoritarian and neoliberal attempt of the government to consume the natural environment serve as a case study.

Munzur Valley

The Munzur Valley of Munzur Mountains is located within Dersim (Tunceli) province of eastern Turkey. The Munzur Valley was listed as a national park in 1971 because of its unique and diverse fauna and flora. However, the law that was enacted by the state to protect the valley has been breached many times by the state itself through the neoliberal policies that included the dam-building projects. As mentioned above, Turkey adopted neoliberal policies in 1980s, but use of these neoliberal policies increased exponentially since the JDP took power (Göçek 2018). In 2004, under JDP rule, the law on national parks, whose aim was to protect nature, the landscape and biodiversity, was amended to allow private companies to conduct mining operations, build dams and other forms of construction projects within protected lands. Dams were planned in the region of Dersim where the Munzur Valley is located. The valley is 85km long, stretching from the centre of Munzur Mountain, which is also considered significant for the Alevis (see Figure 5.10). In the region of Dersim, which contains many rivers and streams, more dams have also been built under the aegis of economic development. The Keban Dam which was built in Dersim area (away from the Munzur Valley) was perhaps the biggest dam in the region that changed the whole ecosystem and landscape (see Figure 5.11). In Dersim three of the dams became operational by 2009 (Figure 5.12). In the case of Munzur Valley, the top-down planned dam construction policies clashed with the persistence and resistance of the Alevi communities, whose identity construction is developed on the cultural and natural landscapes of the valley.

Alevis are a sub-minority group in Turkey, whose cultural values and identities have never been recognized by the state because they do not fit with the Turkish ideology. Although many scholars, who have carried out research on Alevis, describe them as 'orthodox Islam' or part of Islam, here I would like to follow the Dersim local community members' interpretations of their belief system, which is distinct to practice and theory of Islam (also see Deniz 2019, 2012). Most of the studies on Alevis indicate that the Alevis derived mainly from Anatolia and they are unique to this region (Shankland 2003). The Alevi belief system is based on oral tradition in which Alevi cultural values and identity is constructed on and passed to next generations. These oral traditions are mostly poems, music and dance called *Semah* (listed as UNESCO Intangible Cultural Heritage[11]), which have been passed down in the Alevi community (see Gezik and Gültekin 2019; Weineck 2015). *Semah*, a ritual dance, is one of the most important cultural practices of Alevis. During the Ottoman period and most of the twentieth century it was held secretly by Alevis who were scared of authorities who restricted this practice. It is usually held at *Cems* (a ritual ceremony) at *Cem Evi* (a house or community centre today) where Alevi community members come together periodically to join the ceremony. It is often considered as a place and time where all community members come together and practise their rituals through songs and dancing *Semah*, and it is sometimes when young members are introduced to the Alevi path. Therefore, this cultural practice is not only significant for engendering a sense of belonging and community, cultural memory and collective identity, it is also very significant for survival of Alevi cultural values. However, since many Alevis were dispersed into the big cities of Turkey as well as across Europe (Shankland 2010; Kaya 2016), this has become an endangered cultural practice, as without communities it cannot be practised. This is also

Figure 5.10 Overview of Munzur Valley and River. © Cenk Gökalp/Istock by Getty Images.

Figure 5.11 Keban Dam water reservoir. Built in the 1970s. © Veysel Apaydin.

Figure 5.12 Uzunçayir Dam in Dersim. © sadikgulec/Istock by Getty Images.

one of the main reasons that dam construction has a great danger to eliminate this intangible cultural practice which is strongly linked to Munzur Valley for Dersim Alevis.

The main foundation of Alevi philosophy is based on the important principles of 'humanism and love and respect for all people, tolerance, sharing and science'. The values of Alevis are developed on the idea at the essence of human rights: they believe every individual is responsible for their actions, self-realization is very important and, most importantly, there is no religious dogma (Deniz 2019; Gezik and Gültekin 2019). Alevi culture is developed within a very limited geographical area that is usually defined as being in Anatolia (modern Turkey), which had been very multicultural and home to many ethnic and religious groups until the purification process that Turkey began in the 1920s to create the one-nation state. Particularly in the region of Dersim, where Alevism is better preserved compared to the rest of Turkey, how people in the region develop values, cultural practices and beliefs, through using the landscape and natural environment, can clearly be seen. One of the local members, who lives in the city centre of Dersim, says:

we are completely different from the rest of Turkey, even from the rest of Alevis in other parts of the country ... People of Dersim have managed to preserve the authenticity of Alevi values even though they faced massacres and forced displacements in the past.

The number of Alevis in Turkey is between 15 and 20 million; however, they have never been recognized as a minority and their rights never been acknowledged by Turkey and the Ottoman Empire. Both used different tools to eliminate or assimilate them under Islamic and Turkish values and erase the heritage, principles and philosophy of this minority cultural group. Alevis can be found in all parts of Turkey because they have been dispersed to different regions over time. Dersim, an area that managed to preserve Alevi values and practices highly linked to nature and the landscape and sourced to Alevi oral tradition and heritage (similar to indigenous cultural practices and belief systems: see Estes 2019), has faced destruction through dam construction over the last couple of decades (Ronayne 2005, 2006). One of the main differences between Dersim Alevis and other Alevis is that they are also ethnically Zaza, a sub-group of Kurdish ethnicity (Gezik and Gültekin 2019); other Alevis describe themselves as Turkish.

While nature and the landscape are valuable for the Alevis, whose identity is based on an intangibility that uses nature and landscape as a resource, their struggle and their persistence to continue with their heritage for centuries, from the Ottoman periods to the Republic of Turkey, has also become an oral history and intangible heritage in itself for the Alevis in Dersim. Because of Dersim Alevis' distinct values and cultural identity from the majority of Turkey and the state's official ideology, they have also been treated as a threat since Ottoman times. In Chapter 2, I mentioned the demographic restructuring of Turkey following the foundation of the Turkish Republic as part of a nation-building process when Kurdish people were relocated into areas where they could be assimilated. This was also legalized in 1934 with the Law on Resettlement, which gave the Turkish government power to enact the lands where they saw communities as a threat to Turkish national unity. Therefore, as part of this repopulation programme, the Turkish government began to purify the region of Dersim and assimilate its Alevi Kurdish population through deportation and Turkifying the region. Although some Alevi groups resisted this move, it resulted in the massacre of Alevis in 1938 when tens of thousands of Alevis were killed, along with the Armenian population of Dersim (Tunceli) by Turkish forces in the name of the idea of 'one nation, one state' (Van Bruinessen 1994; Törne 2015).

In the last two decades, the conflict between the Kurdistan Workers' Party, Marxist militias and Turkish forces (Dissard 2018) has also had a devastating impact on local communities whose houses were destroyed, with others forced to leave their lands after access was restricted by the military for security reasons. The recent conflict has also led to environmental destruction because forests have been systematically burnt. One of the local community members, who has lived in Dersim all his life, states:

> the destruction has never ended in Dersim through history ... my parents and their parents, all, lived under oppression and have faced destruction which had human costs as well as nature. Now we are facing the same through conflict and dam constructions.

I discussed above, in the case of Ilisu Dam and its impact on communities and cultural landscape, how dam building leads to interrupt memory and heritage making by dispersing communities. Many local people in Dersim region say that dam building is ideologically motivated along with making profit to disperse the Alevis because their cultural identity does not fit with Turkish ideology. However, in spite of this, the long history and the persistence of Alevis has seen them continue in heritage making and undertake determined efforts to preserve their sense of place and belonging today. For example, a local Alevi community member, who lives in the city centre, points out:

> All Alevis know the fact that the state wants to eliminate us and obey its ideology. However, we have a history of struggle that we learnt from our great grandparents and we'll pass this heritage struggle to next generations. Dersim is everything for us, its air, river, mountain and all are sacred for us.

This statement contains three different discourses but these are all linked to each other. The first incorporates the insistence that local community members are aware of the fact that the aim of dam constructions is for Turkey to impose its nationalistic ideology under the guise of economic development; as the above commentary points out, the people of Dersim have long resisted this authoritarian approach and continue to do so. The second discourse relates to how the history of the struggle itself becomes heritage and that leads to reinforcement and enduring persistence rather than defeat or acceptance of more dominant narratives. Lastly, the third discourse – and strongly supporting the first two – places emphasis on the importance of the natural landscape as the basis and resource for the intangible heritage of Alevis (Figure 5.13, 5.14, 5.15).

In relation to this emphasis on the natural landscape, in Dersim Alevism is far more linked to nature than Alevis in other parts of the country. In the case of the Munzur River (*Munzur Suyu*), where dams are also planned, it is not just a river that is important environmentally, but it is also considered as sacred by the local Alevis. Dersim Alevis believe that the Munzur River gives life to Munzur Baba (Munzur father), a 'force' or spirit in the valley, where it has a visiting place (*ziyaret*[12]), as one of the Alevi community members who lives near Munzur river points out. The planned dam projects also affects many other aspects of their intangible heritage. For instance, the god Xizir (Deniz 2019) is significant for the Alevis and it is also linked to the Munzur Valley. It should be noted, however, that most Alevis in Dersim do not believe that Xizir is a god that is linked to a religion but, like Munzur Baba, it is a 'power' or 'force' that helps people when they need it. An academic, who is also from Dersim, points out:

> Xizir doesn't have space and time but its spirit lives in nature. This is why it is so much attached to Munzur Valley and significant for Alevis who consider these spaces as sacred and they take significant place for Alevi cultural, religious memory and heritage.

This clearly shows that the whole valley represents the values of the Dersim Alevis who consider it as a cultural space where they used nature for heritage making, similar to Amazonia where all aspects of the environment are considered as social partners (Descola 2013) and the Whanganui River in New Zeland where the Maori indigenous community consider the river as part of their community

Figure 5.13 Munzur Mountain and national park. © Veysel Apaydin.

Figure 5.14 Munzur River springs from the Munzur Mountain. © Thankful Photography/Istock by Getty Images.

Figure 5.15 Munzur River and Valley. © Veysel Apaydin.

and cultural life, and it is their duty to protect the river and the landscape. The long struggle of Maori people resulted in legal protection of the river, as New Zeland granted legal personhood to the river (Charpleix 2017; BBC 2020). Similarly, the Munzur Valley is not only significant as part of the spiritual beliefs of Alevis, but also, along the river itself, natural structures like rocks are considered to be sacred and have an important place for intangible heritage that is linked to nature. For instance, the sacred site of Fatma Ana (mother Fatma) on the edge of the Munzur River, in Ovacik, a small town of Dersim, is also under threat from one of the planned dams (this is just one of the sacred sites under threat from dam constructions: Ronayne 2005). The site consists of two rocks around a natural spring. The natural spring is considered to be Fatma Ana, who gives life to nature. One of the local community members states:

> Fatma Ana is a water goddess and spiritual being for us. The site attracts too many visitors from Alevi communities throughout the year.

Some trees are also sacred for Alevis and considered to be forms of spirits. I visited one of these sacred sites that is also considered to be a pilgrimage site for Alevis. The site has a large tree in which visitors put candles (Figure 5.16). Similar examples where rocks, water and the general landscape is considered as sacred can be seen in the indigenous lands of North Dakota (Estes 2019) as well as in Brazil where sacred rocks are demolished for Amazon dams. The Munzur Valley and Dersim region do not only have importance for Alevis but there are also significant traces of Christian architectural heritage, mostly monasteries and churches (Sinclair 1989), demonstrating the multicultural and diverse past of the region.

Thus, dam development projects do not only impact people and their intangible and tangible heritages, as in the case of the Ilisu Dam impact area, they also greatly impact the ecology. The Munzur Valley was listed as a national park in 1971 because of its unique ecology and biodiversity, which is often reflected in Alevi songs and poetry. It is important to point out that the flora and fauna are also as important as the landscape and nature for Alevis, particularly for Dersim Alevis. They value the flora and fauna of the valley both as natural heritage and as a resource which is used for intangible heritage practices such as cooking and Alevis' cultural practices are being developed on a specific natural biogeography. Doga Dernegi,[13] a leading nongovernmental organization in Turkey, carried out a detailed assessment of the Munzur Valley and state that the whole valley, the mountain and the river are home to a wide variety of birds including falcons and eagles, some of which are endangered and some of which are unique. The whole valley is home to a broad array of wild animals, including wild goats and pigs, lynx (Ronayne 2005) and many more. The World Wildlife Fund[14] similarly states that the region is 'considered one of the most important areas of plant biodiversity in Turkey with 3,200 vascular plant species and 725 of them are endemic to Turkey'. The diversity of species is without doubt very important for nature and the ecosystem here, but they are also an important part of the cultural landscape that gives resources for heritage making. In relation to this, one of the community members told me that:

> the Munzur means for us that it is a life, the mountain, the valley and the river that gives life to all species including people. They are all linked to each other. We are all sharing the same resources of the Munzur Valley.

The above quote and the belief system of Dersim Alevis both attest to the fact that the Alevi philosophy is strongly linked to the natural environment. Alevis consider that every species has the right to live freely and share the natural resources. For instance, wild goats are considered sacred and they can be seen everywhere in the valley. This is the main reason that the recent regulation by the government that allowed hunting Dersim goats faced a strong backlash from the local communities in the Dersim (Cumhuriyet 2021). One of the Dersim Alevi community members talks about the link between wild goats and Alevi belief system:

> wild goats are very significant for Dersim Alevis who consider them as sacred. The main reason for this is that they are associated with the Xizir [a spiritual force/power] and we believe that wild goats are the herds of Xizir and represent Xizir.

The natural environment of Munzur Valley is also very significant for intangible heritage making for the Dersim Alevis, playing a key role in the development and continued practice of poetry, dance and music – key elements in local Alevi identity construction (Neyzi 2002). As I pointed out above, the Dersim Alevis differ from the Alevis in other parts of Turkey, who have been dispersed and gone through an assimilation process. Because of the historical and traditional resistance and persistence, the Dersim Alevis have relatively managed to keep their own authentic values and cultural resources (Gezik and Gültekin 2019) compared to Alevis in other parts of Turkey. This is related to geography and identity construction because the Dersim Alevis have managed to retain the ability to govern their own territory and this made their identity construction distinct (Donnan and Wilson

Figure 5.16 Sacred tree. © Veysel Apaydin.

1999) and helped to preserve local meanings and values (Appadurai 2003). However, this dogged persistence has brought more oppression upon them from the dominant power (the nation state) because it considers such 'localities' a threat to itself. While geographical distinction and locality have provided the basis for the Dersim Alevis to preserve the authenticity of Alevi culture, locality and geographical distinction bring their own issues, as Appadurai (2003, 338) points out:

> The production of locality, as a dimension of social life, as a structure of feeling and in its material expression in lived 'compresence', faces two challenges in a postnational order ... the production of locality challenges the order and orderliness of the nation-state.

The intangible cultural production of the Dersim Alevis is a result of their historical interaction with the local environment, as one of the local members pointed out above. However, it is both their 'material expression', as Appadurai discusses, and the intangible manifestation in the forms of poetry, song and dance that consolidate its locality and collective identity. In this case, poetry, songs and dance are of the utmost importance for Alevis, who express their cultural orientation through an oral tradition (Neyzi 2002). The poetry, songs and dances that are performed as cultural activities and rituals are created and ascribed to the natural features of Munzur Valley. For example, Munzur Baba or Xizir, the 'forces' that I mentioned above, and which are attached to the Munzur Valley and River, can often be seen in the intangible production, such as songs and poetries of Dersim Alevis.

Arjun Appadurai (2003) points out the pitfalls and potentials of 'nationality and locality' and how locality can be a threat for the idea of nation state or, in the words of Anderson (1983), the 'imagined community'. In the case of Turkey, which constructed and consolidated itself on the idea of 'one nation, one state', the state does not recognize the production of local cultural practices of the Kurds and Alevis. As a nation state, to protect its sovereignty and territoriality, building dams is an unarguably good opportunity to erase 'locality', landscape and environment that would otherwise provide the basis for a threateningly local minoritarian identity production.

Locality here also means producing unique values, meanings, memories and identities that are linked to landscape, river and nature. This also demonstrates emotional engagement of Alevis with this natural landscape, as can be seen in every anecdotes of local community members of Dersim. In Amarna Kearney's (2009) study of the Yanyuwa indigenous community of northern Australia, she emphasizes that it was the group's emotional engagement with and relationship to the landscape and sea as playing a crucial in the development of intangible elements that shape the cultural value of Yanyuwa people and play a crucial role in how this area is conceptualized as their homeland. She also emphasizes 'love, nurturance, concern, fear, anger, bewilderment, sadness and loneliness' as emotions that Yanyuwa people engage in with their homelands. From an emotional engagement perspective, a similar range of emotions can also be seen in Dersim for the Alevi people as they engage with the valley, river and the mountain. For example, the spiritual characteristic of the valley, with its difficult history which includes massacres of Alevis in the past, created fear and concerns as well as anger among Alevi people who may think this may happen again or it happens through other methods such as dam projects. The valley also represents love for nurturance for Alevis, as it is a physical space that with its natural spiritual places provides care, and, therefore, Alevi people show emotional care in turn for the protection of the valley. As I have demonstrated, it is this autochthonous emotional engagement with the valley that is at the core of Dersim Alevis' cultural identity.

The destructive impacts of megadam constructions are unquestionably far-reaching. As we have seen, these impacts only grow greater in the long term because the violence occurs slowly, deteriorating the natural environment and landscape that is used by the inhabitants who had previously transformed it into a cultural terrain. In the Dersim region, three dams have already been constructed and many others are planned for its rivers, despite their importance as a cultural resource for the Alevis. The State Water Institution (DSI), which is responsible for all dam construction in Turkey, justifies the dam constructions in Dersim and the Munzur Valley by stating that 'we are bringing water of life to Dersim'.[15] They also proudly announced that the dams are successful economic and social developments that will help to aggregate the lands for better farming. At the beginning of the twenty-first century, a cultural and environmental impact assessment project was carried out by Kurdish Human Rights Project and National University of Ireland, which focused on ethnographic data collection along with other sources (Ronayne 2005). The report indicated that before the first two dams were built, no detailed assessments in terms of their impact were carried out by the state and communities were not consulted about the dams. As I have discussed, such a top-down approach was not new in Turkey; similar approaches can be seen in other parts of the country, for instance in the Black Sea region where many dams were developed with still others planned by the State Water Agency.

The cultural landscape is a 'common good', as I pointed out at the beginning of this chapter. It should therefore be considered as part of the rights of local people who must have the power to manage and use it as part of the representation dimension of social justice. However, decisions regarding managing cultural landscapes are usually taken using a top-down approach and on a national level, which excludes local opinions and localities. This not only happens at the national level but is also very common at the international level. UNESCO management guidelines also neglect locality and the local meaning of landscape and heritage; rather it frames its management around 'Outstanding Universal Values', which in practice are enacted by dominant state parties at the expense of sub-national groups and minorities. This approach frequently fails to capture the local conceptions and perceptions of *local* landscapes, whose populations have distinct interpretations of cultural landscapes and nature (Peluso 1995; King and Eoin 2014; Byrne 2008a, 2008b; Byrne and Nugent 2004; Harrison 2011).

The main reason for this top-down approach is that locality is seen as a threat to hegemonic powers, particularly for nation states, as Appadurai (2003) also emphasized. Similar to the Ilisu Dam construction, the Munzur Valley dam projects also excluded excluded local community members from the decision-making process (Ronayne 2005). Most community members in Dersim point out that no consultation had been carried out with local community members about the dams built in the past or currently being planned.

Of course, including local communities and recognition of the localities of the region into the decision-making process would have brought a series of issues for the Turkish state, which has a strict authoritarian and neoliberal approach. However, the negative approach of the state which has destructive methods also brings positivity for Alevis, who remain motivated to protect their heritage against the state. Since the dam projects began in the Munzur Valley, there have been large national and international campaigns against the dam projects (Figure 5.17). Estes (2019) discusses the similarly destructive impact of pipelines in indigenous lands and sacred sites and historical resistance of indigenous people. In the same way, a historical resistance can be seen in the case of the Dersim Alevis against authoritarian and neoliberal policies to protect indigenous lands and cultural resources. As the Alevi community members pointed out above, the people of Dersim have learned how to resist when it comes to their 'right to landscape', their 'right to heritage', their 'right to perform culture' and 'right to use and manage the natural environment'. These four points are the main bases for the resistance and persistence of the Dersim Alevis against authoritarianism and neoliberalism to protect their heritage making through cultural performance, a 'basic human right' that has been breached repeatedly by Turkey.

Figure 5.17 A banner in Munzur Festival [Stop all dam projects]. © Veysel Apaydin.

we owe life to these lands that gives us life. We won't allow looting of our nature.
(Munzur Culture and Nature Festival)

The above quote was taken from the banner of the Munzur Festival, which was initially started to protest against the dam construction in the Munzur Valley. The festival has been held every year since 2000, with a large number of people from local communities, and Alevis from Turkey and Europe. During the three days of the festival, people gather together, perform traditional songs and dances, and visit sacred places (*ziyarets*) in the Munzur Valley. The large number and diverse attendees from all over Turkey and Europe demonstrate the importance of Munzur for the Alevi cultural memory and heritage as well as collective identity. The people of Dersim show their persistence and resistance against authoritarian and neoliberal policies by attending the festival and taking part in the solidarity campaigns.

As discussed earlier in this book, neoliberal policies have accelerated and become more destructive in Turkey in the last few decades (Göçek 2018); this tends to make the ideology of Turkey more Islamic combined with more traditional notions of Turkishness (Zencirci 2014). These policies of 'economic development' are particularly used in the contested regions of Turkey (Göçek 2018) where minority groups live, who do not fit with this mainstream Turkish ideology, and are deployed to erase these groups' cultural resources.

As discussed above, the resistance of the Dersim Alevis against the dam construction has also been assisted by many NGOs and lawyers, who have made court applications against the dam constructions. In 2020, following two decades of local, national and international campaigns, the dams' construction in the Munzur Valley have finally been stopped through court action.[16] For now however, campaigners and local community members also point out that 'we will continue our struggle and protect our nature'. In the case of the Munzur Valley resistance, the Alevi community demonstrate that the 'negativity' of the Turkish state actually motivated the Alevis to become more persistent in carrying on their cultural activities by protecting and preserving their natural environment, organizing new cultural activities and carrying intangible performances to consolidate and transform their collective identity, cultural memory and heritage for future generations. The Munzur Festival has become a symbol of persistence and heritage making; it is a cultural event as well as heritage itself – a heritage in which protests become heritage. Such acts of resistance becoming rapidly 'heritagized' are seen more broadly in other cases across Turkey and are particularly in evidence in the well-known example of Gezi Park, to which I now turn.

6

Resistance

In the early morning of 27 May 2013, bulldozers suddenly entered Gezi Park, Taksim Square in Istanbul – one of the rare green spaces in the city centre – to cut down trees in order to build shopping malls and the Ottoman barracks. This had been planned years ago, without any legal or public consent and approval. This authoritarian, top-down action led to protests, which quickly spread to other parts of the country. In May and June 2013, there were weeks of protests and occupations at the park, with the aim to protect green and public spaces. These were the biggest environmental protests seen, with millions of people reclaiming the public space (Arat 2013; Moudouros 2014; Baydar 2014).

On the third day of protests, following two nights of heavy clashes between protesters and the Turkish police, hundreds of thousands of protesters entered the park and occupied it for weeks. The tension was very high in the city and in the rest of the country as protests spread to almost every city in Turkey (Figure 6.1). In Taksim Square and Gezi Park, tens of thousands of people were chanting and demonstrating, using the creative arts, music, dance, plays, even doing yoga, as forms of creative protest (Figures 6.2, 6.3).

In the previous chapter I demonstrated forms of resistance to authoritarian power over heritage uses and abuses in the rural areas of Turkey. Here, I will attempt to demonstrate how the collective resistances of people, who were from different backgrounds in terms of ethnicity, class, education and political views, came together to protect a space that was significant for memory, identity and the environment. By demonstrating the violent authoritarian decision-making process in Turkey's biggest city, Istanbul. I will discuss how the importance of space for memory also creates tension, and collective resistance and peaceful protest in turn creates dialogue and constructs bridges between different groups who had once been opposed to and held prejudices about each other and how this creative protest led to building dialogues between socially, culturally and politically different groups and generated art, social production and democratic platforms for people.

Figure 6.1 Gezi Park protests in Taksim Square, Istanbul. © CelilKirnapci/Istock by Getty Images.

Figure 6.2 Protesters doing yoga and sport at Gezi Park. © Yunlutas/Istock by Getty Images.

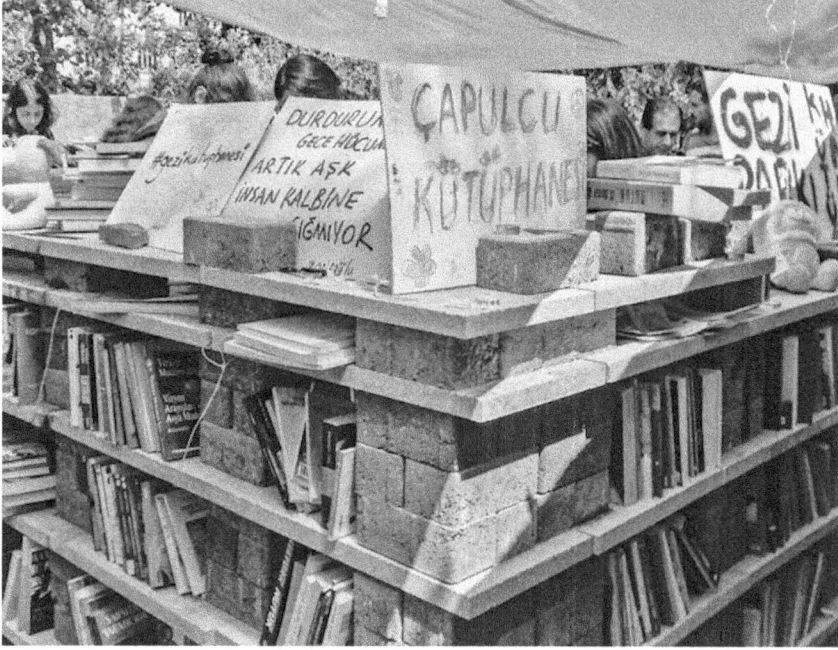

Figure 6.3 A library that was created by the protestors. Free for everyone.
© Yunlutas/Istock by Getty Images.

Memory and space

In his book, *The Book of Laughter and Forgetting* (1980, 4), Milan Kundera points out that 'the struggle of man against power is the struggle of memory against forgetting'. So, why do these two concepts create tension? Why is the concept of *remembering* of memory so important for some and a threat for others, especially for those who have power? Why does this lead to conflict?

Gezi Park, located in Taksim Square in the centre of Istanbul, is one of those public spaces that created this form of tension over cultural and collective memory and it is one of those spaces that has symbolic and powerful meanings; it is a space that acts as a repository for memories and is very significant for the collective identity of groups. The square has monumental symbols, monuments and architecture that commemorate the Turkish War of Independence following the collapse of the Ottoman Empire and symbols of secularism for Turkey, such as the Atatürk Cultural Centre, which represents secular modern Turkey. As such, particularly the secularist communities of Turkey ascribe great meanings to Taksim Square.

The secularists of Turkey are not only the claimants of Taksim Square and Gezi Park: it also has great significance as a space for the labour rights movements (Baykan and Hatuka 2010). Gezi Park is also significant for the memories and sense of belonging for the Armenian minority, who had a graveyard located within the space of the park (later moved; Watenpaugh 2013). Historically, the neighbourhood around the square and the park were also very multicultural, and Turkish, Armenian, Greek and Jewish communities all left architectural heritage in the area, including churches and synagogues. The strong representation of power of Taksim Square and Gezi Park for the people, whose identity and worldview opposed that of the JDP, played a significant role in the JDP's attempt to demolish these old identities and memories and establish its own identity through new architecture. The JDP aimed to demolish Gezi Park in order to reconstruct an Ottoman barracks and to build a shopping mall to symbolize its own new identity based on the idea of *Yeni Turkiye* (New Turkey) (Zencirci 2014) as well as make economic profit. The idea of building the Ottoman barracks, to impose a new ideology based on Turkish, Ottoman and Islamic ideology, and to build shopping malls as part of its heavy destructive neoliberal policies all clearly represent the ideology of 'New Turkey' under the control of the JDP.

As I discussed in previous chapters, memory, architecture and spaces are all strongly linked to each other, and architecture and space as tangible heritage are powerfully representative of the memories and collective identities of communities (Apaydin 2020b). Memory is often described as something that is developed in the past and remembered in the present or as something that is used in the present for different purposes (Nora 1989; Ricoeur 2004). Memory certainly has great importance for individuals and groups of people who share a common past and heritage to construct a collective identity. Although memory is often discussed as something abstract, it is embodied in material culture and, therefore, it is often very tangible. What is also significant is the way memories are developed and their meanings in the present for groups and communities. Meanings and the ways of developing memories and uses differ, of course, because there are different circumstances and communities have socially and culturally unique dynamics. However, what is common in memory development across different societies is that memories are developed in a space, a physical space, and embodied in tangible and intangible heritage.

What I am trying to argue is that while memory itself is significant for people, the *space* where it is developed is also as important for the people whose identity is constructed and who use that space as part of their sense of belonging as a community (see Assman and Czaplicka 1995) more on cultural memory and cultural identity. However, that space, which includes the landscape, natural environment and urban areas, where memories are developed by groups becomes a space to control by other groups whose aims are to dominate and to (ab)use resources of others, as in the case of the JDP. Therefore, the JDP, as an oppressor, uses its power to interrupt the memory making that is there and to develop new memories, its memories, linked to its own economic and political ideology. Contrary to this, the resistance and struggle of the oppressed is based on remembering, remembering consciously or unconsciously, as in the case of Malaysian villagers' everyday resistance (Scott 1985) and the conservation of cultural memory, identity and the space where they were attached.

As in the cases of dam projects (Chapter 5) and conflict in Sur (Chapter 4), the JDP used neoliberalism as a powerful tool to implement its own ideology as part of an authoritarian approach that excludes the public from the decision-making process. This top-down decision-making process that excludes public views and opinions on matters of the transformations of spaces and cultural landscapes under the guise of economic development is quite common across the world. Although the struggle to protect and preserve resources for heritage making and to control these resources is not new, what we are seeing, particularly in the twenty-first century, are new forms and tools to control these resources and spaces. We are certainly in a new political age, but it is difficult to define and name it, as Brown (2019, 2) points out:

> We even have trouble with the naming – is this authoritarianism, fascism, populism, illiberal democracy, undemocratic liberalism, right-wing plutocracy? Or something else?

The struggle against the abuse of power has perhaps been around for centuries, with different forms of preserving and transforming memories through the strong resilience of communities. While the form of resistance changes to protect memory and heritage that construct the identities of people, the forms of the abuse of power changes as well, with social and political transformations. The twenty-first century is witnessing new forms of politics following on from post-capitalism, embodied in far-right and right-wing populist politics (Brown 2019). White nationalism has increased, even in the heart of Europe where democracy and human rights are embodied in their constitutions. Hungary, Poland and Turkey are led by right-wing populist governments, which are abusing their power to consolidate their control on the one hand, and profit through the use of neoliberal policies on other (Kaya 2019).

The move to demolish Gezi Park and build a shopping mall and Ottoman barracks was not only politically motivated but there were economic motives as well. As Brown (2019) discusses, authoritarianism often uses strong neoliberal policies to support its ideological interests. JDP is an authoritarian government that aims to implement its own ideology everywhere, from state institutions to rural areas to public spaces; it sees these spaces, such as Gezi Park, as threats because they are memory stores and social, cultural and economic resources for those who oppose the ideology of the JDP. These resources can be natural resources that have importance for local and indigenous people and different identity groups, as in the case of the Alevi and Kurdish minorities in Turkey. Resources can also be the spaces that have great importance for public life, not only for interactions and social activities, but also spaces that provide a physical place for identity construction, memory and heritage – in other words, spaces that are used as a resource for social and cultural production for individuals as well as collective identities. Therefore, spaces have substantial impact and are significant because of their symbolic meanings, values, memories and impact on social and individual behaviours as well as cognitive development (Harvey 2009, 36). The plan to transform Gezi Park indeed reveals the importance of space for power sharing and controlling as well as the connection between use of the authoritarian and heavy neoliberal policies, as Lefebvre (Butler 2009, 321) emphasizes:

> Social spaces are a recognition that the political dimensions of space extend beyond its management and use as a political tool by the state. Space is itself a site of political conflict in which the class struggle has increasingly been transformed into forms of conflict which are spatial as well as political and economic.

In the case of Gezi Park, the space was certainly being used as a 'political tool' by the Turkish state, and in other parts of the world, a space can certainly be a symbol or 'site' of 'class struggle', as Lefebvre points out. However, what Gezi Park represents is not a class struggle but rather a collective struggle of people who come from economically, socially and politically different backgrounds. Therefore, the experience of the struggle for the space of Gezi Park also shifts our classical understanding of the relationship between power, space and class struggle. While public spaces in today's world have many different functions and meanings for people, they also have political and economic dimensions, as Henry Lefebvre (1991) points out in his substantial book, *The Production of Space*:

a product that is consumed as a commodity and as a productive resource in the social reproduction of labor power; a political instrument that facilitates forms of social control … reproduction of property relations through legal and planning regimes which order space hierarchically; a set of ideological and symbolic superstructures; … a means of human re-appropriation through the development of counter spaces forged through artistic expression and social resistance.

Gezi Park demonstrates this kind of function of space, in terms of heritage making, uses and abuses. It also shows how people resist power to protect their memory and heritage. In terms of neoliberal consumerism, Gezi Park and the surrounding Taksim Square is considered a 'commodity' and 'productive resource', facilitating profit making and social, political and economic control. Highly linked to this is that neoliberal consumerism also serves as a tool to establish boundaries between people and to use space to demonstrate the power of the state and to consolidate its own ideology symbolically. Most importantly, however, the Gezi Park protests themselves became a heritage and cultural memory through the collective actions of people who also developed a shared value. It went through a cultural process: the millions of protesters who reclaimed Gezi Park transformed into a struggle discourse in terms of personal, collective and sociopolitical empowerment against authoritarian and neoliberal consumerist approaches.

Building dialogue

The Gezi Park protests brought people together from many different backgrounds, political views and classes, and they displayed a sociopolitical and collective solidarity against the park's demolition. The diversity of protesters was easily noticed in terms of politics, demographics, gender and age (Baydar 2014), with all these groups also representing the different identities. This diverse resistance against authoritarianism manifested itself in different forms. In Turkey, historically, conservatives (as this group called themselves 'anti-capitalist Muslims' who joined the protests) and seculars would not have stood side by side for the same aim or goal. The Gezi Park resistance started a conversation between these two ideologically opposed groups. Similarly, secular nationalists had always been biased against pro-Kurdish groups, but at Gezi Park, they all stood together against authoritarianism. Many other groups also joined: LGBTQ, environmentalists, Alevis, football fans, working-class and middle-class people. Everyone started talking to each other around shared values regarding protecting the public space.

The diverse participants in the demonstrations prove that public spaces have a great significance for people, even if from different backgrounds. What makes this process more significant is that a multicultural representation of space also creates dialogues between groups, and this can be argued as a way to bridge gaps and create paths for sustainability. Although I often emphasize (Apaydin 2020b, 2018c) that heritage is also an embedded reason for conflict and can be divisive rather than positive, in the case of Gezi Park, the multicultural representation of space represents positivity rather than negativity for people who are from different social, economic and ethnic backgrounds. According to the intergroup group contact theory (Allport 1954), the majority of prejudices and biases are developed against other groups because these groups are not in contact with each other. Gezi Park provided a platform where groups with prejudices and biases came into contact and began to accept each other, recognize and acknowledge others with their backgrounds, providing a social experience for all these groups.

Of course, Gezi Park and other public spaces are built upon social experiences, either by multiple or single-identity groups. They are, therefore, closely associated with lived experiences. However, what is clear in the case of Gezi Park is that social experience was built on diversity because the demonstrators were politically diverse and from different ethnic, social and economic backgrounds (Konda 2014) and they established different forms of relationships and experiences by removing the boundaries between themselves. What is also important is that Gezi Park provided 'contact' in an equal and cooperative platform for diverse backgrounds. For instance, during the occupation, every group and each individual had a chance to express themselves and share their opinions regarding the space. In other words, all groups, regardless of their backgrounds, were equal in making decisions.

Their new experience led to the creation of different social values and developed memories that became the heritage of people who valued and ascribed meaning to the protests. The diverse background of protesters at Gezi Park also demonstrated that people, at the grassroots level, have shared values. In this case, the shared value was 'rights': all those people and groups from different backgrounds valued the fact that everyone has a right to have a voice in issues relating to their social, cultural and economic daily life, space and heritage. The motivation behind the high attendance and weeks of persistence of protesters to prevent the demolition of the park was more about the breach of their rights rather than any ideological or political protest. According to the poll conducted by Konda (2014), the majority of people who attended the protests stated that they were there 'for freedom', 'to demand for rights', and were 'against dictatorship and oppression'. However, the most striking response among protesters for joining protests (close to nine out of ten respondents) was to 'oppose the government policies' (Konda 2014) that violated people's right to use and manage public spaces.

In my previous discussion of the case of Munzur Valley, I argued how the systematic and destructive policies of the state through dam constructions faced a backlash of strong resistance and systematic persistence by the Alevi communities. This resistance changed the meaning of the valley through the development of another intangible heritage event: the Munzur Festival and protests. In the case of Gezi Park, it already had a heritage symbolized with values and meanings. It had a significant role in identity constructions for secular communities and the labour movement, and provided a sense of belonging for Armenians. The grassroots resistance by the public demonstrates another level of heritage building through the transformation of the space and heritage with the bottom-up people-centred resistance against authoritarianism. In other words, while Gezi Park and Taksim Square were already significant for specific communities, cultural, social and 'non-hegemonic' resistance created new memories, added new values and ascribed new meanings to the identity and value of the square and park. Through dialogue, people who are dissimilar in terms of their identity backgrounds developed a new heritage at Gezi Park that has opened new ways for the reconciliation process for a sustainable society.

Of course, heritage is a social production that is made by individuals and groups through social interactions that develop social value. Certainly, social values are very complex because they are developed with different dynamics and meanings. In heritage studies, it has often been pointed out that they are mostly related to identity, attachment and a sense of belonging (Jones 2017; Byrne et al. 2003) of specific ethnic or local groups and communities. In contrast to this traditional way of interpreting social values, what Gezi Park demonstrates is that social values are not necessarily developed by a specific group and do not necessarily represent one identity group or community which shares similar values. Instead, it also shows that social values are part of social production in space and can be produced by people who do not share similar values but are able to make a new community that is open to developing multicultural values. A detailed survey conducted among the protesters indicates the variety of participants who do not have similar backgrounds or values but who have the same purpose and motivation: they see Gezi Park as a significant space that is highly linked to their rights. Of course, weeks of protest and occupation by many different individuals and groups whose backgrounds vary also developed memories, common values and meanings that also reflected heavily on and embodied social production that is made through social interaction of people during the protest and occupation.

The social interaction of people from different groups also embodied itself in art as part of social production. Perhaps one of the most effective and significant impacts of Gezi Park as a public space was that using art as a communication tool created the basis for critical dialogue between the diverse groups, whose values and identity constructions were different. Or, vice versa, through dialogue people created different forms of street art during and following the Gezi Park occupation.

> Art is more moral than moralities. For the latter either are or tend to become, consecrations of the status quo, reflections of custom, reinforcements of the established order ... Art has been the means of keeping alive the sense of purposes that outrun evidence and of meanings that transcend indurated habit.
>
> John Dewey (1934, 362), *Art as Experience*

Weeks of occupation and social interactions of people who have different backgrounds resulted in social production and created a new culture as Gezi Park protests resisted authoritarianism through art and developed social production that embodied tangible and intangible art. As Dewey points out above, art is more about morals and can come out with the oppression of the power and always has a purpose. This purpose has been embodied in street art in many parts of the world as part of protests, as in the case of the financial crisis of Greece, or Latin America when people rose up against dictatorship (Chaffe 1993). In the case of Gezi Park, different forms of art (graffiti, paintings, music, plays, dance) can be seen from different but creative perspectives to challenge the authoritarian order. In other words, art as a social production comes out of resisting oppression by becoming a voice of people.

Political scientist and anthropologist James C. Scott (1995) formulates 'resistance' into two categories: 'formal resistance', which is organized, and 'everyday resistance', which can be considered as an informal way of resistance that can happen spontaneously. Perhaps the latter better explains Gezi Park, because it happened informally (see Barnstone and Otto 2019). Scott (1995) also points out three characteristics of resistance, which can be a reaction to injustice, linking it to 'ideological struggle' and response to 'appropriation of symbols' (also see Barnstone and Otto 2019). All these characteristics share creativity in the acts of resistance. In many parts of the world, resistance can be linked to Scott's point, as it usually happens spontaneously and from the bottom up to engage with authoritarian political decisions; art is often used as a form of expression and protest itself. Barnstone and Otto (2019, 6) point out that in Germany, resistance or activism has always been linked with artistic production and art has been used to respond to politics as part of protest.

These social productions made during the protests and occupation became visible. In fact, in the case of Gezi Park, making different forms of art became a form of communication as how the protesters expressed themselves through art. Niklas Luhmann (2000, 22) in his book *Art as a Social System*, points out that:

> Art can exist only when there is language – this is less trivial than it sounds. Art is unique in that it makes possible a type of communication that, in the strict sense of the word, avoids language along with the routines involved in language use. The forms of art are understood as communications, but without language, without argumentation. Instead of using words and grammatical rules, people employ works of art to communicate information in ways that can be understood.

The art through social interaction as a result of resistance at Gezi Park embodied itself in different forms and years to come have had an impact on people, as well as opened new ways of protesting. For instance, music was one of the artistic approaches in the resistance to and main collective response to the authoritarian approach of the government. Not only did musical groups and musicians join the protest and play music, but also the protest itself became a resource for poetry and song making (Bianchi 2018). Music was not only a production but also it was a communication tool to build dialogue between groups. While pop and rock musicians were often in the scenes, the traditional music of the Alevis, for example, was a form of tool to protest. Similarly, Sufi music, which is normally considered more conservative, and mystic music and dance were also performed at Gezi Park (Bianchi 2018). The combination of different genres of music and musicians also demonstrated how music from an artistic perspective can lead to dialogue and become a social production.

Other common expression and communication tools at Gezi Park were graffiti, murals and paintings that were very popular even after the protests. These graffiti and paintings were commonly shared on social media (Chrona and Bee 2017); the posts went viral and got the attention of the international media. Gezi Park certainly transformed the way people protest in Turkey through creative means, but it also brought new insights into how democratic processes for decision making can be established.

Representation and participation

The city and its public spaces are very complex in terms of its uses and management the public spaces have many different claimants and are always contested spaces (Mitchell 2003b, 4); they have often been a point of conflict between different identity groups (Bevan 2016; Walasek 2015; Herscher 2010). These spaces are constantly transformed and new meanings are attached. However, what makes a transformation destructive is when it is top-down, using an authoritarian neoliberal approach as I demonstrated in previous chapters. Developing material culture or intangible heritage is, of course, something that needs to be considered as a progressive, dynamic cultural production and with new developments, meanings and memories; it needs to be open for transformation. The main issue in those countries that have imposed heavy authoritarian neoliberal policies, however, is that this process is led from a top-down, destructive perspective and it is not managed at the bottom-up, grass-roots level.

Holtorf (2018, 644) points out that 'cultural heritage, just like nature, is a continuously evolving process, not a legacy in any part already complete ... people and buildings, like mountains, clouds and waves in the ocean, are considered to be crystallizations of persistent processes that continually carry on (also see Ingold 2010). Heritage, including buildings, monuments, and any other tangible heritage, as well as intangible heritage, is certainly a process and cannot be preserved as it is forever. It regenerates itself through new memories and meanings, and new values are attached. However, the neoliberal authoritarian approach towards space that uses it as s a cultural resource interrupts this natural process of heritage making because it is imposed top-down rather than implemented bottom-up. Public spaces can be transformed, of course, and this can be considered as a progressive ontology. However, the questions should be, as Harvey (2003, 2007) discusses, whether this process is *creative* or *destructive*, who benefits from this transformation, is the transformation consensual and ethical, and what are the long-term impacts? And most importantly, who decides how to transform? By ethical or transformation, I refer to the 'representation' dimension of social justice (see Fraser 2009). Fraser (2009) discusses the importance of the representation dimension of social justice, which aims to give a voice to people regarding making decisions, rather than only the authorities, through a top-down approach. Fraser discusses the necessity of 'representation' for democratizing the process, though she also points out the difficulties of this process because one group can dominate the other.

During the occupation of Gezi Park, democratic platforms were established to make decisions regarding the occupation and the park and everyone was included in the decision-making process. Following the end of occupation, these platforms turned into 'people's assemblies' (forums or *Halk Meclisi*) in many cities and neighbourhoods of Turkey. These assemblies were perhaps one of the most important contributions of the Gezi Park protests: democratic decision making was established regarding the future of public spaces where heritage is made and memories developed. After the occupation at Gezi Park, people began to get together every week in small parks in their neighbourhoods to discuss actions not only about Gezi Park but also about authoritarian decisions and how they can have a voice in these decisions about their public space, parks and cities. In the summer of 2013, one of these assemblies was established in the Beşiktaş neighbourhood, which is in walking distance of Taksim Square and Gezi Park (Figure 6.4) here. I had the chance to observe how these assemblies were held and how they functioned.

The residents of Beşiktaş, including its famous football club fans, were one of the main drivers of the protest. In the crowd, people of all age groups were visible and they were all very eager to participate in these new assemblies. In the assembly, NGO and labour union representatives and journalists and writers also took part. While there were organizers and speakers, who may have appeared to be dominating the decision-making process, people from the crowd also had the microphone and contributed to the discussions. It may have not been the most democratic platform but it was the beginning of a new era for many people who were taking initiative to contribute to the decisions of their cities. In the following years, these forums/people's assemblies turned into local organizations that aim to deal with local issues, such as 'Istanbul City Defence' which was established in 2014 (Zihnioglu 2019).

In *The Right to the City,* David Harvey (2009, 315) points out that desires, lifestyles, values and social relationships are extremely significant for people who develop these aspects out of social experiences. Particularly if this kind of change comes with an authoritarian and profit-making approach, people usually resist because it is a top-down social and political transformation (see Hall 2005). Considering that space is physical and provides a basis for social production, as

Figure 6.4 A forum that was established in Beşiktaş neighbourhood following the protests. © Veysel Apaydin.

Lefebvre (1991) pointed out, it is the people's right to change or preserve themselves. Therefore, it is not only a space, it is also the people's right to experience and carry out social activities and to take part in cultural performance.

Making decisions through people's assemblies is a creative transformation in contrast to the authoritarian destructive forms. Space and heritage can be transformed through the actions of people who have the right to claim space for heritage making, as the Gezi Park protests and occupations demonstrate. The Gezi Park protests show not only resistance against authoritarian policies and profit making, but they also demonstrate an ethical way to transform space and heritage making by developing new memories, attaching new values and ascribing new meanings during the protests through the production of the resistance of people. What Gezi Park protests also show is that the destructive, authoritarian attempts of changing values of spaces leads to grassroot resistance to protect values, meanings, memories and identities.

7

Conclusion: Right to Heritage

Throughout the twentieth century there was a rise in nation states and nationalism, inequality and injustice increased, the distinction between the rich and the poor grew, particularly following heavy use of neoliberal policies, and power structures shifted away from the people to dominant powers, especially following the Second World War. Authoritarian regimes became more common; oppression increased, in particular for many minority groups across the world whose rights as individuals and groups were often breached in mostly undemocratic nation states. In the twenty-first century, we see the continuation and increase of inequalities, the devastating impact of climate change through the consumption of natural resources in order to make profit, combined with wars and conflicts that have displaced people. Within these changing and devastating political and global issues, as heritage scholars, we have the moral responsibility to contribute to the reduction of inequalities and injustices, the development of dialogues between communities, and to helping in the prevention of conflicts between groups using heritage. As heritage scholars, we need to develop new theoretical approaches and methods to reflect on these issues and help to make positive changes; to provide ways to sustain communities through developing more democratic approaches to people and communities, landscapes and nature, and biodiversity. These elements should not be considered separately because they are intricately linked with each other in terms of cultural practices and heritage making. The democratic approach would not only prevent human rights breaches but it can also create a path towards justice for both human and non-human participants of the world and help to prevent dramatic climate change through the prevention of the destruction of landscapes and biodiversity.

The democratic approach not only brings positive change for the rights of people but it also has the potential to contextualize and implement social justice dimensions: redistribution, recognition and representation. The three components of social justice are significant for basic human rights, from the right to live to the right to participate in cultural activities and develop heritage without restrictions, exclusion and misrecognition, and having an equal share in the social, economic and cultural capitals regardless of background, i.e. identity, ethnicity, religion, sexual orientation and/or class. In other words, the three dimensions of social justice create a path to protect the rights of people, in contrast to authoritarian regimes that undermine all of these basic human rights.

In Turkey, as an authoritarian state, and in many other modern and ancient nation states, different means have been used to oppress and erase the identities, memories and heritage of minoritized groups. These different means include preventing minority groups from learning about their own heritage, past and history; restricting the use of their landscape; consuming and destroying the natural resources of those communities; forced displacement through mega-construction projects; and conflict. While all of these means have been used in nationalist discourses (that is, for the 'good' of the nation state), I argue that the main embedded discourse is to cut off communities from resources needed for developing, preserving, transferring and transforming heritage, and to be the dominating power. These resources are, in the case of Turkey: education that transfers heritage knowledge developed through cultural activities and participation of communities; homes, neighbourhoods or, in other words, the physical space where people carry out their everyday lives despite oppression; and the landscape and natural environment that are the sources for tangible and intangible heritage.

The conflict over the management of resources, perhaps, is a never-ending story because resource management, resource control is power. However, these resources are also the sources for communities to carry out cultural activities that develop heritage and memories and preserve their identities; and these are at the centre of human rights and social justice. The concepts of 'rights' and 'social justice' that I discuss throughout this book are very significant for community survival and performing culture and participating in heritage making. They are also closely related to the hegemonic discourses that have been developed by the elites who hold the power in undemocratic societies, that breach rights and aggravate injustices to suppress others and conserve their own identity. These hegemonic discourses are being developed on top of 'cultural, political and economic' discourses, where conflicts arise over power sharing and exercising rights. The three discourses, cultural, political and economic, have a strong relationship and are applied well in learning and education, managing the landscape and natural environment and space. They also motivate the oppressed to resist and persist.

Right to learn. Access to knowledge is perhaps one of the most significant aspects for communities who develop heritage and transfer it to next generations. In modern societies, this access is provided mostly through formal education in schools, which is usually controlled by the state. The strict control of education and content also leads to unequal distribution of knowledge, knowledge that is usually selected by the state, which often manipulates the content through discourses (Fairclough and Wodak 1997) in textbooks. These discourses are, of course, deliberately developed by the dominant power to prevent learning about minority cultures and the multicultural heritage of the country, such as what happens in Turkey. The strict centralized and controlled education system not only prevents minority groups from learning about their own heritage and the past but it also makes them the 'other' through discourses in the textbooks, which leads to oppression. Not only are the minorities oppressed through the one-sided education but students who are from dominant groups are also prevented from learning about those cultures and their access to wider knowledge is restricted by the oppressor.

In his classic book *Pedagogy of the Oppressed*, Paulo Freire (1970) calls this oppressive education system the *Banking Education* model. In this system, he says, teachers are active agents and students are passive and only receivers of the knowledge. This model is a one-way and informative system that does not allow students to question and participate in learning. It is not experiential and constructive learning (Dewey 1934) where students are encouraged to learn and resources are provided. It is an oppressive education model that dictates certain knowledge and excludes others. The most important part of Freire's critique is that this kind of oppressive education system is in the nature of capitalist society. Education and learning are supposed to free and to liberate people, as he often points out in his other books, such as in *Pedagogy of Freedom* (1998). This type of oppressive education system becomes even worse in authoritarian nation states like Turkey, which combines heavy neoliberal policies with its authoritarian approach, becoming a very class-structured society. This reflects in a different way in Turkey – not from a classical way of understanding class structure that is based on economic background, but rather, in the Turkish case, based on ethnic identities developed through tangible and intangible heritage. The dominant power, Turkey, becomes the oppressor and the students and minority groups who are being excluded from learning about other cultures in the education system become the oppressed. The education system that is supposed to be a learning mechanism becomes an exclusive and discriminative tool rather than an inclusive one.

Exclusive, discriminative and oppressive education is also a great obstacle for the redistribution dimension of social justice. The 'redistribution' concept of social justice seeks justice for an equal distribution of wealth and resources, as I discussed in Chapter 1 and exemplified with the concepts of Global North and Global South, whereby the Global South is exploited by the Global North and is discriminated against getting an equal share of its own resources. Here, I consider knowledge as a resource that communities should be able to equally access through schools or other forms of informal learning spaces, such as museums, galleries and other informal public spaces. Formal and informal education institutions need to make sure that communities are getting an equal share of knowledge as a resource, which I strongly argue to be one of the ways of sustaining communities. Equal share of knowledge is also directly linked to inequalities and injustices that have created great barriers between communities through class structures. This is because increasing economic wealth is also directly linked to education that provides the skills that increase the cultural capital of people, as Bourdieu (1986) outlines and argues in his 'cultural capital' theory. Equal share and redistribution of knowledge will enable especially unprivileged communities to develop skills. These skills can be anything that helps them have a specialism in daily and economic life, therefore they can participate equally in social, cultural and political life, and thus decrease the inequalities and discrimination for those who have been deprived of these resources.

One of the other pitfalls of oppression and exclusion of knowledge in textbooks is that they increase division in society and undermine diversity. In Chapter 2, I discussed how this type of exclusion has impacted Turkish community members who do not recognize other heritages and histories outside of the Turkish one. The oppression is not only leading to misrecognition and exclusion of other people's heritage but also to not knowing about other cultures and their heritage, and this leads to conflict, as can be seen in many examples (see Bilmez et al. 2017). Growing up with selected and manipulated knowledge because of the formal education system leads students to not being able to develop empathy towards other cultures that are neglected in the textbooks and curriculum. Or in other words, students are not able to have contact with other cultures in the schooling process. Formal education is the only place, perhaps, where all individuals can learn about the world and different cultures. This may be abstract knowledge; however, it is important to know about other cultures to prevent prejudices and biases.

In *The Nature of Prejudice* (1954), social psychologist Gordon Allport reflects on prejudice and details the importance of contact. He points out that no one is born with prejudice but it is learned and it leads to prejudgement even before people know anything about others. It is the total opposite of truth. It becomes worse with religious, ethnic or racial prejudices because it can lead to discrimination and violence against people and groups. His research on the nature of prejudice led to his *intergroup contact theory*, which he argues is one of the most effective ways to decrease or totally eliminate prejudice between majority and minorities in societies. Brown et al. (2003) conducted a study based on the intergroup contact theory to examine interactions between Black and White Americans in order to reduce white people's prejudice. Their findings indicate that white students who are in groups with black students have a high positive attitude towards black students (also see Savelkoul et al. 2010 for a Netherlands case). What I am arguing here is that an inclusive and diverse learning system, especially one that is inclusive about heritage and past material culture, although indirect or abstract, has a high potential to reduce prejudices and biases; reduce hatred against certain groups such as Armenians who are portrayed in Turkish textbooks as enemies; or increase knowledge about Kurdish culture and heritage. Therefore, conflict and division between cultures can be decreased. I pointed out earlier that tangible architectural and monumental heritage is the main reason for many conflicts from ancient times to today, as it is a visible symbol that stores memories for different cultures that are often not recognized as part of national discourses. Non-prejudiced learning and education platforms that recognize all diversities and which can bring people in contact through heritage, I argue, have an important role in decreasing tension between groups and communities.

Right to recognition. The intergroup contact theory that is proven to reduce prejudice, discrimination and violence may also be strongly linked to recognition. I discussed recognition in a heritage context at the beginning of this book. The recognition that I am emphasizing here is not only that which acknowledges one's existence, which is very important, but also which recognizes people with their social and cultural values, practices, and their own unique identities – in other words, recognizing people with their unique heritage and material culture. However, many nation states, especially undemocratic ones, do not recognize individual cultures and cultural productions within their borders. The (mis) recognition in the heritage context is framed by the individual countries' national interests and narratives that draw the lines of 'authorized heritage discourse'. As in the case of Turkey, the lines of authorized heritage discourse strictly only recognize the majority group's heritage, its past and history and exclude minority heritage. The main reason for this is that, I argue, recognition of heritage and identity is also linked to giving back ownership rights and rights to use resources, especially in the case of Turkey. Misrecognition provides the basis for the dominant power to abuse the cultural and economic resources of those minority groups. This kind of misrecognition and abuse also increases inequality in the society. This is, of course, not something new to Turkey or to the twentieth and twenty-first centuries; it has a history of thousands of years (Graeber and Wengrow 2018, 2021) but increased in the last couple of centuries. During the course of post-capitalism and neoliberalism in the twentieth century, inequality has more dramatically and rapidly increased, combined with the need and increased demand for resources, for example, landscapes and natural environments, for consumerism. The Global North, which dominates, has very effectively (ab)used the resources of the Global South, where communities are more impoverished because of the unequal distribution of wealth and resources (Fraser 1998).

Of course, using one's economic resources is not just about economics but it is also about politics and social justice when one's rights have also been breached. As I demonstrated in Chapters 4 and 5, neoliberal economic policies have been used as a tool for authoritarian regimes to oppress people. This is more visible for minorities who are being assimilated through the erasing of their heritage and the restriction of cultural performances and access to lands and resources. Access and use of resources and the recognition of minorities by the dominant power are strongly linked to each other. Dominant powers refuse to recognize the cultural norms and values of minorities in order to use their resources or, as in the case of Turkey, to preserve and consolidate its national narratives. Nancy Fraser (1998, 6) discusses the discourses of distribution and recognition in today's world and says redistribution and recognition should not be separated as they both sit in the centre of justice:

> Some proponents of redistribution reject the politics of recognition outright, casting claims for the recognition of difference as 'false consciousness', a hindrance to the pursuit of social justice. Conversely, some proponents of recognition see distributive politics as part and parcel of an outmoded materialism, simultaneously blind to and complicit with many injustices. In such cases, we are effectively presented with what is constructed as an either/or choice: redistribution or recognition? class politics or identity politics? multiculturalism or social democracy? … Justice today requires both redistribution and recognition. Neither alone is sufficient.

Recognizing one's heritage and cultural identity is also tightly linked to one's access and right to use one's cultural resources, which is also economically significant for those minorities whose identity is not recognized or misrecognized by the dominant power. The case of the Kurdish and Alevi communities in Turkey is a good example to demonstrate this link. Both minority groups' heritage and cultural rights have never been recognized and their right to practise cultural norms are often breached through access restriction and other forms of oppressive use of power. Particularly, the Kurdish region of Turkey is also economically deprived for decades (Yadirgi 2017, 2020) for political reasons. The embedded discourse that lies behind the misrecognition and deprivation of those minorities from using economic resources are political, as recognition of identity means also recognition of the right to use cultural and natural resources. In such countries, like Turkey, that have an authoritarian approach combined with heavy neoliberal policies and that are ideologically constructed on a single ethnicity, this kind of recognition has the potential to break their national narratives and unity. The ruling elites of Turkey also see this as a great threat to their use of power. The recognition of minorities' identities and recognition of minorities' rights to use their natural resources freely without restriction sits at the centre of social justice and power sharing, which is complex and closely linked to politics and economics.

From an authoritarian state perspective – in this case the current government in Turkey is a good example – the right to recognition brings great danger to its hegemony in every state institution as well as in social, cultural and economic life. This is because right to recognition also means recognizing the right to management of landscapes and natural resources to tangible and intangible heritage by people themselves. However, to create a path for a sustainable future, we, as heritage scholars, need to pay more attention and find ways to bring communities into management and decision-making processes for their heritage and natural resources. This is strongly linked to the 'representation' dimension of social justice that seeks to include people and communities at every stage of the decision-making process related to their social, cultural, economic and political lives. The case studies of this book are strongly related to people's and communities' resources not only for heritage making but also their survival and they should be the ones who make decisions from an ethical perspective. The power relationship between the state and the people – or, in other words, the reason why the state does not want to share the power with the communities – also links to landscapes and natural environment as a resource.

Right to landscape and natural environment. Landscape and the natural environment as a whole are not only about physical spaces but they are also resources for social and cultural production that contributes to the culture and economy of people. As in the case of southeast and east Turkey, where Kurdish and Alevi communities live, the landscapes and natural environments have also become more important for the communities' identity construction because they use these spaces for producing tangible and intangible heritage along with their daily activities. In other words, space also has importance for its representational role for its inhabitants, as Lefebvre (1991) points out. The main reason is that the landscape and natural environment provide space for communities to interact with each other to develop a sense of place and sense of community. In a way, it represents power because it is a *symbolic* but powerful *capital*, as it is being used for economic, social and cultural practices (Bourdieu 1986).

According to Bourdieu (1986), *economic capital* represents materiality and is a resource that can be traded; *social capital* represents resources of different social relationships of individuals in the community; and *cultural capital* is a different manifestation of human activity and skills. Consider the landscape and natural environment of southeast and east Turkey, where dam construction projects have been initiated: they represent all economic, social and cultural capitals that are the basic rights of local Kurdish and Alevis to survive as a community and preserve their sense of community and collective identity. They use the landscape and natural environment for economic, social and cultural activities. In other words, the landscape and natural environment as a space provides resourceful power to those communities. This, on the other hand, creates a threat to a dominant power that does not want to share its power and wants to consume all resources to protect its own ideology and national narratives. In other words, conflict over ownership rights of power creates discourses for opposition that are taken as an opportunity by the dominant power. Max Weber (1976 [1922]) explains this power opposition as 'any opportunity within a social relationship to assert one's own will against opposition, regardless of what this opportunity is based on' (Kühne 2019, 74). Sur, in Chapter 4, was in the middle of this type of conflict over controlling power, which led to heavy consequences from destruction and displacements as both sides aimed at controlling ownership rights of the town and its heritage.

Years of access restriction to landscape and homes in the Kurdish region can be explained with these power negotiations. I argue that this is the embedded and obvious reason that Turkey has been using heavy neoliberal policies through the megadam construction projects in the contested lands. These lands for the minorities, who are not recognized, have been excluded and have had their access restricted to use these resources effectively to develop economic, social and cultural capital, and carry out their social interactions, also represent power. A physical space itself does not represent power but the social interactions that are carried out by people within that particular space represent power. In this case, the landscape and natural environment represent the power as a space itself that provides the basis for power of social interactions (Foucault 1977; Popitz 1992; Kühne 2019).

Therefore, considering the landscape and natural environment as a resource for developing power also explains Turkey's political and economic motivation, which is combined with authoritarianism and heavy neoliberal policies that implement hundreds of dam construction in these regions. First, building dams in the short term brings economic profit in terms of making energy for the state. At the same time, it destroys the daily economic capital of local communities, such as the Kurdish and Alevi communities whose economy is based on using the landscape and rivers for farming and animal grazing. Second, this type of extensive destruction, like the Ilisu Dam and the dams in Munzur Valley, restricts interactions of individuals and groups within the community. As a result of this restriction and breaches of one's right to use the landscape and natural environment, the process of heritage making stops because people no longer continue taking part in cultural activities using the landscape and natural environment. Further, this leads to memory interruption and traumas and this is one of the great impacts of displacement. Third, as cultural participation and activities are no longer taking place, people are not able to make heritage as individuals, and groups no longer not share common resources, cultural capital as a human activity and skills development – or, in other words, the cultural identity of those minority groups – begins to decay and this leads to the forgetting of memory and cultural values. However, this type of oppression against certain groups also leads to counter-resistance to take back power on many occasions.

Right to resistance. It is part of the natural dialectic that oppression also brings resistance for those oppressed. I am not only pointing out economic and political oppression but also cultural oppression, as I discuss above. This type of heavy oppression by hegemonic powers makes cultural, economic and political resistance inevitable because people want to protect their collective and cultural identity as part of their rights. In his 1920s and 1930s writings, Anthony Gramsci (1971) analyses discourses of power and resistance between classes in which the capitalist class dominates, rules, controls and uses resources of subaltern groups. He terms this dialectic as *cultural hegemony* in which the state controls everything. Gramsci describes the state as:

> which is usually thought of as political society – i.e., a dictatorship or some other coercive apparatus used to control the masses in conformity with a given type of production and economy [is] a balance between political society and civil society, by which ... the hegemony of one social group over the entire nation, exercised through so-called private organizations. (Lears 1985)

He emphasizes that within this class-structured hierarchical society, where power is controlled by dominant culture, subaltern groups can always show resistance, but it totally depends on or is subject to the dominant cultural group or ruling class which holds the power. This kind of oppression also leads to counter-hegemony through 'everyday resistance'. The concept, *everyday resistance*, was coined by anthropologist James Scott (1985), who built his theory on ethnographic work that supports the idea that the everyday form of the peasants' resistance in Malaysia is more related to the argument that I am making in the heritage context. Scott's argument in everyday resistance is not dependent on negotiations between hegemonic powers but rather that people show this resistance by engaging in day-to-day activities, as in the case of peasants' everyday work in Malaysia. In everyday resistance, Scott builds his argument that the response to dominant power or oppressor does not have to be always organized in a rebellion form, but it can certainly be in forms of 'cultural resistance' that are based on a non-organizational structure. In other words, Scott does not consider resistance as organization but rather as not obeying the dominant power or its order. For the case studies of this book, both Scott's argument with everyday resistance and Gramsci's hegemony and resistance apply well: Turkey is the dominant power that wants to control society by controlling the natural resources of people who often use right to resist through developing tangible and intangible heritage every day through the organizational resistance as a community.

In the case of Gezi Park resistance against abuse of public resources by the Turkish government, what we see is organizational community resistance rather than the form of 'everyday resistance'. The Gezi Park resistance was not a class struggle as Gramsci discusses, but it was a collective struggle in which different classes and cultural groups came together. The Gezi Park resistance was also a type of power negotiation and that was allowed by the dominant power, as per Gramsci. The right to resist and the collective action in Gezi Park forced the dominant power to allow people to exercise their right to resist. The Alevi community in Munzur Valley, in contrast, resists the abuse of power in both ways: organizational resistance through campaigning and creating solidarity platforms, such as the Munzur Festival, which also becomes a form of heritage of resistance to carry on cultural performances; and the persistence in using the landscape and characteristics of a sacred valley as part of their belief system fits with the idea of everyday cultural resistance.

Southeast Turkey, where the Ilisu Dam was built, however, represents a totally different picture. Although the Kurdish people resisted the dominant power through using their landscape, river and natural environment in their daily activities – or, in Scott's term 'everyday resistance' – which was significant for tangible and intangible heritage making, this right of exercising cultural activities or counter-hegemony was ended by the dominant power by building the dam. As Gramsci points out, the power has hidden discourses that are often in conflict between hegemonic power that dominates society and subordinate groups whose right to resist often depends on the dominant power.

Throughout this volume, I discuss several important points that are highly related to social justice and human rights. I discuss the importance of practising heritage as part of the human rights approach, which is closely linked to social justice for communities, particularly minorities, and I demonstrated how the right to learn about heritage has been abused, how the public's heritage perception is formed through national discourses; and how the landscape, space and natural environment, where heritage is constructed, has been restricted and destroyed by the dominant power.

In the case of Turkey, the 'cultural', 'political' and 'economic' discourses have been developed and applied in every part of the country to promote the idea of 'one nation state', which has often been in conflict with the reality of the country's multicultural structure and identity. Although this kind of nationalist approach and especially authoritarianism in the last decade seems to have protected Turkey's national narratives, it has led to unsustainability, as in the case of southeast Turkey. This unsustainability is not only about communities but is also reflected in Turkey's economy, as many communities were displaced and had to move to cities and therefore large farming lands were left to decay or flooded through dams. Therefore, in the long term, Turkey is not getting much benefit from nationalist, authoritarian and heavy neoliberal approaches. Rather, having a democratic approach that recognizes people with their rights, backgrounds, ethnic identities, religious or spiritual beliefs; allowing and supporting their cultural activities and heritage making; supporting them to protect what is valuable for them; giving them a voice to make their decision regarding social, cultural, economic and political life, would make Turkey and many other countries more sustainable. This form of people-centred, ethic-based democratic approach is not only beneficial for people but also for nature, which is the resource for heritage making and therefore for people.

Throughout this book, based on case studies from Turkey, I developed an interlinkage between practising cultural, social and economic activities as well as developing heritage, the right to heritage and social justice, and often pointed out, with examples, how the rights of practising cultural heritage have often been breached by the dominant power. I argue that heritage itself is very cultural as well as political. It is not only about material culture and objects and other forms of tangible and intangible heritage, but it is about people who construct, reconstruct and transform it through the active participation in space, landscape and natural environment. We, as heritage scholars, need to rethink heritage from a much wider perspective and this includes the interlinkage of social, cultural, economic and political components of everyday life. We need to pay more attention to heritage beyond its materiality and reconsider landscape and natural environment as its main resources. We also need to remember that heritage is created by people, but non-human participants of the natural environment, including landscapes, river, flora and fauna, also have a great contribution to tangible and intangible heritage making. As such, the protection of the environments also means preserving heritage but, most importantly, their protection also contributes to slowing down the dramatic change in the climate, which is a global problem.

Notes

1 Reflections

1 See https://www.horniman.ac.uk/wp-content/uploads/2020/02/horniman-climate-manifesto-final-29-jan-2020.pdf
2 See http://www.unesco.org/new/en/culture/themes/armed-conflict-and-heritage/convention-and-protocols/1954-hague-convention/
3 https://www.ohchr.org/en/professionalinterest/pages/cescr.aspx
4 See https://rm.coe.int/1680083746
5 https://en.unesco.org/themes/right-to-education/convention-against-discrimination
6 See https://www.un.org/en/about-us/universal-declaration-of-human-rights
7 https://www.coe.int/en/web/culture-and-heritage/faro-convention
8 https://www.ohchr.org/en/professionalinterest/pages/ccpr.aspx
9 See http://portal.unesco.org/en/ev.php-URL_ID=13179&URL_DO=DO_TOPIC&URL_SECTION=201.html

2 Oppression

1 See https://whc.unesco.org/en/list/377/
2 See https://whc.unesco.org/en/criteria/
3 See https://www.ohchr.org/en/instruments-mechanisms/instruments/declaration-rights-persons-belonging-national-or-ethnic
4 See https://www.un.org/en/about-us/universal-declaration-of-human-rights

4 Conflict

1 See https://whc.unesco.org/en/list/1488/
2 See https://www.unesco.org/en/articles/ukraine-over-150-cultural-sites-partially-or-totally-destroyed
3 See https://www.hrw.org/news/2020/10/21/turkey-justice-rights-lawyers-killing
4 See https://whc.unesco.org/uploads/nominations/1488.pdf
5 https://whc.unesco.org/en/list/1488/documents/

6   https://www.ohchr.org/en/professionalinterest/pages/ccpr.aspx

7   https://www.ohchr.org/en/professionalinterest/pages/ccpr.aspx

8   https://www.echr.coe.int/documents/convention_eng.pdf

9   https://whc.unesco.org/en/list/1488/documents/

5   Slow Violence

1   See https://whc.unesco.org/en/culturallandscape/#1

2   See https://rm.coe.int/1680080621

3   See https://rm.coe.int/1680080621

4   https://rm.coe.int/16806b0867

5   See https://whc.unesco.org/en/news/943

6   See http://www.dsi.gov.tr/faaliyetler/hessu-kullanim-anlasmalari

7   See https://ich.unesco.org

8   See 'Hasankeyf Survey Report,' http://www.dogadernegi.org/wp-content/
uploads/2015/10/ HASANKEYF-SURVEY-REPORT-Summary.pdf accessed

9   See https://whc.unesco.org/en/guidelines/

10 See Universal Declaration of Human Rights, UN Doc. A/810, 10 December 1948
See United Nations Declaration on the Rights of Indigenous Peoples, GA Res 61/295,
UN GAOR, UN Doc A/RES/61/295

11 See https://ich.unesco.org/en/RL/semah-alevi-bektasi-ritual-00384

12 Ziyaret is a general term among Alevis who consider these specific places as sacred.

13 See https://www.dogadernegi.org/mercan-munzur-daglari/

14 See https://www.worldwildlife.org/ecoregions/pa0420

15 See http://www.dsi.gov.tr/haberler/2020/03/04/tunceli-nin-bereketli-
topraklar%C4%B1na-can-suyu-oluyoruz-

16 See https://www.dw.com/tr/munzur-vadisinde-hes-projesi-iptal-edildi/a-50846748

Bibliography

Adams, M. and Bell, L. B. (eds) (2016). *Teaching for Diversity and Social Justice*. Third edition. New York: Routledge, Taylor & Francis, 2016. Print.

Akçam, T. (2004). *From Empire to Republic: Turkish Nationalism and the Armenian Genocide*. London: Zed Books.

Akçam, T. (2012). *The Young Turks' Crime against Humanity: The Armenian Genocide and Ethnic Cleansing in the Ottoman Empire*. Princeton, NJ: Princeton University Press.

Akçayöz, V., T. Çakaş, Y. Oztürkkan, S. Yazıcı, and O. Yurdalan (2007). *Kars Kent Rehberi*. Istanbul: Kars Kent Konseyi.

Akdar, A. (2000). *Varlık Vergisi Ve Türkleştirme Politikaları*. Istanbul: İletişim Yayınları.

Aksoy, A. (2012). 'Riding the storm: "New Istanbul"'. *City,* 16(1–2): 93–111. DOI: 10.1080/13604813.2012.662373.

Allison, C. (1996). 'Old and New Oral Traditions in Badinan'. In P. Kreyenbroek and C. Allison (eds) *Kurdish Culture and Identity*. London: Zed Books. 29–47.

Allport, G. W. (1954). *The Nature of Prejudice*. Reading, Mass.: Addison-Wesley.

Amir, S. (2015). 'Food Sovereignty and the Agrarian Question: Constructing Convergence of Struggles within Diversity'. In Rémy Herrera and Kin Chi Lau (eds) *The Struggle for Food Sovereignty: Alternative Development and the Renewal of Peasant Societies Today*. London: Pluto Press. 14–34.

Amnesty International (2016). *Displaced and Dispossessed: Sur Residents' Right to Return*. London. https://www.amnesty.org/en/documents/eur44/5213/2016/en/ (accessed September 2021).

Anderson, B. (1983). *Imagined Communities: Reflections on the Origin and Spread of Nationalism*. London: Verso.

Andrews, P. A. (ed.) (1989). *Ethnic groups in the Republic of Turkey (Vol. 1)*. Wiesbaden: Reichert.

Apaydin, V. (2016a). 'The Challenge of Neoliberalism and Archaeological Heritage in Turkey: Protection or Destruction?' In P. Aparicio-Resco (ed.) *Archaeology and Neoliberalism*. Madrid: JAS Arqueología Editorial. 341–52.

Apaydin, V. (2016b). 'Economic rights, heritage sites and communities: sustainability and protection'. *Complutum* 27(2): 369–84.

Apaydin, V. (2016c). 'Effective or not? Success or failure? Assessing heritage and archaeological education programmes – the case of Çatalhöyük'. *International Journal of Heritage Studies* 22(10): 1–16. DOI: 10.1080/13527258.2016.1218912.

Apaydin, V. (2018a). 'Critical Community Engagement in Heritage Studies'. In C. Smith (ed.) *Encyclopaedia of Global Archaeology*. New York and London: Springer. 1–12.

Apaydin, V. (ed.) (2018b). *Shared Knowledge Shared Power: Engaging Local and Indigenous Heritage*. Cham: Springer.

Apaydin, V. (2018c). 'The Entanglement of the Heritage Paradigm: Values, Meanings and Uses'. *International Journal of Heritage Studies* 24(5): 491–507. DOI: 10.1080/13527258.2017.1390488.

Apaydin, V. and Hassett, B. (2019). 'Should I Stay or Should I Go? Ideals and Realities of Archaeology in the Conflict Regions'. *Journal of Community Archaeology & Heritage* 6(1): 36–50. DOI: 10.1080/20518196.2018.1549821.

Apaydin, V. (2020a). *Critical Perspectives on Cultural Memory and Heritage: Construction, Transformation and Destruction*. London: UCL Press.

Apaydin, V. (2020b). 'The interlinkage of cultural memory, heritage and discourses of construction, transformation and destruction'. In Veysel Apaydin (ed.) *Critical Perspectives on Cultural Memory and Heritage: Construction, Transformation and Destruction*. London: UCL Press. 13–30.

Apaydin, V. (2022). *Heritage, Education and Social Justice*. Cambridge: Cambridge University Press.

Aparicio-Resco, P. (ed.) (2016). *Archaeology and Neoliberalism*. Madrid: JAS Arqueología Editorial.

Appadurai, A. (1986). *The Social Life of Things: Commodities in Cultural Perspective*. West Nyack: Cambridge University Press.

Appadurai, A. (1988). 'How to Make a National Cuisine: Cookbooks in Contemporary India'. *Comparative Studies in Society and History* 30 (1): 3–24.

Appadurai, A. (1995). 'The production of locality'. In Richard Fardon (ed.) *Counterworks: Managing the diversity of knowledge*. London: Routledge. 204–25.

Appadurai, A. (1996). 'Sovereignty without Territoriality: Notes for a Postnational Geography'. In P. Yaeger (ed.) *The Geography of Identity*. Arbor: University of Michigan Press. 40–59.

Apple, M. W. (2004). 'Democratic education in neoliberal and neoconservative times'. *International Studies in Sociology of Education* 21(1): 21–31. DOI: 10.1080/09620214.2011.543850.

Apple, M. W. (2009). *Ideology and Curriculum*. New York: Routledge.

Arat, Y. (2013). 'Violence, Resistance, and Gezi Park'. *International Journal of Middle East Studies*, 45(4): 807–9.

Arendt, H. (1958). *The Origins of Totalitarianism* New York: Meridian Books.

Aristotle (384–322 BC). *The Politics*. English translation with introduction and notes by C. D. C. Reeve. Indianapolis/Cambridge: Hackett Publishing Company, 1998.

Armstrong-Fumero, F. and Hoil Gutierrez, J. (2017). 'Introduction'. In F. Armstrong-Fumero and J. Hoil Gutierrez (eds) *Legacies of Space and Intangible Heritage: Archaeology, Ethnohistory, and the Politics of Cultural Continuity in the Americas*. Boulder: University of Colorado. 3–13.

Ashworth, G. J. and Graham, B. (eds) (2005). *Senses of Place: Senses of Time*. Aldershot: Ashgate.

Ashworth, G. J., Graham, B. and Tunbridge, J. E. (2007). *Pluralising Pasts: Heritage, Identity and Place in Multicultural Societies*. London: Pluto Press.

Assmann, J. and Czaplicka, J. (1995). 'Collective Memory and Cultural Identity'. *New German Critique* 65, Cultural History/Cultural Studies (Spring–Summer, 1995): 125–33.

Assi, E. (2012). 'World Heritage sites, human rights and cultural heritage in Palestine'. *International Journal of Heritage Studies* 18(3): 316–23.

Association of Critical Heritage Studies (ACHS) (2011). 'Association of critical heritage studies manifesto' [online]. Available from: http://archanth.anu.edu.au/heritage-museum-studies/association-criticalheritage-studies (accessed May 2020).

Atakuman, C. (2008). 'Cradle or Crucible: Anatolia and Archaeology in the Early Years of the Turkish Republic (1923–1938)'. *Journal of Social Archaeology* 8: 214–35.

Atkinson, D. (2007). 'Kitsch Geographies and the Everyday Spaces of Social Memory'. *Environment and Planning* A 39: 521–40. DOI:10.1068/a3866

Aydın, S. and Y. Taşkın. (2014). *1960'dan Günümüze Türkiye Tarihi*. Istanbul: Iletişim Yayınları.

Aydin, D. (2013). 'Moblising the Kurds in Turkey: Newroz as a myth'. In C. Günes and W. Zeydanlioglu (eds) *The Kurdish Question in Turkey: New Perspectives on Violence, Representation and Reconciliation*. London: Routledge. 84–104.

Aydin, S. (2020). 'Survey of the Roots and History of Kurdish Alevism: What are the Divergences and Convergences between Kurdish Alevi Groups in Turkey?'. *Kurdish Studies* 8(1): 17–42.

Aykan, B. (2018). 'Saving Hasankeyf: Limits and Possibilities of International Human Rights Law'. *International Journal of Cultural Property* 25:11–34. Printed in the USA.

Badiou, A. (2001). *Ethics: An Essay on the Understanding of Evil*. Translated and introduced by Peter Hallward. London: Verso.

Baird, M. (2014). 'Heritage, Human Rights, and Social Justice'. *Heritage & Society* 7(2): 139–55, DOI: 10.1179/2159032X14Z.00000000031.

Bakhtin, M. M. (1981). *The Dialogic Imagination: Four Essays by M.M. Bakhtin*. Edited by Michael Holquist; Translated by Caryl Emerson. Austin: University of Texas Press.

Balsom, E. (2014). 'Against the Novelty of New Media: The Resuscitation of the Authentic'. In O. Kholeif (ed.) *You Are Here: Art After the Internet*. Manchester: Cornerhouse Publications. 66–77.

Barkey, H. and Fuller, G. (1998). *Turkey's Kurdish question*. Maryland: Rowman & Littlefield.

Barth, F. (1969). *Ethnic Groups and Boundaries: The Social Organization of Cultural Difference*. Boston: Little, Brown and Company.

Bauman, Z. (2001). *Community: Seeking Safety in an Insecure World*. Cambridge: Polity.

Barnstone, A. D. and Otto, E. (2019). 'How Art Resists'. In D. Ascher Barnstone and E. Otto (eds) *Art and Resistance in Germany*. New York: Bloomsbury Visual Arts. 1–20.

Başol, S., Yıldırım, T., Koyuncu, M., Yıldız, A. and Evirgen, O. F. (2013). *Türkiye Cumhuriyeti Inkilap Tarihi ve Atatürkçülük. Öğretmen Kılavuz Kitabı 8* [Primary Education Curricula for 8th level] MEB: Milli Eğitim Bakanlığı Yayınları.

Baydar, G. (2014). 'Gender, Public Space and Resistance'. *Architecture, Media, Politics, Society* 5(3): 1–8.

Baykan, A. and Hatuka, T. (2010). 'Politics and Culture in the Making of Public Space: Taksim Square, 1 May 1977'. *Istanbul, Planning Perspectives* 25(1): 49–68. DOI:10.1080/02665430903421734.

BBC (2010). 'Turkish nationalists rally in Armenian holy site at Ani'. BBC. October 1. http://www.bbc.co.uk/news/world-europe-11454014 (accessed September 2020).

BBC (2020). 'The New Zealand River that became a legal person'. BBC. January 2020. https://www.bbc.com/travel/article/20200319-the-new-zealand-river-that-became-a-legal-person (accessed June 2021).

Bell, L. A. (2016). 'Theoretical Foundations for Social Justice Education'. In M. Adams and L. Anne Bell with D. J. Goodman and K. Y. Joshi (eds) *Teaching for Diversity and Social Justice*. Third edn. New York: Routledge.

Bennett, T. (2004). *Pasts Beyond Memory: Evolution, Museums, Colonisation*. London and New York: Routledge.

Bennett, T., Dibley, B. and Harrison, R. (2014). 'Introduction: Anthropology, Collecting and Colonial Governmentalities'. *History and Anthropology* 25(2): 137–49, DOI: 10.1080/02757206.2014.882838.

Berkol, N. A., Neset Ömer Irdelp, Aime Mouchet, Süreyâ Ali Kayacan and Ismail Hakkı Celebi (1927). 'Türk Irkı Hakkında Antropoloji Tedkikâtı'. *Türk Antropoloji Mecmuası* 5 (Oct.): 6–16.

Berkol, N. A., Neset Ömer Irdelp, Aime Mouchet, Süreyâ Ali Kayacan and Hamza Vahit Gögen (1928). 'Türk Irkının Antropolojisi Hakkında, (Mâ-ba'd)'. *Türk Antropoloji Mecmuası* 6 (March): 5–14.

Bevan, R. (2016). *The Destruction of Memory: Architecture at War*. London: Reaktion.

Bianchi, R. (2018). 'Istanbul sounding like revolution: the role of music in the Gezi Park Occupy movement'. *Popular Music* 37(2): 212–36. DOI: 10.1017/S0261143018000016

Bianet (2019). 'They Said "We Will Cut 2.5 Million Trees for 3rd Airport", They Cut 13 Million Instead'. https://bianet.org/english/environment/209630-they-said-we-will-cut-2-5-million-trees-for-3rd-airport-they-cut-13-million-instead (accessed February 2022).

Bilmez, B., K. Cayir, O. Caykent, P. Gamaghelyan, M. Karapetyan, and P. Sayan (2017). *History Education in Schools in Turkey and Armenia: A Critique and Alternatives*. Istanbul and Yerevan: History Foundation (Tarih Vakfı) and Imagine Center for Conflict Transformation.

Binter, J. T. S. (2019). 'Beyond Exhibiting the Experience of Empire?'. *Third Text* 33(4–5): 575–93. DOI: 10.1080/09528822.2019.1651510.

Blake, J. (2011). 'Taking a Human Rights Approach to Cultural Heritage Protection'. *Heritage & Society* 4(2): 199–238.

Bourdieu, P. (1986). 'The forms of capital'. In J. Richardson (ed.) *Handbook of Theory and Research for the Sociology of Education*. New York: Greenwood. 241–58.

Bourdieu, P. (2005). 'Habitus'. In J. Hillier and E. Rooksby (eds) *Habitus: A sense of place.* Aldershot: Ashgate. 43–52.

Bozarslan, H. (1996). 'Political Crisis and the Kurdish Issue in Turkey'. In Robert Olson (ed.) *The Kurdish Nationalist Movement in the 1990s: Its Impact on Turkey and the Middle East.* Lexington: The University Press of Kentucky. 135–53.

Bozarslan, H. (2008). 'Kurds and the Turkish State'. In Resat Kasaba (ed.) *The Cambridge History of Turkey, Volume 4: Turkey in the Modern World.* Cambridge: Cambridge University Press. 333–56.

Borck, L. (2019). 'Constructing the Future History: Prefiguration as Historical Epistemology and the Chronopolitics of Archaeology'. *Journal of Contemporary Archaeology* 5(2): 229–38.

Brown, M. F. (2005). 'Heritage Trouble: Recent Work on the Protection of Intangible Cultural Property'. *International Journal of Cultural Property* 12(1): 40–61.

Brown, K. T., Brown, N. T., Jackson, J. S., Seller, R. M. and Manuel, J. W. (2003). 'Teammates On and Off the Field? Contact With Black Teammates and the Racial Attitudes of White Student Athletes'. *Journal of Applied Social Psychology* 33(7): 1379–403.

Brown, W. (2019). *In the Ruins of Neoliberalism: The Rise of Antidemocratic Politics in the West.* New York: Columbia University Press.

Brulotte, R. L. and Michael A. Di Giovine (eds) (2016). *Edible Identities: Food as Cultural Heritage.* London: Routledge.

Bulmer, M. and Solomos, J. (eds) (2012). *Nationalism and National Identities.* London: Routledge.

Buğra, A. and O. Savaşkan (2014). *New Capitalism in Turkey: The Relationship Between Politics, Religion and Business.* Cheltenham: Edward Elgar Publishing.

Butler, B. (2006). 'Heritage and the Present Past'. In C. Tilley, W. Keane, S. Kuechler, M. Rowlands and P. Spyer (eds) *Handbook of Material Culture.* London: Sage Publications. 463–79.

Butler, B. (2009). 'Palestinian Heritage "to the moment": Archival Memory and the Representation of Heritage in Conflict', *Conservation and Management of Archaeological Sites* 11(3–4): 236–61. DOI: 10.1179/175355210X12747818485402.

Butler, C. (2009). 'Critical Legal Studies and the Politics of Space'. *Social and Legal Studies* 18: 313–32.

Byrne, D., Brayshaw, H. and Ireland, T. (2003). *Social Significance: A Discussion Paper.* Second edition. Hurstville: New South Wales National Parks and Wildlife Service.

Byrne, D. R. (2008a). 'Heritage as social action'. In G. J. Fairclough, R. Harrison, J. H. Jameson and J. Schofield (eds) *The Heritage Reader.* London: Routledge. 149–73.

Byrne, D. (2008). 'Counter-mapping: New South Wales and Southeast Asia'. *Transforming Cultures eJournal* 3(1): 256–64.

Byrne, D. and Nugent, M. (2004). *Mapping Attachment: A Spatial Approach to Aboriginal Post-Contact Heritage.* Bathurst: Department of Environment and Conservation (NSW).

Calvert, A. and Warren, M. (2014). 'Deliberative democracy and framing effects: Why frames are a problem and how deliberative mini-publics might overcome them'. In K. Grönlund, A. Bächtiger and M. Setälä (eds) *Deliberative mini-publics: Involving citizens in the deliberative process*. Colchester: ECPR Press. 203–24.

Chaffee, Lyman G. (1993). *Political Protest and Street Art: Popular Tools for Democratisation in Hispanic Countries*. Westport, CT: Greenwood.

Charpleix, L. (2017). 'The Whanganui River as Te Awa Tupua: Place-based law in a legally pluralistic society'. *The Geographical Journal* 1819(1): 19–30.

Chomsky, N. (2003). *Objectivity and Liberal Scholarship*. London: New Press.

Chatterjee, H. J., Clini, C., Butler, B., Al-Nammari, F., Al-Asir, R. and Katona, C. (2020). 'Exploring the psychological impact of cultural interventions with displaced people'. In E. Fiddian-Qasmiyeh (ed.) *Refuge in a Moving World: Tracing refugee and migrant journeys across disciplines*. London: UCL Press. 323–40

Chrona, S. and Bee, C. (2017). 'Right to public space and right to democracy: The role of social media in Gezi Park'. *Research and Policy on Turkey* 2(1): 49–61. DOI: 10.1080/23760818.2016.1272267.

Clifford, J. (1994). 'Diasporas'. *Cultural Anthropology* 9(3): 302–38.

Clifford, J. (1997). 'Palenque Log'. In J. Clifford (ed.) *Routes*. Cambridge: Harvard University Press. 220–37.

Cohen, A. (1985). *The Symbolic Construction of Community*. London and New York: Routledge.

Convery, I., G. Corsane and W. Davis (eds) (2012). *Making Sense of Place: Multidisciplinary Perspectives*. Woodbridge: Boydell & Brewer.

Copeaux, E. (1998a). *Tarih Ders Kitaplarında (1931–1993): Türk Tarih Tezinden Türk Islam Sentezine*. Istanbul: Tarih Vakfı Yurt Yayınları.

Copeaux, E. (1998b). 'Türkiye'de Kimlik Söyleminin Topografyasi ve Kronografisi'. In *Tarih Eğitimi ve 'Öteki' Sorunu 2. Uluslararasi Tarih Kongresi. 8–10 Haziran 1995 Istanbul*. Istanbul: Tarih Vakfı Yurt Yayınları. 70–85.

Council of Europe (2000a). 'European Landscape Convention (ETS 176)'. Strasbourg: Council of Europe. http://conventions.coe.int/Treaty/EN/Treaties/Html/176.htm. (accessed May 2021).

Council of Europe (2000b). 'Explanatory Report to the European Landscape Convention (ETS 176)'. Strasbourg: Council of Europe.

Council of Europe (2005). 'Framework Convention on the Value of Cultural Heritage for Society'. Faro. https://rm.coe.int/1680083746 (accessed August 2020).

Council of Europe (2008). 'Recommendation CM/Rec (2008)3 of the Committee of Ministers to member states on the guidelines for the implementation of the European Landscape Convention'. *European Landscape Convention Guidelines*. Strasbourg: Council of Europe.

Council of Europe (2021). 'Convention for the Protection of Human Rights and Fundamental Freedoms'. https://www.echr.coe.int/documents/convention_eng.pdf (accessed August 2021).

Cowe, P. S. (ed.) (2001). *Ani: World Architectural Heritage of a Medieval Armenian Capital*. University of Pennsylvania Armenian Text and Studies; 16. Peeters, Leuven, Sterling, Virginia.

Crooke, E. (2008). *Museums and community: ideas, issues and challenges*. London: Routledge.

Cumhuriyet (2021). 'Tunceli'de yaban hayvanlarını katletmek isteyen avcılara tepki gösterildi'. https://www.cumhuriyet.com.tr/turkiye/tuncelide-yaban-hayvanlarini-katletmek-isteyen-avcilara-tepki-gosterildi-1890938 (accessed February 2022).

Da Rocha, B. C. (2017). 'Ipi Ocemumuge: A Regional Archaeology of the Upper Tapajós River'. Doctoral thesis, UCL (University College London).

Da Rocha, B. C. (2020). '"Rescuing" the ground from under their feet? Contract archaeology and human rights violations in the Brazilian Amazon'. In V. Apaydin (ed.) *Critical Perspectives on Cultural Memory and Heritage: Construction, Transformation and Destruction*. London: UCL Press. 156–69.

Davidson, J. and C. Milligan (2004). 'Embodying Emotion Sensing Space: Introducing Emotional Geographies'. *Social and Cultural Geography* 5(4): 523–32.

Davidson, J., L. Bondi and M. Smith (eds) (2005). *Emotional Geographies*. Aldershot: Ashgate.

Davies, C. A. (2012). *Reflexive Ethnography a Guide to Researching Selves and Others*. London: New York: Routledge.

Davis, P. (1999). *Ecomuseums: A Sense of Place*. London: Leicester University Press.

Demossier, M. (2016). 'The Politics of Heritage in the Land of Food and Wine'. In W. Logan, M. N. Craith and U. Kockel (eds) *A Companion to Heritage Studies*. West Sussex: Wiley-Blackwell. 87–100.

Descola, P. (2013). *Beyond Nature and Culture*. Chicago: University of Chicago Press.

Deniz, D. (2012). *Yol/Rê: Dersim İnanç Sembolizmi. Antropolojik Bir Yaklaşım* [Yol/Rê: Belief Symbolism of Dersim. An Anthropological Perspective]. Istanbul: İletişim Yayınları.

Deniz, D. (2019). 'Kurdish Alevi belief systems, Rêya Heqî/Raa Haqi: structure, networking, ritual, and function'. In E. Gezik and A. K. Gültekin (eds) *Kurdish Alevis and the Case of Dersim: Historical and Contemporary Insights*. Lanham, Maryland Lexington Books.

DeSilvey, C. (2017). *Curated Decay: Heritage Beyond Saving*. Minneapolis, MN: University of Minnesota Press.

Deutsche Welle (DW) (2019). 'Munzur Vadisi'nde HES Projesi iptal edildi'. https://www.dw.com/tr/munzur-vadisinde-hes-projesi-iptal-edildi/a-50846748 (accessed May 2021).

Dewey, J. (1934). *Art as Experience*. New York: Perigee.

Dewey, J. (1997). *Experience and Education*. New York: Touchstone. (Original work published 1938.)

Diaz-Andreu, M. (1995). 'Archaeology and Nationalism in Spain'. In P. Kohl and C. Fawcett (eds) *Nationalism, Politics and the Practice of Archaeology*. Cambridge: Cambridge University Press. 39–56.

Diaz-Andreu, M. (2007). *A World History of Nineteenth-Century Archaeology: Nationalism, Colonialism and the Past*. Oxford: Oxford University Press.

Diaz-Andreu, M. and Champion, T. C. (eds) (1996). *Nationalism and Archaeology in Europe*. Boulder: Westview Press.

Dissard, L. (2018). 'From Shining Icons of Progress to Contested Infrastructures: "Damming" the Munzur Valley in Eastern Turkey'. In F. M. Göçek (ed.) *Contested Spaces in Contemporary Turkey: Environmental, Urban and Secular Politics*. London and New York: I.B. Tauris.

Dissard, L. (2021). 'Hasankeyf, the Ilisu Dam, and the Kurdish Movement in Turkey'. In S. E. Hunt (ed.) *Ecological Solidarity and the Kurdish Freedom Movement: Thought, Practice, Challenges, and Opportunities*. London: Rowman & Littlefield.

Doga Dernegi (2015). 'Hasankeyf Survey Report'. http://www.dogadernegi.org/wp-content/uploads/2015/10/HASANKEYF-SURVEY-REPORT-Summary.pdf (accessed May 2020).

Donnan, H. and Wilson, T. M. (1999). *Borders: Frontiers of Identity, Nation and State*. Oxford: Berg.

Devlet Su Isleri [State Water Institution] https://www.dsi.gov.tr/Sayfa/Detay/698 (accessed September 2020).

Ekern, S., Logan, W., Sauge, B. and Sinding-Larsen, A. (2012). 'Human rights and World Heritage: preserving our common dignity through rights-based approaches to site management'. *International Journal of Heritage Studies* 18(3): 213–25. DOI: 10.1080/13527258.2012.656253.

Ekern, S., Logan, W., Sauge, B. and Sinding-Larsen, A. (eds) (2015). *World Heritage Management and Human Rights*. London: Routledge.

Erdogan, S. and Sezgin, K. (2020). 'Tunceli Iron Age and Hellenistic Survey – 2018'. *Anatolia Antiqua XXVIII*. 201–18. Istanbul: Ege Yayinlari.

Eriksen, T. H. (2010). *Ethnicity and Nationalism: Anthropological Perspectives*. London and New York: Pluto Press.

Ersanlı, B. (2003). *Iktidar ve Tarih: TüRkiye'de 'Resmi Tarih' Tezinin Oluşumu (1929-1937)*. Istanbul: İletişim Yayınları.

Eoin, L. and King, R. (2013). 'How to Develop Intangible Heritage: The Case of Metolong Dam, Lesotho'. *World Archaeology* 45: 653–69.

Erll, A. (2011). *Memory in Culture*. London: Palgrave Macmillan.

Erll, A. and Nunning, A. (eds) (2008). *Cultural Memory Studies: An International and Interdisciplinary Handbook*. Berlin and New York: Walter de Gruyter.

Erll, A. and Rigney, A. (2009). 'Introduction: Cultural Memory and its Dynamics'. In L. Basu, P. Bijl, A. Erll and A. Rigney (eds) *Mediation, Remediation, and the Dynamics of Cultural Memory*. Berlin: Walter de Gruyter. 1–14.

Estes, N. (2019). *Our History Is the Future: Standing Rock versus the Dakota Access Pipeline, and the Long Tradition of Indigenous Resistance.* London: Verso.

Etten, V. J., Jongerden, J., de Vos, H. J., Klaasse, A. and van Hoeve, E. C. (2008). 'Environmental destruction as a counterinsurgency strategy in the Kurdistan region of Turkey'. *Geoforum* 39(5): 1786–97.

European Convention on Human Rights (1950). 'Convention for the Protection of Human Rights and Fundamental Freedoms'. https://www.echr.coe.int/Documents/Convention_ENG.pdf (accessed June 2020).

European Landscape Convention (2011). 'Évora Declaration on the European Landscape Convention'. Evora, Portugal. https://rm.coe.int/16806b0867 (accessed June 2020).

Fairclough, N. and Wodak, R. (1997). 'Critical Discourse Analysis'. In Dijk, Teun Van (ed.) *Discourse as Social Interaction: A Multidisciplinary Introduction.* Volume 2. Sage: London. 258–84.

Fiddian-Qasmiyeh, E. (2020). *Refuge in a Moving World: Tracing refugee and migrant journeys across disciplines.* London: UCL Press.

Foucault, M. (1977). *Überwachen und Strafen: Die Geburt des Gefängnisses*, Vol. 184. Suhrkamp-Taschenbuch Wissenschaft. Frankfurt a. M.: Suhrkamp.

Foucault, M. (1991). 'Governmentality'. In G. Burchell, C. Gordon and P. Miller (eds) *The Foucault Effect: Studies in Govermentality.* With two lectures by and an interview with Michel Foucault. London: Wheatsheaf Harvester. 87–104.

France24 (2016). 'Destruction of Kurdish sites continues as Turkey hosts UNESCO'. https://www.france24.com/en/20160714-turkey-unesco-heritage-sites-damage-kurdish-diyarbakir-sur (accessed February 2022).

Fraser, N. (1989). *Unruly Practices: Power, Discourse and Gender in Contemporary Social Theory.* Cambridge: Polity.

Fraser, N. (1998). 'Social justice in the age of identity politics: redistribution, recognition, participation'. https://www.ssoar.info/ssoar/bitstream/handle/document/12624/ssoar-1998-fraser-social_justice_in_the_age.pdf?sequence=1 (accessed May 2021).

Fraser, N. (2000). 'Rethinking Recognition'. *New Left Review* 3: 107–20.

Fraser, N. (2003). 'Social justice in the age of identity politics: Redistribution, recognition and participation'. In N. Fraser and A. Honneth (eds) *Redistribution or recognition? A political-philosophical exchange.* London: Verso. 7–28.

Fraser, N. (2009). *Scales of justice: Reimagining political space in a globalizing world.* New York, NY: Columbia University Press.

Fraser, N. (2013). *Fortunes of feminism: From state-managed capitalism to neoliberal crisis.* London, UK: Verso.

Freire, P. (1970). *Pedagogy of the Oppressed.* London, UK: Penguin.

Freire, P. (1998). *Pedagogy of Freedom: Ethics, Democracy, and Civic Courage.* London: Rowman & Littlefield Publishers.

Freud, S. (1920). 'Beyond the pleasure principle'. *The Standard Edition of the Complete Psychological Works of Sigmund Freud.* 18: 1–64.

Gabaccia, D. (1998). *We Are What We Eat: Ethnic Foods and the Making of Americans.* Cambridge, MA: Harvard University Press.

Gambetti, Z. (2009). 'Decolonizing Diyarbakir: Culture, identity and the struggle to appropriate urban space'. In K. A. Ali and M. Rieker (eds) *Comparing cities: The Middle East and South Asia.* Oxford University Press. 97–129.

Gambetti, Z. and Jongerden, J. (2011). 'The spatial (re)production of the Kurdish issue: multiple and contradicting trajectories – introduction'. *Journal of Balkan and Near Eastern Studies* 13(4): 375–88. DOI: 10.1080/19448953.2011.621785.

Gambetti, Z. and Jongerden, J. (2015). *The Kurdish issue in Turkey: A spatial perspective.* London: Routledge.

Gellner, E. (1983). *Nation and Nationalism.* Oxford: Blackwell.

Gentry, K. and Smith, L. (2019). 'Critical heritage studies and the legacies of the late-twentieth century heritage canon'. *International Journal of Heritage Studies* 25(11): 1148–68. DOI: 10.1080/13527258.2019.1570964.

Gezik, E. and Gültekin, K. A. (2019). *Kurdish Alevis and the Case of Dersim: Historical and Contemporary Insights.* Lanham, Maryland Lexington Books.

Gilbert, J. (2010). 'Custodian of the Land: Indigenous Peoples, Human Rights and Cultural Diversity'. In W. Langfield, W. Logan and M. N. Craith (eds) *Cultural Diversity, Heritage and Human Rights: Intersections in Theory and Practice.* London and New York: Routledge. 31–44.

Gordillo, G. R. (2014). *Rubble: The Afterlife of Destruction.* Durham NC: Duke University Press.

Gourlay, W. (2018). 'Oppression, Solidarity, Resistance: The Forging of Kurdish Identity in Turkey'. *Ethnopolitics* 17(2): 130–46. DOI: 10.1080/17449057.2017.1339425.

Göçek, F. (ed.) (2018). *Contested Spaces in Contemporary Turkey: Environmental, Urban and Secular Politics.* London and New York: I.B. Tauris.

Göçek, F. M. (2018). 'Introduction: Contested Spaces in Neo-liberal Turkey'. In F. M. Göçek (ed.) *Contested Spaces in Contemporary Turkey: Environmental, Urban and Secular Politics.* London and New York: I.B. Tauris. 1–38.

Göç-Der (2002). *The Research and Solution Report on the Socio-Economic and Socio-Cultural Conditions of the Kurdish Citizens Living in the Turkish Republic Who Are Forcibly Displaced Due to Armed-Conflict and Tension Politics.* Istanbul: Göç-Der.

Graf, L. W. (1999). 'Dam nation: A geographic census of American dams and their large-scale hydrologic impacts'. *Water Resources Research* 35(4): 1305–11.

Graham, B., Ashworth, G. J. and Tunbridge, J. E. (2000). *A Geography of Heritage.* London: Arnold.

Graham, B. and Howard, P. (eds) (2008). *The Ashgate Research Companion to Heritage and Identity.* Aldershot: Ashgate Publishing.

Graeber, D. and Wengrow, D. (2018). 'How to change the course of human history'. *Eurozine.* https://www.eurozine.com/change-course-human-history/?pdf (accessed June 2020).

Graeber, D. and Wengrow, D. (2021). *The Dawn of Everything: A New History of Humanity*. London: Allen Lane.

Gramsci, A. (1971). *Selections from the Prison Notebooks*. Translated by Q. Hoare and G. N. Smith. New York: International Publishers.

Greenberg, R. and Hamilakis, Y. (2022). *Archaeology, Nation, and Race: Confronting the Past, Decolonizing the Future in Greece and Israel*. Cambridge: Cambridge University Press.

Greenfield, A. (2017). *Radical Technologies: The Design of Everyday Life*. Verso: London

Güler-Biyikli, S. and C. Aslan. (2013). 'A Review of Cultural Heritage Education in Turkish Schools (1962–2011)'. *Public Archaeology* 12(4): 255–70.

Guroian, V. (1994). 'Religion and Armenian National Identity: Nationalism Old and New'. *Occasional Papers on Religion in Eastern Europe* 14(2): Article 3.

Hackman, H. (2005). 'Five essential components for social justice education'. *Equity & Excellence in Education* 38: 103–9.

Halbwachs, M. (1950). *La Mémoire collective*. Paris: Presses Universitaires de France.

Halilovich, H. (2013). *Places of Pain: Forced Displacement, Popular Memory and Trans-local Identities in Bosnian War-torn Communities*. New York: Berghahn

Hall, S. (2005). 'Whose Heritage? Un-settling "The Heritage": Re-imagining the post-nation'. In J. Litter and R. Naidoo (eds) *The Politics of Heritage: The Legacies of Race*. London: Routledge. 23–35.

Hemmerechts, K., Smets, K. and Timmerman, C. (2017). 'Perceived Human Rights in Van Merkez, Eastern Turkey'. *Journal of Balkan and Near Eastern Studies* 19(4): 388–402. DOI: 10.1080/19448953.2017.1280979.

Hollowell, J. and Nicholas, G. (2009). 'Using Ethnographic Methods to Articulate Community-Based Conceptions of Cultural Heritage Management'. *Public Archaeology* 8(2–3): 141–60. DOI: 10.1179/175355309X457196.

Hamilakis, Y. (2007). *The Nation and Its Ruins: Antiquity, Archaeology and National Imagination in Greece*. Oxford and New York: Oxford University Press.

Hamilakis, Y. and Duke, P. (eds) (2008). *Archaeology and capitalism: from ethics to politics*. Walnut Creek, CA: Left Coast Press.

Hanks, W. (1990). *Referential Practice: Language and Lived Space among the Maya*. Chicago: University of Chicago Press.

Hardt, M. and Negri, A. (2001). *Empire*. Cambridge: Harvard University Press.

Harrison, R. (2008). 'The Politics of the Past: Conflict in the Use of Heritage in the Modern World'. In G. Fairclough, R. Harrison, J. Jameson and J. Schofield (eds) *The Heritage Reader*. Abingdon and New York: Routledge. 177–90

Harrison, R. (2011). 'Counter-mapping' heritage, communities and places in Australia and the UK'. In J. Schofield and R. Szymanski (eds) *Local Heritage, Global Context: Cultural Perspectives on Sense of Place* (Heritage Culture and Identity). Farnham: Ashgate. 79–98.

Harrison, R. (2013a). *Heritage: Critical Approaches*. Abingdon; New York: Routledge.

Harrison, R. (2013b). 'Forgetting to Remember, Remembering to Forget: Late Modern Heritage Practices, Sustainability and the 'Crisis' of Accumulation of the Past'. *International Journal of Heritage Studies* 19(6): 579–95. DOI: 10.1080/13527258.2012.678371.

Harrison, R. (2015). 'Beyond "Natural" and "Cultural" Heritage: Toward an Ontological Politics of Heritage in the Age of Anthropocene'. *Heritage & Society* 8: 24–42. DOI:1 0.1179/2159032X15Z.00000000036.

Harrison, R. (2016). 'Archaeologies of Emergent Presents and Futures'. *Historical Archaeology* 50(3): 165–80.

Harvey, C. D. (2001). 'Heritage Pasts and Heritage Presents: Temporality, Meaning and the Scope of Heritages Studies'. *International Journal of Heritage Studies* 7(4): 319–38.

Harvey, D. (2003). 'The Right to the City'. *International Journal of Urban and Regional Development* 27(4): 939–41.

Harvey, D. (2005). *A Brief History of Neoliberalism.* Oxford: Oxford UP.

Harvey, D. (2007). 'Neoliberalism as Creative Destruction'. *The Annals of the American Academy of Political and Social Science* 610(1): 22–44.

Harvey, D. (2009). *Social Justice and the City.* Athens, GA; London: University of Georgia Press.

Harvey, D. (2011). 'The Future of the Commons'. *Radical History Review* 109: 101–7. DOI: 10.1215/01636545-2010-017.

Hassan, F. (2007). 'The Aswan High Dam and the International Rescue Nubia Campaign'. *The African Archaeological Review* 24(3/4): 73–94.

Hawke, S. (2012). 'Heritage and Sense of Place: Amplifying Local Voice and Co-constructing Meaning'. In I. Convery, G. Corsane and P. Davis (eds) *Making Sense of Place: Multidisciplinary Perspectives.* Woodbridge: Boydell & Brewer. 235–48.

Henson, D. (2004). 'Archaeology in Schools'. In D. Henson et al. (eds) *Education and Historic Environment.* London: Routledge. 23–32.

Herscher, A. (2010). *Violence Taking Place: The Architecture of the Kosovo Conflict.* Stanford, CA: Stanford University Press.

Heese, V. M. (2018). 'The War Over Nagorno-Karabakh and Its Lasting Effects on Cultural Heritage'. In P. Wagenaar and J. Rodenberg (eds) *Cultural Contestation: Heritage, Identity and the Role of Government.* (Palgrave Studies in Cultural Heritage and Conflict). London: Palgrave Macmillan. 177–96. DOI: 10.1007/978-3- 319-91914-0_1.

Hobbes, T. (1963). *Leviathan.* Introduction by John Plamenatz. Meridian Books: Cleveland and New York.

Hobsbawm, E. J. and Ranger, T. O. (1983). *The Invention of Tradition.* Cambridge: Cambridge University Press.

Hodder, I. (2014). 'Çatalhöyük: The Leopard Changes Its Spots. A Summary of Recent Work'. *Anatolian Studies* 64: 1–22.

Hodder, I. and Pels, P. (2010). 'History houses: a new interpretation of architectural elaboration at Çatalhöyük'. In I. Hodder (ed.) *Religion in the Emergence of Civilization: Çatalhöyük as a Case Study.* Cambridge: Cambridge University Press. 163–86

Hodgkin, K. and Radstone, S. (2003). *Contested Past: The Politics of Memory*. London: Routledge.

Hofmann, D., Hanscam, E., Furholt, M., Baca, M., Reiter, S. S., Vanzetti, A., Kotsakis, K., Petersson, H., Niklasson, E., Hølleland, H. and Frieman, C. J. (2021). 'Forum: Populism, Identity Politics, and the Archaeology of Europe'. *European Journal of Archaeology* 24(4): 519–55.

Holtorf, C. (2015). 'Averting Loss Aversion in Cultural Heritage'. *International Journal of Heritage Studies* 214: 405–21. DOI:10.1080/13527258.2014.938766.

Holtorf, C. (2018). 'Embracing Change: How Cultural Resilience is Increased Through Cultural Heritage'. *World Archaeology* 50(4): 639-50. DOI: 10.1080/00438243.2018.1510340.

Holtorf, C. (2020). '"Cultural heritage is concerned with the future": a critical epilogue'. In V. Apaydin (ed.) *Critical Perspectives on Cultural Memory and Heritage: Construction, Transformation and Destruction*. London: UCL Press. 309–12

Hollowell, J. and Nicholas, G. (2009). 'Using Ethnographic Methods to Articulate Community-Based Conceptions of Cultural Heritage Management'. *Public Archaeology* 8(2–3): 141–60. DOI: 10.1179/175355309X457196.

Horniman Museums and Gardens (2020). 'Horniman Museum and Gardens Climate and Ecology Manifesto January 2020'. https://www.horniman.ac.uk/wp-content/uploads/2020/02/horniman-climate-manifesto-final-29-jan-2020.pdf (accessed April 2021).

Howard, P. and Graham, B. (eds) (2016). *The Ashgate Research Companion to Heritage and Identity*. Boca Raton, FL: Taylor and Francis.

Human Rights Watch, HRW (2015). 'Turkey: Mounting Security Operation Deaths: Scores of Civilians Among Hundreds Killed in Southeast'. https://www.hrw.org/news/2015/12/22/turkey-mounting-security-operation-deaths. (accessed March 2022).

Human Rights Watch (2020). 'Turkey: Justice for Rights Lawyer's Killing'. https://www.hrw.org/news/2020/10/21/turkey-justice-rights-lawyers-killing (accessed February 2022).

ICCPR (1966). 'International Covenant on Civil and Political Rights'. Articles 12 and 17. https://www.ohchr.org/Documents/ProfessionalInterest/ccpr.pdf (accessed June 2020).

ICESCR (1966). 'International Covenant on Economic, Social and Cultural Rights'. https://www.ohchr.org/en/professionalinterest/pages/cescr.aspx (accessed April 2021).

Ingold, T. (2010). 'No More Ancient; No More Human: The Future Past of Archaeology and Anthropology'. In D. Garrow and T. Yarrow (eds) *Archaeology and Anthropology*. Oxford: Oxbow. 160–70.

Ireland, T. and Schofield, J. (eds) (2015). *The Ethics of Cultural Heritage*. London: Springer.

Ishay, M. R. (2004). 'What Are Human Rights? Six historical Controversies'. *Journal of Human Rights* 3(3): 359–71.

Johnston, R. and Marwood, K. (2017). 'Action heritage: research, communities, social justice'. *International Journal of Heritage Studies* 23(9): 816–31. DOI: 10.1080/13527258.2017.133911.

Jokilehto, J. (2012). 'Human rights and cultural heritage: Observations on the recognition of human rights in the international doctrine'. *International Journal of Heritage Studies* 18(3): 226–30. DOI: 10.1080/13527258.2012.651741.

Jones, S. (2017). 'Wrestling with the Social Value of Heritage: Problems, Dilemmas and Opportunities'. *Journal of Community Archaeology & Heritage* 4: 21–37. DOI: 10.1080/20518196.

Jongerden, J. (2007). *The settlement issue in Turkey and the Kurds: An analysis of spatial policies, modernity and war.* Leiden: E.J. Brill.

Jongerden, J. (2010). 'Village Evacuation and Reconstruction in Kurdistan (1993–2002)'. *Ètudes rurales* 186: 77–100.

Joy, C. (2020). *Heritage Justice.* Cambridge: Cambridge University Press.

Kaika, M. (2006). 'Dams as Symbols of Modernization: The Urbanization of Nature between Geographical Imagination and Materiality'. *Annals of the Association of American Geographers* 96(2): 276–301.

Kamash, Z. (2019). 'On Well-Being, Activism and Ethical Practice: Response to Trentin, Lisa. Sharing Histories: Teaching and Learning from Displaced Youth in Greece'. *Humanities* 8(3): 149.

Karabekir, K. (1988). *Istiklal Harbimiz.* Istanbul: Merk Yayıncılık.

Karimova, N. and Deverell, E. (2001). 'Minorities in Turkey'. Stockholm: Utrikespolitiska institutet: The Swedish Institute of International Affairs 19.

Kaya, A. (2019). 'Populism as a neo-liberal form of governmentality: Resorting to Heritage, Culture and Past'. In Lia Galani, Evangelia Mavrigaki and Kostas Skordulis (eds) *Geographical Literacy and European Heritage: A Challenging Convention in the field of Education.* Limassol: Solva-tech. 64–94.

Kaya, A. (2016). 'The Alevi-Bektashi order in Turkey: syncreticism transcending national borders'. *Southeast European and Black Sea Studies* 16(2): 275–94. DOI: 10.1080/14683857.2015.1120465.

Kaya, A. (2020). 'Right-wing populism and Islamophobism in Europe and their impact on Turkey–EU relations'. *Turkish Studies* 21(1): 1–28. DOI: 10.1080/14683849.2018.1499431.

Kearney, A. (2009). 'Homeland Emotion: An Emotional Geography of Heritage and Homeland'. *International Journal of Heritage Studies* 15(2–3): 209–22. DOI: 10.1080/13527250902890746.

Kınıkoğlu, N. C. (2021). 'Displaying the Ottoman past in an "old" museum of a "new" Turkey: The Topkapi Palace Museum', *Southeast European and Black Sea Studies* 21(4): 549–69.

Kiddey, R. (2017). *Homeless Heritage: Collaborative Social Archaeology as Therapeutic Practice.* Oxford: Oxford University Press.

Kimmerer, W. R. (2003). *Gathering Moss: A Natural and Cultural History of Mosses.* London: Penguin Books.

Kimmerer, W. R. (2013). *Braiding Sweetgrass: Indigenous Wisdom, Scientific Knowledge and the Teachings of Plants.* Minneapolis, Minnesota: Milkweed Editions.

Kimmerer, W. R. (2014). 'Mishkos Kenomagwen: The Teachings of Grass'. https://www.youtube.com/watch?v=cumEQcRMY3c 8.37 (accessed December 2022).

Kimmerer, W. R. (2021). *The Democracy of Species*. London: Penguin Books.

King, L., Stark, J. and Cooke, P. (2016). 'Experiencing the Digital World: The Cultural Value of Digital Engagement with Heritage'. *Heritage & Society* 9(1): 76–101. DOI: 10.1080/2159032X.2016.1246156.

King, R. (2020). 'Mega-structural violence: considering African literary perspectives on infrastructure, modernity and destruction'. In V. Apaydin (ed.) *Critical Perspectives on Cultural Memory and Heritage: Construction, Transformation and Destruction*. London: UCL Press. 31–44.

King, R. and Eoin, L. N. (2014). 'Before the Flood: Loss of Place, Mnemonics, and "Resources" Ahead of the Metolong Dam, Lesotho'. *Journal of Social Archaeology* 14: 196–223.

Kinross, L. (1954). *Within the Taurus: A Journey in Asiatic Turkey*. London: Murray.

Kinsley, R. P. (2016). 'Inclusion in Museums: A Matter of Social Justice'. *Museum Management and Curatorship* 31(5): 474–90.

Kitchen, W. H. and Ronayne, M. (2002). 'The Ilisu Dam Environmental Impact Assessment Report: Review and critique'. *Public Archaeology* 2(2): 101–16. DOI: 10.1179/pua.2002.2.2.101.

Kizilkan-Kisacik, Z. B. (2013). *Europeanization of Minority Norms in Turkey*. Baden: Nomos.

Kohl, C. and Fawcett, P. (eds) (1995). *Nationalism, Politics, and the Practice of Archaeology*. Cambridge and New York: Cambridge University Press.

Konda (2014). 'Gezi Report: Public perception of the "Gezi protests": Who were the people at Gezi Park?' https://konda.com.tr/wp-content/uploads/2017/03/KONDA_Gezi_Report.pdf (accessed June 2020).

Kreyenbroek, P. and Allison, C. (eds) (1996). *Kurdish Culture and Identity*. London: Zed Books.

Kundera, M. (1980). *The Book of Laughter and Forgetting*. Translated by Aaron Asher. London: Faber.

Kühne, O. (2019). *Landscape Theories: A Brief Introduction*. Wiesbaden: Springer.

Labadi, S. (2007). 'Representations of the nation and cultural diversity in discourses on world heritage'. *Journal of Social Archaeology* 7(2): 147–70.

Labadi, S. (2013). *UNESCO, Cultural Heritage, and Outstanding Universal Value: Value-based Analyses of the World Heritage and Intangible Cultural Heritage Conventions*. Plymouth: AltaMira.

Labadi, S. (2018). *Museums, Immigrants, and Social Justice*. London: Routledge.

Labrador, A. M. and Silberman, N. A. (2018). 'Introduction: Public Heritage as Social Practice'. In A. M. Labrador and N. A. Silberman (eds) *The Oxford Handbook of Public Heritage Theory and Practice*. 1st edn. Oxford: Oxford University Press. 1–19.

Latour, B. (1993). *We Have Never Been Modern*. New York: Harvester Wheatsheaf.

Latour, B. (2004a). 'Why Has Critique Run out of Steam? From Matters of Fact to Matters of Concern'. *Critical Inquiry* 30(2): 225–48.

Latour, B. (2004b). *Politics of Nature: How to Bring the Sciences into Democracy*. Cambridge, Mass.: Harvard University Press.

Lears, J. T. T. (1985). 'The Concept of Cultural Hegemony: Problems and Possibilities'. *The American Historical Review* 90(3): 567–93.

Lefebvre, H. (1991). *The Production of Space*. Oxford: Blackwell

Levitsky, S. and Way, A. L. (eds) (2010). *Competitive Authoritarianism: Hybrid Regimes after the Cold War*. New York; Cambridge: Cambridge University Press.

Logan, W. S. (2008). 'Cultural diversity, heritage and human rights'. In B. Graham and P. Howard (eds) *The Ashgate Research Companion to Heritage and Identity*. Aldershot, UK: Ashgate. 439–54.

Logan, W. S. (2010). 'States, governance and the politics of culture: World Heritage in Asia'. In P. Daly and T. Winter (eds) *The Routledge Handbook of Heritage in Asia*. London: Routledge. 113–28.

Logan, W. S. (2012). 'Cultural diversity, cultural heritage and human rights: towards heritage management as human rights-based cultural practice'. *International Journal of Heritage Studies* 18(3): 231–44. DOI: 10.1080/13527258.2011.637573.

Logan, W. S. (2014). 'Heritage Rights – Avoidance and Reinforcement'. *Heritage & Society* 7(2): 156–69. DOI: 10.1179/2159032X14Z.00000000032.

Langfield, M., Logan, W. and Craith, M. N. (2010). 'Intersecting Concepts and Practices'. In W. Langfield, W. Logan and M. N. Craith (eds) *Cultural Diversity, Heritage and Human Rights: Intersections in Theory and Practice*. London and New York: Routledge. 3–20.

Lowenthal, D. (1985). *The Past Is a Foreign Country*. Cambridge: Cambridge University Press.

Lowenthal, D. (1998). *The Heritage Crusade and the Spoils of History*. Cambridge: Cambridge University Press.

Lowenthal, D. (2006). 'Natural and Cultural Heritage'. *International Journal of Heritage Studies* 11(1): 81–92.

Lowenthal, D. (2015). *The Past Is a Foreign Country – Revisited*. Cambridge: Cambridge University Press.

Luhmann, N. (2000). *Art as a Social System*. Translated by Eva M. Knodt. Stanford, Calif.: Stanford University Press.

Mack, G. R. and Surina, A. (2005). *Food Culture in Russia and Central Asia*. Westport, CT: Greenwood Press.

MacKenzie, R. and Stone, P. G. (1990). 'Introduction: The concept of the past'. In P. G. Stone and R. MacKenzie (eds) *The Excluded Past: Archaeology in Education*. London: Routledge. 1–11.

Maksudyan N. (2005). 'The Turkish Review of Anthropology and the Racist Face of Turkish Nationalism'. *Cultural Dynamics* 17(3): 291–322. DOI: 10.1177/0921374005061992.

Marty, P. F. (2008). 'Museum websites and museum visitors: digital museum resources and their use'. *Museum Management and Curatorship* 23(1): 81–99. DOI: 10.1080/09647770701865410.

Mason, R. (2004). 'Conflict and Complement: An Exploration of the Discourses Informing the Concept of the Socially Inclusive Museum in Contemporary Britain'. *International Journal of Heritage Studies* 10(1): 49–73. DOI: 10.1080/1352725032000194240.

May, S. (2019). 'Heritage, endangerment and participation: alternative futures in the Lake District'. *International Journal of Heritage Studies* 26(1): 71–86. DOI: 10.1080/13527258.2019.1620827.

McDowall, D. (2000). *A Modern History of the Kurds.* London: I.B. Tauris

McDowell, S. (2016). 'Heritage, Memory and Identity'. In P. Howard and B. Graham (eds) *The Ashgate Research Companion to Heritage and Identity.* Boca Raton, FL: Taylor & Francis.

McGuire, R. H. (2008). *Archaeology as Political Action.* Berkeley; London: University of California Press.

Mels, C., Derluyn, I., Broekaert, E. and Rosseel, Y. (2010). 'The psychological impact of forced displacement and related risk factors on Eastern Congolese adolescents affected by war'. *Journal of Child Psychology and Psychiatry* 51(10): 1096–104.

Menatti, L. (2017). 'Landscape: from common good to human right'. *International Journal of the Commons* 11(2): 641–83.

Merriman, N. (ed.) (2004). *Public Archaeology.* London: Routledge.

Meskell, L. (ed.) (1998). *Archaeology Under Fire: Nationalism, Politics and Heritage in the Eastern Mediterranean and Middle East.* London; New York: Routledge.

Meskell, L. and Pells, P. (eds) (2005). *Embedding Ethics.* London: Berg Press.

Meskell, L. (2010). 'Human Rights and Heritage Ethics'. *Anthropological Quarterly* 83(4): 839–60.

Meskell, L. (2014). 'States of Conservation: Protection, Politics, and Pacting within UNESCO's World Heritage Committee'. *Anthropological Quarterly* 87(1): 217–43.

Meskell, L. (2018). *A Future in Ruins: UNESCO, World Heritage, and the Dream of Peace.* New York: Oxford University Press.

Meskell, L., Liuzza, C., Bertacchini, E. and Saccone, D. (2015). 'Multilateralism and UNESCO World Heritage: Decision-making, States, Parties and Political Processes'. *International Journal of Heritage Studies* 21(5): 423–40. DOI: 10.1080/13527258.2014.945614.

Minority Groups International Report (MGIR) (2007). 'A Quest for Equality: Minorities in Turkey'. London: MRG.

Mitchell, T. J. W. (1994). *Landscape and Power.* Chicago and London: The University of Chicago Press.

Mitchell, D. (2003a). 'Cultural landscapes: Just landscapes or landscapes of justice?'. *Progress in Human Geography* 27(6): 787–96.

Mitchell, D. (2003b). *Cultural Geography: A Critical Introduction*. Oxford: Blackwell.

Mohamed, A.-N. and C. Holtorf (2017). 'The Challenges of Somali Cultural Heritage for the Dominant Heritage Discourse in Sweden.' Manuscript based on a presentation given at the Second Annual Meeting of the Association of Critical Heritage Studies, Montreal, Canada (June 2016).

Mortensen, L. (2006). 'Copán: The Authenticity of Stone.' In H. Silverman (ed.) *Archaeological Site Museums in Latin America*. University Press of Florida, Gainesville. 47–63.

Moshenska, G. (2017). *Key Concepts in Public Archaeology*. London: UCL Press.

Moudouros, N. (2014). 'Rethinking Islamic Hegemony in Turkey through Gezi Park.' *Journal of Balkan and Near Eastern Studies* 16(2): 181–95. DOI: 10.1080/19448953.2014.910394.

Muller, M. (1996). 'Nationalism and the Rule of Law in Turkey: The Elimination of Kurdish Representation during the 1990s.' In Robert Olson (ed.) *Kurdish Nationalist Movement in the 1990s*. Kentucky: University of Kentucky Press. 173–99.

Neimark, A. (2013). 'The Infrastructural Monument: Stalin's Water Works under Construction and in Representation.' *Future Anterior* 9(2): 1–14.

Neyzi, L. (2002). 'Embodied Elders: Space and Subjectivity in the Music of Metin-Kemal Kahraman.' *Middle Eastern Studies* 38: 89–109.

Nixon, R. (2009). 'Neoliberalism, Slow Violence, and the Environmental Picaresque.' *MFS Modern Fiction Studies* 55(3): 443–67.

Nixon, R. (2011). *Slow Violence and the Environmentalism of the Poor*. Cambridge, MA: Harvard University Press.

Nora, P. (1989). 'Between Memory and History: Les Lieux de Mémoire.' *Representations* 26(26): 7–24.

Nuri, K. (ed.) (2013). *Ilkögretim Sosyal Bilgiler Ögretmen Kılavuz Kitabı 6* [Primary Education Soscial Sciences Curricula for 6th level]. MEB: Milli Eğitim Bakanlığı Yayınları.

OHCHR (United Nations Human Rights Office of the High Commissioner) (2017). 'Report on the human rights situation in South-East Turkey.' July 2015 to December 2016. https://www.ohchr.org/Documents/Countries/TR/OHCHR_South-East_ TurkeyReport_10March2017.pdf (accessed July 2020).

Okur, Y., Genç, I., Özcan, T., Yurtbay, M. and Sever, A. (2013a). *Ortaöğretim TARIH 9* [History 9th level]. MEB: Milli Eğitim Bakanlığı Yayınları.

O'Lear, S., Furlong, K., Akhter, M., Forest, B. and Sneddon, C. (2018). 'Concrete Revolution: Large Dams, Cold War Geopolitics, and the US Bureau of Reclamation.' *The AAG Review of Books* 6(1): 41–9.

Olwig, K. R. (2003). 'Commons and Landscape.' In E. Berge and L. Carlsson (eds) *Commons Old and New*. Oslo: Centre for Advanced Study, Norwegian University of Science and Technology. 15–22.

Olwig, K. R. (2011). 'The Right Rights to the Right Landscape.' In S. Egoz, J. Makhzoumi and G. Pungetti (eds) *The Right to Landscape: Contesting landscape and human right*. Farnham: Ashgate. 39–50.

Ozbudun, E. (2012). 'Turkey – plural society and monolithic state'. In A. Kuru and A. Stepan (eds) *Democracy, Islam and secularism in Turkey*. New York: Columbia University Press. 61–94.

Panayi, P. (2000). *Ethnic Minorities in 19th and 20th Century Germany Jews, Gypsies, Poles, Turks and Others*. London, New York: Routledge.

Parr, A. (2013). *The Wrath of Capital: Neoliberalism and Climate Change Politics*. New York: Columbia University Press.

Pamuk, O. (2004). *Snow*. New York: Knopf

Parry, R. (2007). *Recoding the Museum: Digital Heritage and Technologies of Change*. Oxford: Routledge.

Pearson, M. and Sullivan, S. (1995). *Looking After Heritage Places*. Carlton, Victoria: Melbourne University Press.

Peluso, N. L. (1995). 'Whose woods are these? Counter-mapping forest territories in Kalimantan, Indonesia'. *Antipode* 27(4): 383–406.

Perry, S. (2019). 'The Enchantment of the Archaeological Record'. *European Journal of Archaeology* 22(3): 354–71. DOI: 10.1017/eaa.2019.24.

Philp, J. (2010). 'The political appropriation of Burma's cultural heritage and its implications for human rights'. In M. Langfield, W. Logan and M. N. Craith (eds) *Cultural diversity, heritage and human rights: Intersections in theory and practice*. London: Routledge. 83–100.

Popitz, H. (1992). *Phänomene der Macht* (2., stark erweiterte Aufl.). Tübingen: Mohr.

Posocco, L. (2018). 'Nationalism, Politics, and Museums in Turkey under the Justice and Development Party (AKP): The Case of the Panorama Museum 1453'. *Contemporary Southeastern Europe* 5(1): 35–55.

Ricoeur, P. (1973). 'Ethics and Culture'. *Philosophy Today* 17(2) 153–65.

Ricoeur, P. (2004). *Memory, History, Forgetting*. Chicago: University of Chicago Press.

Ronayne, M. (2005). 'The Cultural and Environmental Impact of Large Dams in Southeast Turkey'. London: Kurdish Human Rights Project and National University of Ireland, Galway.

Ronayne, M. (2006). 'Archaeology against Cultural Destruction: The Case of the Ilısu dam in Southeast Turkey'. *Public Archaeology* 5(4): 223–36.

Rowlands, M. (2004). 'Cultural Rights and Wrongs: Uses of the Concept of Property'. In K. Verdery and C. Humphrey (eds) *Property in Question: Value Transformation in the Global Economy*. Oxford: Berg. 207–26.

Ruggles, D. F. and Silverman, H. (eds) (2009). *Intangible Heritage Embodied*. New York: Springer.

Rusk, R. R. (1965). *The Doctrines of the Great Educators*. Melbourne, London, Toronto: Macmillan.

Rutland, P. (1994). 'Democracy and Nationalism in Armenia'. *Europe-Asia Studies* 46(5): 839–61.

Rüsen, J. T. (2007). 'Introduction'. In J. Rüsen (ed.) *Time and History: The Variety of Cultures*. New York and Oxford: Berbabn Books.

Saadi, S. (2021). 'Waiting for justice amidst the remnants: urban development, displacement and resistance in Diyarbakir'. *Social Anthropology* 29(3): 847–61.

Saglamtimur, H. (2014). 'A Castle and a River Port From the Late Roman Period on the Shores of Tigris'. *Maritime Archaeology Periodical* 2: 8–25.

Saglamtimur, H. (2015). 'Mezopotamya'da Nehir Tasimaciligi, Kelek Kullanimi ve Hasankeyf'. *Metro Gastro* 77: 8–15.

Sakellariadi, A. (2011). 'Archaeology for the People? Greek Archaeology and its Public: An Analysis of the Socio-Political and Economic Role of Archaeology in Greece'. Unpublished PhD Thesis. University College London.

Sandell, R. (1998). 'Museums as Agents of Social Inclusion'. *Museum Management and Curatorship* 17: 401–18. DOI: 10.1080/09647779800401704.

Sandell, R. (2007). 'Museums and the Combating of Social Inequality: Roles, Responsibilities, Resistance'. In S. Watson (ed.) *Museums and Their Communities*. London: Routledge. 95–111.

Sandell, R. and Nightingale, E. (eds) (2012). *Museums, Equality and Social Justice*. New York: Routledge.

Savelkoul, M., Tolsma, J., Scheepers, P. and Hagendoorn, L. (2010). 'Anti-Muslim Attitudes in The Netherlands: Tests of Contradictory Hypotheses Derived from Ethnic Competition Theory and Intergroup Contact Theory'. *European Sociological Review* vol. X: 1–18.

Savran, A. (2020). 'The Peace Process between Turkey and the Kurdistan Workers' Party, 2009–2015'. *Journal of Balkan and Near Eastern Studies* 22(6): 777–92. DOI: 10.1080/19448953.2020.1801243.

Schäfers, M. (2015). 'Being sick of politics: The production of dengbêjî as Kurdish cultural heritage in contemporary Turkey'. *European Journal of Turkish Studies*. Online. DOI: 10.4000/ejts.5200.

Schäfers, M. (2023). *Voices That Matter: Kurdish Women at the Limits of Representation in Contemporary Turkey*. Chicago: The University of Chicago Press.

Schofield, J. (2015). 'Forget About "Heritage": Place, Ethics and the Faro Convention'. In T. Ireland and J. Schofield (eds) *The Ethics of Cultural Heritage*. Ethical Archaeologies: The Politics of Social Justice, vol. 4. New York: Springer. DOI: 10.1007/978-1-4939-1649-8_12.

Schofield J. and Szymanski, F. (eds) (2011). *Local Heritage, Global Context: Cultural Perspective on a Sense of Place*. Farnham: Ashgate.

Schofield, J. and Ireland, T. (2015). *The Ethics of Cultural Heritage*. Ethical Archaeologies: The Politics of Social Justice, vol 4. New York: Springer. DOI: 10.1007/978-1-4939-1649-8_12.

Scott, J. C. (1985). *Weapons of the weak: Everyday forms of peasant resistance*. New Haven, CT: Yale University Press.

Scott, J. C. (1995). *Domination and the Arts of Resistance: Hidden Transcripts*. New :Haven and London: Yale University Press.

Sgard, A. (2010). 'Le paysage dans l'action publique: du patrimoine au bien commun'. *Développement durable et territoires* 1(2): 1–15.

Shafak, E. 2019. 'How to remain sane in the age of populism, pessimism and political uncertainty'. Talk on 20 June 2019.

Shankland, D. (2003). *The Alevis in Turkey: The Emergence of a Secular Islamic Tradition.* London: Routledge Curzon.

Shankland, D. (2010). 'Maps and the Alevis: On the Ethnography of Heterodox Islamic Groups'. *British Journal of Middle Eastern Studies* 37(3): 227–39. DOI: 10.1080/13530194.2010.543307.

Shepherd, N., and Haber, A. (2011). 'What's up with WAC? Archaeology and "Engagement" in a Globalized World'. *Public Archaeology* 10(2): 96–115. DOI: 10.117 9/175355311X13086617126567.

Shoup, D. (2006). 'Can Archaeology Build a Dam? Sites and Politics in Turkey's Southeast Anatolia Project'. *Journal of Mediterranean Archaeology* 19(2): 231–58.

Silberman, A. N. (2007). '"Sustainable" Heritage? Public Archaeological Interpretation and Marketed Past'. in Hamilakis, Y. and Duke, P (eds) *Archaeology and Capitalism: From Ethics to Politics.* Walnut Creek: Left Coast Press. 179–94.

Silberman, A. N. (2012) 'Heritage interpretation and human rights: documenting diversity, expressing identity, or establishing universal principles?'. *International Journal of Heritage Studies* 18(3): 245–56. DOI: 10.1080/13527258.2012.643910.

Silverman, H., and Ruggles, D. F. (eds) (2007). *Cultural Heritage and Human Rights.* London; New York: Springer.

Silverman, H. (ed.) (2010). *Contested Cultural Heritage: Religion, Nationalism, Erasure, and Exclusion in a Global World.* London; New York: Springer.

Sinclair, T. A. (1989). *Eastern Turkey: An Architectural and Archaeological Survey III.* London: The Pindar Press.

Smith, C. E. and Jackson, G. T. (2008). 'The Ethics of Collaboration. Whose Culture? Whose Intellectual Property? Who Benefits?' In C. Colwell-Chanthaphonh and T. J. Ferguson (eds) *Collaboration in Archaeological Practice: Engaging Descendent Communities.* Walnut Creek, CA: AltaMira Press, 171–91.

Smith, C. and Wobst, M. H. (eds) (2005). *Indigenous Archaeologies: Decolonizing Theory and Practice.* London: Routledge.

Smith, C., Burke, H., Ralph, J., Pollard, K., Gorman, A. . . . Jackson, G. (2019). 'Pursuing Social Justice Through Collaborative Archaeologies in Aboriginal Australia'. *Archaeologies* 15: 536–69.

Smith, C., Copley, V. and Jackson, G. (2018). 'Intellectual Soup: On the Reformulation and Repatriation of Indigenous Knowledge'. In V. Apaydin (ed.) *Shared Knowledge, Shared Power: Engaging Local and Indigenous Heritage.* Cham: Springer, 9–28.

Smith, C., Jackson, G., Ralph, J., Brown, N., Rankin, G. and Barunga Community (2021). 'An engaged archaeology field school with a remote aboriginal community:

Successes, failures, and challenges'. *Journal of Community Archaeology & Heritage* 8(2): 105–26. DOI: 10.1080/20518196.2020.1804112.

Smith, C., Ralph, J., Pollard, K. and De Leiuen, C. (2022). 'Social Justice: Material Culture as a Driver of Inequality'. In L. De Cunzo and C. Roeber (eds) *The Cambridge Handbook of Material Culture Studies (Cambridge Handbooks in Anthropology)*. Cambridge: Cambridge University Press. 100–27. DOI: 10.1017/9781108622639.005.

Smith, L. (2006). *Uses of Heritage*. London; New York: Routledge.

Smith, L. (2010). 'Ethics or Social Justice? Heritage and the Politics of Recognition'. *Australian Aboriginal Studies* 2: 60–8.

Smith, L. (2012). 'The Cultural "Work" of Tourism'. In L. Smith, E. Waterton and S. Watson (eds) *The Cultural Moment of Tourism*. London: Routledge. 210–34.

Smith, L. (2013). 'Taking the Children: Children, Childhood and Heritage Making'. In K. Darian-Smith and C. Pascoe (eds) *Children, Childhood and Cultural Heritage*. London: Routledge. 107–25.

Smith, L. (2020). *Emotional Heritage: Visitor Engagement at Museums and Heritage Sites*. Abingdon, Oxon, New York, NY: Routledge

Smith, L. and Akagawa, N. (eds) (2009). *Intangible Heritage*. Abingdon: Routledge.

Smith, L. and Waterton, E. (2009). 'The Envy of the World? Intangible Heritage in England'. In L. Smith and N. Akagawa (eds) *Intangible Heritage*. Abingdon: Routledge. 289–302.

Smith, T. W. (2005). 'Civic Nationalism and Ethnocultural Justice in Turkey'. *Human Rights Quarterly* 27(2): 436–70.

Sommer, U. (2017). 'The Appropriation or the Destruction of Memory? Bell Beaker "Re-Use" of Older Sites'. In R. Bernbeck, K. P. Hofmann and U. Sommer (eds) *Between Memory Sites and Memory Networks: New Archaeological and Historical Perspectives*. Berlin: Edition Topoi. 33–70.

Soyukaya, N. (2017). 'SUR – The Walled City of Diyarbakir Conflict, Dispossession and Destruction Damage Assessment Report'. https://www.hlrn.org/img/documents/ NSoyukaya_SUR_REPORT_1-8-2017.pdf (accessed July 2020).

Stall, A., Flores, M. B., Aguiar, D. A. P., Bosmans, J. H. J., Fetzer, I. and Tuinenburg, A. (2020). 'Feedback between drought and deforestation in the Amazon'. *Environmental Research Letters* 15(4). DOI: 10.1088/1748-9326/ab738e.

Sterling, C. (2020). 'Critical heritage and the posthumanities: problems and prospects'. *International Journal of Heritage Studies* 26(11): 1029–46. DOI: 10.1080/13527258.2020.1715464.

Stone, P. G. and Farchakh Bajjaly, J. (eds) (2008). *The Destruction of Cultural Heritage in Iraq*. Woodbridge, Suffolk: Boydell Press.

Stone, P. G. and MacKenzie, R. (eds) (1990). *The Excluded Past: Archaeology in Education*. London: Routledge.

Stone, P. (2012). 'Human rights and cultural property protection in times of conflict'. *International Journal of Heritage Studies* 18(3): 271–84. DOI: 10.1080/13527258.2012.651737.

Summerfield, D. (2000). 'Childhood, war, refugeedom and "trauma": Three core questions for mental health professionals'. *Journal of Transcultural Psychiatry* 37(3): 417–33. DOI: 10.1177/136346150003700308.

Swann, L. S. A., Longo, M., Knox, G. R., Lee, E. and Moorcroft, R. P. (2015). 'Future deforestation in the Amazon and consequences for South American climate'. *Agricultural and Forest Meteorology* vols 12–24. DOI: 10.1016/j.agrformet.2015.07.006.

Taylor, K. and Lennon, J. (2011). 'Cultural landscapes: a bridge between culture and nature?'. *International Journal of Heritage Studies* 17(6): 537–54. DOI: 10.1080/13527258.2011.618246.

The Hague Convention (1954). '1954 Hague Convention for the Protection of Cultural Property in the Event of Armed Conflict'. http://www.unesco.org/new/en/culture/themes/armed-conflict-and-heritage/convention-and-protocols/1954-hague-convention/ (accessed April 2021).

Thomas, S. and Thomas, S. (2004). 'Displacement and health'. *British Medical Bulletin* 69: 115–27.

Tobias, S. (2009). 'An eclectic appraisal of the success or failure of constructivist instruction'. In S. Tobias and T. M. Duffy (ed.) *Constructivist instruction: success or failure?* New York: Routledge. 335–50.

Tourle, P. K. (2020). 'Sound, heritage and homelessness in the age of noise'. Doctoral Thesis (PhD). University College London.

Törne, A. (2015). '"On the grounds where they will walk in a hundred years' time" – Struggling with the heritage of violent past in post-genocidal Tunceli'. *European Journal of Turkish Studies* 20. DOI: 10.4000/ejts.5099.

Trigger, B. G. (2006). *A History of Archaeological Thought*. 2nd edn. Cambridge: Cambridge University Press.

Tunbridge, J. E. and G. J. Ashworth (1995). *Dissonant Heritage: The Management of the past as a Resource in Conflict*. Chichester: Wiley.

Tunçel, H. (2000). 'Türkiye'de İsmi Değiştirilen Köyler'. *Fırat Üniversitesi Sosyal Bilimler Dergisi* 10(2): 23–34.

Turan, V., Genç, I., Çelik, M., Genç, C. and Turedi, S. (2013). *Ortaöğretim TARIH 10* (History 10th level). MEB: Milli Eğitim Bakanlığı Yayınları.

Tureli, I. (2014). 'Heritagisation of the "Ottoman/Turkish House" in the 1970s: Istanbul-Based Actors, Associations and Their Networks'. *European Journal of Turkish Studies* 19: 1–32.

United Nations Human Rights Council (2011). 'Meeting with independent expert in the field of cultural rights'. 1 June 2011. Geneva, Switzerland: UNHR.

United Nations Organization (1995). 'Our creative diversity: Report of the World Commission on Culture & Development'. Paris, France: EGOPRIM. https://unesdoc.unesco.org/ark:/48223/pf0000101651 (accessed August 2020).

Universal Declaration of Human Rights, UN (1948). http://www.un.org/Overview/rights.html. (accessed August 2020).

UNESCO (1960). 'Convention against Discrimination in Education'. https://en.unesco.
org/themes/right-to-education/convention-against-discrimination (accessed August
2020).

UNESCO (1972). 'Convention concerning the protection of the world cultural and
natural heritage'. Paris, France: UNESCO. https://whc.unesco.org/en/
conventiontext/ (accessed August 2020).

UNESCO (2002). 'Universal declaration on cultural diversity'. Paris, France: UNESCO.
https://unesdoc.unesco.org/ark:/48223/pf0000127162 (accessed August 2020).

UNESCO (1986). 'World Heritage Convention. Hattusha: the Hittite Capital'. https://
whc.unesco.org/en/list/377/ (accessed May 2021).

UNESCO (2003). 'Convention for the safeguarding of the intangible cultural heritage'.
Paris, France: UNESCO. https://ich.unesco.org/en/convention (accessed April
2021).

UNESCO (2004). 'Linking universal and local values'. *World Heritage Papers*, no. 13.
Paris, France: World Heritage Centre. https://whc.unesco.org/en/documents/4969
(accessed August 2020).

UNESCO (2005). 'International convention on the protection of the diversity of
cultural contents and artistic expressions'. Paris, France: UNESCO. https://en.
unesco.org/creativity/sites/creativity/files/passeport-convention2005-web2.pdf
(accessed August 2020).

UNESCO (2005). 'The Operational Guidelines for the Implementation of the
World Heritage Convention'. https://whc.unesco.org/en/criteria/ (accessed
May 2020).

UNESCO World Conference on Cultural Policies (1982). 'Mexico declaration on
cultural policies'. Mexico City, Mexico: UNESCO. https://unesdoc.unesco.org/
ark:/48223/pf0000052505 (accessed May 2020).

Unite Nations (2007). 'United Nations Declaration on the Rights of Indigenous Peoples'.
https://www.un.org/en/genocideprevention/documents/atrocity-crimes/Doc.18_
declaration%20rights%20indigenous%20peoples.pdf (accessed May 2021).

UNESCO (2012). 'UNESCO Florence Declaration on landscape'. http://whc.unesco.
org/en/news/943/ (accessed July 2020).

UNESCO (2010). 'Intangible Cultural Heritage: Semah, Alevi-Bektaşi ritual'.
https://ich.unesco.org/en/RL/semah-alevi-bektasi-ritual-00384 (accessed
February 2022).

UNESCO (2014). 'Diyarbakır Fortress and Hevsel Gardens Cultural Landscape
Nomination for Inscription on The World Heritage List'. https://whc.unesco.org/
uploads/nominations/1488.pdf (accessed February 2022).

UNESCO (2015). 'World Heritage Convention: Diyarbakır Fortress and Hevsel
Gardens Cultural Landscape'. https://whc.unesco.org/en/list/1488/ (accessed
September 2020).

UNESCO (2017). 'Survey report: Intangible Cultural Heritage of Displaced Syrians'.
https://ich.unesco.org/doc/src/38275-EN.pdf (accessed June 2020).

UNHR (United Nations Human Rights) (1992). 'Declarations on the Rights of Persons Belonging to National or Ethnic, Religious and Linguistic Minorities'. https://www.ohchr.org/en/instruments-mechanisms/instruments/declaration-rights-persons-belonging-national-or-ethnic (accessed September 2022).

UNHR (United Nations Human Rights) (1948). 'Universal Declaration of Human Rights'. https://www.un.org/en/about-us/universal-declaration-of-human-rights (accessed June 2021).

Üngör, U. Ü. (2011). *The Making of Modern Turkey: Nation and State in Eastern Anatolia, 1913–50*. Oxford: Oxford University Press.

Urry, J. (2003). *Global Complexity*. Cambridge: Polity.

Van Bruinessen M. (1989). 'The Ethnic Identity of the Kurds'. In P. Andrews (ed.) *Ethnic Groups in the Republic of Turkey*. Wiesbaden: Reichert.

Van Bruinessen, M. (1994). 'Genocide in Kurdistan? The Suppression of the Dersim Rebellion in Turkey (1937–38) and the Chemical War Against the Iraqi Kurds (1998)'. In G. J. Andreopoulos (ed.) *Conceptual and historical dimensions of genocide*. Pennsylvania: University of Pennsylvania Press. 141–70.

Van Bruinessen, M. (1995). 'Forced Evacuations and Destruction of Village in Dersim (Tunceli) and Western Bingol, Turkish Kurdistan'. Nethardlands Kurdistan Society.

Van Bruinessen, M. (1996). 'Kurds, Turks and the Alevi revival in Turkey'. *Middle East Report* 200: 7–10.

Vale, L. (2008). *Architecture, Power and National Identity*. Abingdon: Routledge.

Walasek, H. (2015). *Bosnia and the Destruction of Cultural Heritage*. Farnham, Surrey: Ashgate.

Watenpaugh, Z. H. (2013). 'Learning From Taksim Square: Architecture, State Power, and Public Space In Istanbul'. https://www.huffpost.com/entry/learning-from-taksim-squa_ (accessed June 2020).

Watenpaugh, Z. H. (2014). 'Preserving the Medieval City of Ani: Cultural Heritage between Contest and Reconciliation'. *Journal of the Society of Architectural Historians* 73(4): 528–55. DOI: 10.1525/jsah.2014.73.4.528.

Waterton, E. (2005). 'Whose Sense of Place? Reconciling Archaeological Perspectives with Community Values: Cultural Landscapes in England'. *International Journal of Heritage Studies* 11(4): 309–25. DOI: 10.1080/13527250500235591.

Waterton, E. and Smith, L. (2010). 'The recognition and misrecognition of community heritage'. *International Journal of Heritage Studies* 16(1–2): 4–15. DOI: 10.1080/13527250903441671.

Watts, N. F. (2010). *Activists in office: Kurdish politics and protest in Turkey*. Seattle, WA: University of Washington Press.

Weber, M. (1976 [1922]). *Wirtschaft und Gesellschaft: Grundriß der verstehenden Soziologie*. Tübingen: Mohr.

Weineck, B. (2015). 'Alevi Cultural Heritage in Turkey and Germany: Negotiating "Useable Pasts" in Transnational Space'. *European Journal of Turkish Studies* 20. DOI: 10.4000/ejts.5206.

Wetherell, M. (2007). 'Introduction: community cohesion and identity dynamics: dilemmas and challenges'. In M. Wetherell, M. Lafléche and R. Berkeley (eds) *Identity, ethnic diversity and community cohesion*. London: SAGE Publications. 1–14.

Whelan, Y. (2005). 'Mapping Meaning in the Cultural Landscape'. In G. J. Ashworth and B. Graham (eds) *Senses of Place: Senses of Time*. Aldershot: Ashgate. 61–72.

Williams, R. (1976). 'Base and Superstructure in Marxist Cultural Theory'. In R. Dale, G. Esland and M. MacDonald (eds) *Schooling and Capitalism: A Sociological Reader*. For the Schooling and Society Course at the Open University. London: Routledge and Kegan Paul [for] the Open University Press.

Williams, R. (1973). 'Base and Superstructure in Marxist Cultural Theory'. *New Left Review* 82(3). https://newleftreview.org/issues/i82/articles/raymond-williams-base-and-superstructure-in-marxist-cultural-theory (accessed February 2022).

Winter, T. (2010). 'Heritage Tourism: The Dawn of a New Era?' In S. Labadi and C. Long (eds) *Heritage and Globalisation*. London: Routledge. 117–29.

Winter, T. (2013). 'Clarifying the critical in critical heritage studies'. *International Journal of Heritage Studies* 19(6): 532–45. DOI: 10.1080/13527258.2012.720997.

Winter, T. (2015). 'Heritage and Nationalism: An Unbreachable Couple?' In E. Waterton (ed.) *Palgrave Handbook of Contemporary Heritage Research*. London: Palgrave. 331–45.

Winter, T. and Waterton, E. (2013). 'Critical Heritage Studies'. *International Journal of Heritage Studies* 19(6): 529–31. DOI: 10.1080/13527258.2013.818572.

Witcomb, A. and Buckley K. (2013). 'Engaging with the future of "critical heritage studies": Looking back in order to look forward'. *International Journal of Heritage Studies* 19(6): 562–78. DOI: 10.1080/13527258.2013.818570.

Wodak, R. and Meyer, M. (2001). 'Critical Discourse Analysis: History, Agenda, Theory and Methodology'. In R. Wodak and M. Meyer (eds) *Methods of Critical Discourse Analysis*. London: Sage. 1–34.

World Heritage Watch Report (2017). 'Destruction of the Old City (Suriçi) of Diyarbakır Since 2015 and its Current Status'. Berlin. https://world-heritage-watch.org/wp-content/uploads/2019/06/World-Heritage-Watch-Report-2019.pdf (accessed July 2020).

World Wildlife Fund (n.d.). 'Turkey'. https://www.worldwildlife.org/ecoregions/pa0420 (accessed May 2021).

Yadirgi, V. (2017). *The Political Economy of the Kurds of Turkey: From the Ottoman Empire to the Turkish Republic*. Cambridge: Cambridge University Press.

Yadirgi, V. (2020). 'Turkey's Kurdish question in the era of neoliberalism'. *Journal of Balkan and Near Eastern Studies* 22(6): 793–809.

Yegen, M. (1998). 'The Turkish State Discourse and the Exclusion of Kurdish Identity'. In S. Kedourie (ed.) *Turkey: Identity, Democracy, Politics*. London: Routledge. 216–29.

Yeğen, M. (1999). 'The Kurdish Question in Turkish State Discourse'. *Journal of Contemporary History* 34(4): 555–68.

Yeğen, M. (2007). 'Turkish nationalism and the Kurdish question'. *Ethnic and Racial Studies* 30(1): 119–51.

Yegen, M. (2015). 'The Kurdish peace process in Turkey: Genesis, evolution and prospects'. *Global Turkey in Europe* 11: Roma: Istituto affari internazionali. http://www.iai.it/sites/default/files/gte_wp_11.pdf (accessed September 2022).

Young, I. M. (1990). *Justice and the politics of difference*. Princeton, NJ: Princeton University Press.

Zencirci, G. (2014). 'Civil Society's History: New Constructions of Ottoman Heritage by the Justice and Development Party in Turkey'. *European Journal of Turkish Studies* 19: 1–20.

Zihnioglu, Ö. (2019). 'The Legacy of the Gezi Protests in Turkey'. In R. Youngs (ed.) *After Protests: Pathways Beyond Mass Mobilization*. Carnegie Endowment for International Peace. 11–18.

Zhu, Y. (2021). *Heritage Tourism: From Problems to Possibilities*. Cambridge: Cambridge University Press.

Index